T0273546

POCKET **ROUGH GUIDE**
LONDON

This sixth edition was updated by
ANNIE WARREN

CONTENTS

LONDON

London is huge: stretching for more than thirty miles from east to west, it has a population of almost 10 million. Ethnically and linguistically, it's Europe's most diverse metropolis, offering cultural and culinary delights from right across the globe. The city dominates the national horizon, too. This is where most of the country's news and money are made, it's where central government resides and, as far as its inhabitants are concerned, provincial life begins beyond the circuit of the city's orbital motorway.

View from the Sky Garden

On Regent's Canal, Little Venice

For the visitor, it's a thrilling destination. The biggest problem for newcomers is that the city can seem bewilderingly amorphous, with no single predominant focus of interest. Londoners tend to cope with all this by compartmentalizing their city, identifying strongly with the neighbourhoods in which they work or live, just making occasional forays into the West End, London's shopping and entertainment heartland. As a visitor, the key to enjoying London, then, is not to try and do everything in a single visit – concentrate on one or two areas and you'll get a lot more out of the place.

The capital's traditional sights – Big Ben, Westminster Abbey, Buckingham Palace, St Paul's Cathedral and the Tower of London – continue to draw in millions of tourists every year. Things change fast, though, and the regular emergence of new attractions ensures that there's plenty to do even for those who've visited before. London's world-class museums and galleries – of which there are dozens – are generally forward-looking places, often re-designing and re-imagining their spaces, while the tourist and transport infrastructure is generally pretty good, if crowded.

What's new

London is the master of reinvention, with even the most established attractions rolling out new refurbishments, exhibitions and redesigns. The National Portrait Gallery reopened in 2023 after three years of closure to reveal a luminous transformation (see page 26) and the Geffrye Museum in Shoreditch expanded hugely and rebranded itself as the Museum of the Home (see page 89), providing good reasons for revisits even to those who have been before. Additionally, areas including Camden Market and King's Cross are undergoing extensive regeneration, with the addition of the chi-chi Hawley Wharf in Camden (see page 137) and the fancy redevelopments around Granary Square and Coal Drop's Yard in King's Cross (see page 69).

When to visit

Despite the temperateness of the English climate, it's impossible to say with any degree of certainty that the weather will be pleasant in any given month. While always unpredictable, English summer days tend to range from a comfortable 22°C up to 30°C, while the winters (average daily temperature 6–10°C) don't get very cold – though they're often wet. However, whenever you come, be prepared for all eventualities: it has been known to snow at Easter and rain all day on August bank holiday weekend. As far as crowds go, tourists stream into London pretty much all year round, with peak season from Easter to October and in the run-up to Christmas, when you'll need to book your accommodation well in advance.

Monuments from the capital's glorious past are everywhere, from medieval banqueting halls and the great churches of Christopher Wren to the eclectic Victorian architecture of the triumphalist British Empire. There's also much enjoyment to be had from the city's quiet Georgian squares, the narrow alleyways of the City of London, the riverside walks and the assorted quirks of what is still identifiably a collection of villages. And urban London is offset by surprisingly large expanses of greenery: Hyde Park, Green Park and St James's Park are all within a few minutes' walk of the West End, while, further afield, you can enjoy the more expansive parklands of Hampstead Heath and Richmond Park.

You could spend days just shopping in London, too, mixing with the upper classes in the "tiara triangle" around Harrods, or sampling the offbeat weekend markets of Portobello Road, Camden and Spitalfields. The music, clubbing and LGBTQ+ scenes are second to none, and mainstream arts are no less exciting, with regular opportunities to catch first-rate theatre companies, dance troupes, exhibitions and opera in world-famous venues. The city's pubs have always had heaps of atmosphere, but food is a major attraction too, with eighty Michelin-starred restaurants and the widest choice of cuisines on the planet.

Rope Walk, Maltby Street Market in Bermondsey

Where to...

Eat

With thousands of cafés, pubs and restaurants, you're never far from a good place to fill your stomach. For the widest choice, make for **Soho**, nearby **Covent Garden** or **East London**, where you'll find everything from Italian coffee houses to Japanese noodle stands. The city's food scene is global, exciting and ever-changing. Some districts retain distinct specialities, whether Portuguese in **Ladbroke Grove** or Bangladeshi in **Tower Hamlets**. London's also a great place for snacking, with a vibrant street-food culture: **Borough Market**, **Maltby Street**, **Camden Market**, **Spitalfields** and **Shoreditch** are all good hunting grounds.

OUR FAVOURITES: The Ivy Cafe, see page 50. Dishoom, see page 61. Duck and Waffle, see page 84.

Drink

Found on just about every street corner, the pub remains one of the nation's most enduring social institutions and its popularity in London shows no sign of waning. **The City** has probably the best choice of long-established drinking holes – though with the average pint costing over £5, it's worth knowing that you can pay much less at Sam Smith's pubs. **Soho** and the **East End** attract a clubbier crowd, so you'll find a wide choice of bars and clubs alongside good-old-fashioned pubs. For a riverside drink, head for the **South Bank** or **Docklands**, and for a lazy Sunday afternoon mosey on up to **Hampstead** or down to **Greenwich**.

OUR FAVOURITES: The Black Friar, see page 85. George Inn, see page 116. Cutty Sark, see page 151.

Shop

From the folie de grandeur of Harrods to the street markets of Camden and Spitalfields, London is a shopper's playground. In the West End, **Oxford Street** is Europe's busiest shopping street, followed closely by Regent Street – here you'll find pretty much every mainstream shop you could wish for. **Covent Garden** is an appealing focus for fashion and designer wear. **St James's** equips the English gentleman, **Bond Street** deals with the ladies, but for haute couture – and Harrods – head for **Knightsbridge** and Sloane Street. For something more offbeat, or vintage, head out to **Camden Market** or **Spitalfields** and **Brick Lane**.

OUR FAVOURITES: Hamley's, see page 48. Freedom Press, see page 93. Harrods, see page 129.

Go out

As well as two top-class **opera** houses, London has many **theatres**, most of which are centrally located in the West End districts of Soho and Covent Garden, and boasts more **comedy venues** than any other city in the world. Although you'll find **clubs** and **live music venues** all across the capital, East London is the centre of the city's clubland. London is also the **LGBTQ+** capital of Europe, with Soho, the East End and Vauxhall the go-to areas.

OUR FAVOURITES: Ronnie Scott's, see page 65. XOYO, see page 97. Royal Albert Hall, see page 133.

London at a glance

Hampstead and Highgate p.140.
Elegant Georgian backstreets and the wild Heath appeal in Hampstead, while Highgate's gothic cemetery remains one of the city's most atmospheric spots.

Regent's Park and Camden p.134.
A pristine royal park and an enduringly popular street market are connected by a picturesque old canal.

Mayfair and Marylebone p.40.
Two aspirational West End suburbs harbouring some of the city's most exclusive shops and hotels. Mayfair is grander, while Marylebone retains a genteel village-like feel, and has some excellent restaurants.

Soho and Covent Garden p.52.
Bohemian Soho and cultural Covent Garden sit at the heart of the city's West End.

St James's p.34.
Exclusive enclave that's home to traditional menswear shops, upmarket galleries and auction houses – and Buckingham Palace.

Whitehall and Westminster p.24.
Centre of the British government, including the Houses of Parliament and Westminster Abbey.

Kensington and Chelsea p.118.
Stretching west from the centre, and encompassing the majestic Hyde Park, London's wealthiest borough includes South Kensington, with its trio of superb national museums.

◁ Kew and Richmond p.152.
Kew is home to world-renowned botanic gardens and Richmond boasts the perfect riverside setting.

◁ Hampton Court p.158.
Henry VIII's royal palace, accessible by train or boat.

The East End p.88.
You'll find some of London's best bars and clubs (and the Olympic Park) in a series of neighbourhoods to the east of the City: Spitalfields and Brick Lane, Shoreditch and Hoxton, Bethnal Green and Hackney.

The City p.72.
Established by the Romans, the City is London's financial heart and home to St Paul's Cathedral, while on its edges Clerkenwell appeals for its historic pubs, varied dining options and quieter ambience.

Bloomsbury p.66.
The area of leafy Georgian squares is dominated by the British Museum and the University of London, while to its north, the former warehouses along Regent's Canal are now home to some of central London's most enticing new developments.

Bankside and Borough p.110.
Popular riverside neighbourhood, with Tate Modern as its centrepiece, the gourmet Borough Market to tempt you alongside some charming old pubs.

The Tower and Docklands p.98.
The mighty Tower of London is one of London's essential sights. Beyond here, explore the riverside St Katherine's Docks, and the old quays and docks to its east, culminating in London's second financial centre, Canary Wharf.

South Bank and around p.104.
The cultural powerhouse of the Southbank Centre and the lively riverside walk draws in the crowds.

▷ **Greenwich** p.146.
Take the boat along the Thames to Greenwich for a splendid day out, as you explore its colourful royal and maritime sights.

15

Things not to miss

It's not possible to see everything that London has to offer in one trip – and we don't suggest you try. What follows is a selective taste of London's highlights, from the city's famous museums to its eclectic markets.

> **South Bank**
See page 104
Stroll along the riverbank's Thames Path from the London Eye to the Tate Modern and beyond.

< **East London's markets**

See page 89
Start at Columbia Road on a Sunday morning to enjoy the famous flower market, then dig out some vintage finds around Spitalfields and Brick Lane.

∨ **Greenwich**
See page 146
Explore below deck at the *Cutty Sark*, soak up naval history at the National Maritime Museum and climb up to the Royal Observatory in Greenwich Park to enjoy the view over the river.

< **London pubs**
See pages 71, 87, 96 and 117

Choose from one of London's classic drinking holes: Ye Olde Cheshire Cheese near Holborn, and Borough's Royal Oak, are charmingly unchanging; the Euston Tap or Mother Kelly's Tap Room offer large craft brew selections.

∨ **Hampton Court Palace**
See page 158

This sprawling red-brick Tudor edifice is without a doubt the finest of London's royal palaces.

< **Houses of Parliament**
See page 31
See the "mother of all parliaments" at work from the public gallery; visit for Question Time; or take a tour.

∨ **South Kensington's Museums**
See page 123
Three extraordinary museums – the Natural History Museum, Victoria and Albert and Science Museum – stand together, so whatever your interests, you'll find an exhibition to spark your imagination.

∧ **Tate Modern**
See page 111
A wonderful hotchpotch of global contemporary art, from video works to gargantuan installations, and sublime views from its extension roof terrace.

< **London's theatres**
See pages 65, 109 and 133
If you crave the glitz and glamour of a West End musical, try your luck at the TCKTS booth on Leicester Square for discount tickets. For new writing, visit the Royal Court, the National Theatre (particularly the Dorfman space), the Donmar or Old Vic.

∧ **Tower of London**
See page 98
England's most perfectly preserved medieval fortress and safe-deposit box for the Crown Jewels.

∨ **Borough Market**
See page 116
London's upmarket larder, this historic market has an irresistible selection of British and international gourmet goods to sample, plus street food stalls, and some fine neighbourhood restaurants and pubs.

< **British Museum**
See page 66
The oldest and greatest public museum on the planet, with objects from every corner of the globe.

∨ **The view from the Shard**
See page 114
Quite simply the most impressive view in London.

Day One in London

Parliament Square. See page 31. Gaze at two of the capital's most remarkable buildings: the Houses of Parliament and Westminster Abbey.

Westminster Abbey. See page 29. Take time to explore the galleries and graves at this masterpiece of ecclesiastical architecture.

Churchill War Rooms. See page 29. Discover the subterranean rooms used by Churchill and his War Cabinet during World War II.

St James's Park. See page 34. One of London's smartest royal parks, with views across to Buckingham Palace, exotic ducks and even pelicans.

St James's Park

🍴 **Lunch.** See page 61. Picnic in St James's Park or head to Covent Garden's Seven Dials for lunch, grab a slice of gourmet pizza at *Homeslice* or opt for Japanese steamed buns at *Flesh and Buns*.

Trafalgar Square. See page 24. London's finest set-piece square, overlooked by the National Gallery and famous for its fountains, fourth plinth and Nelson's Column.

British Museum. See page 66. One of the world's most amazing (and largest) museums, with everything from Egyptian mummies to Constructivist ceramics from the Russian Revolution.

Trafalgar Square

🍴 **Dinner.** See page 66. Wander up to King's Cross's Granary Square and enjoy cocktails and delicious Indian dishes at *Dishoom* or inventive fresh flavours at *Caravan*.

British Museum

Day Two in London

Harrods. See page 129. The queen of department stores, Harrods is a sight in itself, especially the Art Nouveau food hall.

Hyde Park. See page 119. Stroll along the Serpentine, go for a dip (if you're feeling brave) and check out the Diana Memorial Fountain.

Serpentine Gallery. See page 122. Sample some contemporary art for free and then have tea at the architecturally cutting-edge summer pavilion.

Albert Memorial. See page 122. Stop by this incredible, over-the-top neo-Gothic memorial to Queen Victoria's husband.

Albert Memorial

🍴 **Lunch.** See page 125. Housed in the museum's original refreshment rooms, the *V&A Café* is a visual treat, and serves everything from sandwiches to grilled fish and meat.

V&A. See page 125. South Kensington is home to a trio of fabulous museums, but the V&A's collection of applied arts is head and shoulders above the others.

Kensington Palace. See page 123. Princess Diana's former residence houses a display of her glamorous frocks, as well as some finely frescoed rooms.

Kensington Palace

Portobello Road Market. See page 127. Browse the antique shops or (if Saturday) the busy flea market.

🍴 **Dinner.** See page 131. Treat yourself to outstanding modern cuisine at *The Ledbury* or go for a drink and meal at *The Cow*.

Portobello Road Market

Riverside London

London grew up around the Thames, and a stroll (or a boat ride) along its banks is one of the city's real treats.

London Eye. See page 105. London's graceful millennial observation wheel has become one of the iconic symbols of the city despite its relative youth.

South Bank. See page 104. The views along the river from the South Bank's car-free promenade are some of London's best.

Tate Modern. See page 111. Feast your eyes on contemporary art from across the globe at the world's largest modern art gallery. Don't miss the sweeping vistas from the viewing platform.

Millennium Bridge. See page 110. London's only pedestrian-only river crossing offers great views of St Paul's Cathedral and the City.

Lunch. See page 116. Fill up at the food stalls in Borough Market (daily except Sun).

The Shard. See page 114. Scale London's most famous skyscraper and see the city spread out below you – and the hills and docks far beyond the edge of the city.

The Globe Theatre. See page 112. Loop back along the waterfront, and join the "groundlings" for an afternoon performance at Shakespeare's Globe.

Dinner. See page 116. Enjoy Middle Eastern flavours at *Bala Baya* or a Spanish feast at *Pizarro*, then settle in at one of Borough's fine historic pubs, like the *George Inn*.

London Eye

South Bank

The Globe Theatre

The City

From the Romans to rogue traders, the City has more history than the rest of London combined.

Sir John Soane's Museum. See page 76. The idiosyncratic home of the architect of the Bank of England is crammed with paintings and sculpture.

Temple Church. See page 72. Fascinating medieval round church, famed for its effigy tombs and appearance in *The Da Vinci Code*.

St Paul's Cathedral. See page 57. Climb up to the top of the dome of Wren's masterpiece for a fabulous view across the river.

Lunch. See page 84. Tuck into fresh, seasonal food at *The Café Below*, in the atmospheric crypt of St Mary-le-Bow, or pub grub at the wonderful Art Nouveau *Black Friar*.

Museum of London. See page 78. From Roman mosaics to Wellington's boots, this museum encompasses the whole of London's history.

The London Mithraeum. See page 81. You can see the head of Mithras – dug up at this site – at the Museum of London, then make your way to the location of the original Roman temple in the heart of the city.

City skyscrapers. See page 81. Stand outside Richard Rogers' Lloyds Building for a panoramic view of the City's latest generation of skyscrapers, or visit the Sky Garden for a free eyeful of cityscape.

Dinner. See page 95. Try modern British cooking at the iconic *St John Bread and Wine* or authentic Punjabi food at *Tayyabs*.

St Paul's Cathedral

The Gherkin

Old Spitalfields Market

PLACES

Tower Bridge at night

Whitehall and Westminster

Whitehall is synonymous with the faceless, pinstriped bureaucracy who run the various governmental ministries located here, while Westminster remains home to the Houses of Parliament. Both are popular with visitors thanks to the Changing of the Guard, and familiar landmarks such as Nelson's Column, Big Ben and Westminster Abbey, London's most historic church. Political, religious and regal power has emanated from Whitehall and Westminster for almost a millennium. It was King Edward the Confessor who first established this spot as London's royal and ecclesiastical power base in the eleventh century. He built his palace and abbey some three miles upstream from the City of London, and it was in the abbey that the embryonic English parliament used to meet in the Middle Ages.

Trafalgar Square

MAP PAGE 26, POCKET MAP G16
⊖ Charing Cross.

Nelson's Column, Trafalgar Square

As one of the few large public squares in London, Trafalgar Square has been a focus for political demonstrations since it was laid out in the 1820s. Along with its fountains, the square's central focal point is the deeply patriotic **Nelson's Column**, which stands 170ft high and is topped by a 17ft statue of the one-eyed, one-armed admiral who defeated the French (and died) at the 1805 Battle of Trafalgar. Nelson himself is actually quite hard to see – not so the giant bronze lions at the base of the column, which provide a popular photo opportunity. Stranded on a nearby traffic island is an equestrian statue of Charles I, while in the square's northeastern corner is one of George IV, which he himself originally commissioned for the top of Marble Arch. The **fourth plinth**, in the northwest corner, was built for an equestrian statue of William IV, but remained empty until 1999, since when it's been used to display alternating works of modern sculpture (Ⓦlondon.gov.uk/fourthplinth).

National Gallery

St Martin-in-the-Fields

MAP PAGE 26, POCKET MAP G16
Duncannon St ⊖ Charing Cross
Ⓦ stmartin-in-the-fields.org. Free.
Something of a blueprint for
eighteenth-century churches across
the empire, St Martin-in-the-
Fields is fronted by a magnificent
Corinthian portico and topped
by an elaborate tower and steeple.
Designed by James Gibbs and
completed in 1726, the barrel-
vaulted interior features ornate,
sparkling white Italian plasterwork
and is best appreciated while
listening to one of the church's
candle-lit evening performances.
Down in the large **crypt** –
accessible via an entrance north of
the church – there's a licensed **café**
(see page 33), shop, gallery and
brass-rubbing centre.

National Gallery

MAP PAGE 26, POCKET MAP G16
Trafalgar Square ⊖ Charing Cross
Ⓦ nationalgallery.org.uk. Free.
Despite housing more than 2300
paintings, the main virtue of the
National Gallery is not so much
the collection's size, but its range,
depth and sheer quality. A quick
tally of the **Italian** masterpieces,
for example, includes works by
Uccello, Botticelli, Mantegna,
Piero della Francesca, Veronese,
Titian, Raphael, Michelangelo
and Caravaggio. From **Spain** there
are dazzling pieces by El Greco,
Velázquez and Goya; from the **Low
Countries**, van Eyck, Memling and
Rubens, and an array of Rembrandt
paintings that features some of his
most searching portraits. Poussin,
Claude, Watteau and the only
Jacques-Louis David paintings in
the country are the early highlights
of a **French** contingent, which also
has a particularly strong showing
of Cézanne and the Impressionists.
British art is also well represented,
with important works by Hogarth,
Gainsborough, Stubbs and Turner,
though for twentieth-century
British art – and many more
Turners – you'll need to move on
to Tate Britain on Millbank (see
page 33).

To view the collection chronologically, begin with the **Sainsbury Wing**, the softly-softly, postmodern 1980s adjunct which is linked to – and playfully imitates – the original Neoclassical building. However, with more than a thousand paintings on permanent display, you'll need stamina to see everything in one day, so if time is tight your best bet is to home in on your areas of special interest, having picked up a gallery plan at one of the information desks. Plans and audioguides are available – much better, though, are the gallery's **free guided tours**, which set off from the Central Hall, and focus on a representative sample of works.

National Portrait Gallery

MAP PAGE 26, POCKET MAP G16
St Martin's Place ⊖ Charing Cross ⓦ npg. org.uk. Free.

Founded in 1856 to house uplifting depictions of the good and the great, the National Portrait Gallery has some fine individual works. However, many of the studies are of less interest than their subjects, and the overall impression is of an overstuffed shrine to famous Brits rather than a museum offering any insight into the history of portraiture. Nevertheless, it is fascinating to trace who has been deemed worthy of admiration at any moment: aristocrats and artists in previous centuries, warmongers and imperialists in the early decades of the twentieth century, writers and poets in the 1930s and 1940s, and latterly, sportsmen and women, politicians and film and pop stars. The NPG's audiovisual guide gives useful biographical background information and the gallery's **special exhibitions** (for which there's often an entrance charge) are well worth seeing – the photography shows, in particular, are usually excellent. The gallery

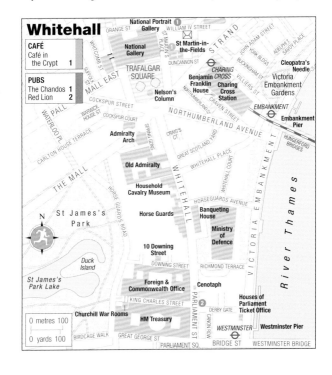

underwent extensive renovations and refurbishment to the tune of £41.3m, and reopened in 2023 transformed, with a new main entrance, step-free access and much more welcoming, open space inside.

Whitehall

MAP PAGE 26, POCKET MAP G17–G18
⊖ Westminster or Charing Cross.

Whitehall, the unusually broad avenue connecting Trafalgar Square to Parliament Square, is associated with the suited politicians charged with the day-to-day running of the country; yet during the sixteenth and seventeenth centuries it served as the chief residence of England's kings and queens. Having started out as the London seat of the Archbishop of York, **Whitehall Palace** was confiscated and embellished by Henry VIII after a fire at Westminster made him homeless; it was here that he celebrated his marriage to Anne Boleyn in 1533, and where he died fourteen years later. Described by one contemporary chronicler as nothing but "a heap of houses erected at diverse times and of different models, made continuous", it boasted some two thousand rooms and stretched for half a mile along the Thames. Not much survived the fire of 1698, and subsequently, the royal residences shifted to St James's and Kensington. Since then, the key governmental ministries and offices have migrated here, rehousing themselves on an ever-increasing scale.

The statues dotted along Whitehall today recall the days when this street stood at the centre of an empire on which the sun never set, while just beyond the Downing Street gates, in the middle of the road, stands Edwin Lutyens' **Cenotaph**, commemorating the dead of both world wars. Eschewing any kind of Christian imagery, the plain monument is inscribed simply

Cenotaph, Whitehall

with the words "The Glorious Dead" and remains the focus of the country's Remembrance Sunday ceremony, held here in early November.

Banqueting House

MAP PAGE 26, POCKET MAP G18
Whitehall ⊖ Westminster Ⓦ hrp.org.uk. Charge.

One of the few sections of Whitehall Palace to escape the 1698 fire, the Banqueting House was among the first Palladian buildings to be built in England. The one room open to the public has no original furnishings, but is well worth seeing for the superlative **Rubens ceiling paintings** commissioned by Charles I in the 1630s, depicting the union of England and Scotland, the peaceful reign of his father, James I, and finally his apotheosis (ask for an audioguide). Charles himself walked through the room for the last time in 1649, when he stepped onto the executioner's scaffold from one of its windows.

Daily inspection at Horse Guards

Horse Guards

MAP PAGE 26, POCKET MAP G18
Whitehall ⊖ **Charing Cross or Westminster.**
Outside this modest building,
built in 1745 and once the old
palace guard house, two mounted
sentries of the **Household Cavalry**
and two horseless colleagues, all
in ceremonial uniform, are posted
daily from 10am to 4pm. With
nothing in particular to guard
nowadays, the sentries are basically
here for the tourists, though they
are under orders not to smile. Try
to coincide your visit with the
Changing of the Guard, when
a squad of mounted Household
Cavalry in full livery arrives to
relieve the guards (Mon–Sat 11am,
Sun 10am) – if you miss it, turn
up at 4pm for the elaborate **daily
inspection** by the Officer of the
Guard.

Household Cavalry Museum

MAP PAGE 26, POCKET MAP G17
Whitehall ⊖ **Westminster**
ⓦ **householdcavalrymuseum.co.uk. Charge.**

Round the back of Horse Guards,
you'll find the Household Cavalry
Museum, where you can try on
a trooper's elaborate uniform,
complete a horse quiz and learn
about the regiments' history. With
the stables immediately adjacent,
it's a sweet-smelling place, and
– horse-lovers will be pleased to
know – you can see the beasts in
their stalls through a glass screen.
Don't miss the pocket Riot Act on
display, which ends with the wise
warning: "must read correctly:
variance fatal".

10 Downing Street

MAP PAGE 26, POCKET MAP G18
⊖ **Westminster.**
Since the days of Margaret
Thatcher, London's most famous
address has been hidden behind
wrought-iron security gates. A
pretty plain, seventeenth-century
terraced house, no. 10 has been the
official home to every British **prime
minister** since it was presented to
Robert Walpole, Britain's first PM,
by George II in 1732.

Churchill War Rooms

MAP PAGE 26, POCKET MAP G18
King Charles St ⊖ Westminster ⓦ iwm.
org.uk. Charge.

In 1938, in anticipation of Nazi
air raids, the basement of the civil
service buildings on the south side
of King Charles Street was converted
into the **Cabinet War Rooms**. It
was here that Winston Churchill
directed operations and held
Cabinet meetings for the duration
of World War II. The rooms have
been left pretty much as they were
when they were finally abandoned
on VJ Day 1945, making for an
atmospheric underground trot
through wartime London. Also in
the basement is the self-contained
Churchill Museum, where you can
hear snippets of Churchill's most
famous speeches and check out his
trademark bowler, spotted bow tie
and half-chewed Havana, not to
mention his wonderful burgundy
zip-up "romper suit".

Westminster Abbey

MAP PAGE 29, POCKET MAP G19
Parliament Square ⊖ Westminster
ⓦ westminster-abbey.org. Charge.

Venue for every coronation since
William the Conqueror, and
burial place of kings and queens,
Westminster Abbey embodies
much of England's history.

Entry is via the north transept,
cluttered with monuments to
politicians. From there you enter
the nave itself, narrow, light and,
at over 100ft in height, the tallest
in the country. The choir leads
through to the central sanctuary,
site of the coronations, and the
wonderful **Cosmati floor mosaic**,
constructed in the thirteenth
century by Italian craftsmen. At
the east end lies the abbey's most
dazzling architectural set piece,
the **Lady Chapel**, added by
Henry VII in 1503 as his future
resting place. With its intricately
carved vaulting and fan-shaped

WHITEHALL AND WESTMINSTER

Westminster Abbey

gilded pendants, the chapel represents the final spectacular gasp of the English Perpendicular style. The public is no longer admitted to the **Shrine of Edward the Confessor**, the sacred heart of the building, except on a guided verger tour, though you get to see Edward I's **Coronation Chair**, a decrepit oak throne from around 1300, and used at every coronation since.

Nowadays, the abbey's royal tombs are upstaged by **Poets' Corner**, in the south transept. The first occupant, Geoffrey Chaucer, was buried here in 1400, not because he was a poet but because he lived nearby. By the eighteenth century, however, this zone had become an artistic pantheon, and since then has been filled with tributes to all shades of talent from William Blake to John Betjeman.

Accessed via a lift, the **Queen's Diamond Jubilee Galleries** inhabit a space 21m above the Abbey floor in the medieval triforium. The museum and viewing gallery displays altarpieces and treasures from the abbey's collections. You can see across to the Houses of Parliament from here and there are dizzying views down into the church.

Doors in the south choir aisle lead to the **Great Cloisters**, rebuilt after a fire in 1298. At the eastern end of the cloisters lies the octagonal **Chapter House**, where the House of Commons met from 1257. The thirteenth-century decorative paving tiles and apocalyptic wall-paintings have survived intact. From the cloisters you can make your way to the little-known **College Garden**, a 900-year-old stretch of green which now provides a quiet retreat.

Houses of Parliament

MAP PAGE 29, POCKET MAP H19
Parliament Square ⊖ Westminster
Ⓦ parliament.uk.

Also known as the **Palace of Westminster**, the Houses of Parliament are one of London's best-known monuments and the ultimate symbol of a nation once confident of its place at the centre of the world. The city's finest example of Victorian Gothic Revival, the complex is distinguished above all by the ornate, gilded clock-tower popularly known as **Big Ben**, after the thirteen-ton main bell that strikes the hour; such is its national status that the news in 2017 that the bongs would be silenced for four years during essential repairs to the tower brought howls of protest from traditionalist MPs (in the end, the clock stayed mute for just over five years).

The original medieval palace burnt to the ground in 1834, but **Westminster Hall** survived, and its huge oak hammerbeam roof – and sheer scale – make it one of the most magnificent secular medieval halls in Europe; you get a glimpse of it en route to the public galleries. For centuries, the hall housed England's highest court of law and witnessed the trials of, among others, William Wallace, Guy Fawkes and Charles I.

To watch the proceedings in either the House of Commons or the Lords, simply join the queue for the **public galleries** (known as Strangers' Galleries) outside the Cromwell Green visitors' entrance. The public is let in slowly; security checks are tight, and the whole procedure can take an hour or more. To avoid the queues, turn up an hour or more later, when the crowds have usually thinned; check online to see the parliamentary schedule.

To see **Question Time**, when the House is at its most raucous and entertaining, UK citizens must book a ticket several weeks in advance from their local MP.

Throughout the year there are audio and guided **tours** in which visitors get to walk through the two chambers, see some of the state rooms and admire Westminter Hall. All year round UK residents are entitled to a free tour of the palace; organize it through your local MP.

Jewel Tower

MAP PAGE 29, POCKET MAP J9
Abingdon St ⊖ Westminster Ⓦ english-heritage.org.uk/visit/places/jewel-tower.
Charge.

The Jewel Tower is another remnant of the medieval palace. It once formed the corner of the original fortifications, and was constructed in around 1365 by Edward III as a giant strongbox for the crown jewels. These days, it houses a small exhibition on the history of the Jewel Tower, and a model of the old Palace of Westminster.

Big Ben

Westminster Cathedral

MAP PAGE 29, POCKET MAP G9
Victoria St ⊖ Victoria
Ⓦ westminstercathedral.org.uk. Free.

Begun in 1895, the stripy neo-Byzantine, Roman Catholic Westminster Cathedral is one of London's most surprising churches, as well as one of the last – and the wildest – monuments to the Victorian era. Brick-built, and decorated with hoops of Portland stone, it culminates in a magnificent 274ft tapered **campanile**, served by a lift. The interior is only half finished, so to get an idea of what the place should eventually look like, explore the side chapels whose rich, multicoloured decor uses over one hundred types of marble from around the world. Be sure, too, to check out the low-relief Stations of the Cross, sculpted by Eric Gill during World War I.

Tate Britain

MAP PAGE 29, POCKET MAP J10
Millbank ⊖ Pimlico Ⓦ tate.org.uk. Free.

A purpose-built gallery founded in 1897 with money from sugar baron Henry Tate, Tate Britain is devoted almost exclusively to British art from 1500 to the present day. In addition, the gallery showcases contemporary British artists and sponsors the Turner Prize, the country's most prestigious modern-art award.

The pictures are displayed chronologically, with fairly regular re-hangs, but always include a fair selection of works by British artists such as Hogarth, Constable, Gainsborough, Reynolds and Blake, plus foreign artists like van Dyck who spent much of their career over here. The ever-popular **Pre-Raphaelites** are well represented, as are established twentieth-century greats including Stanley Spencer, Francis Bacon and Lucian Freud and living artists such as David Hockney. Lastly, don't miss the Tate's outstanding **Turner collection**, displayed in the Clore Gallery.

Inside Westminster Cathedral

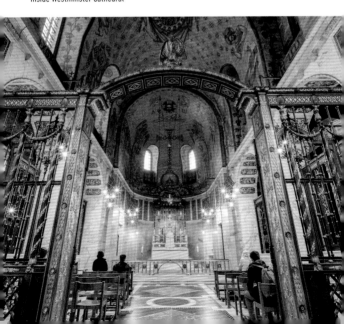

Shops

Houses of Parliament shop

MAP PAGE 29, POCKET MAP G19
12 Bridge St ⊖ Westminster. Ⓦ shop.
parliament.uk.
Pick up copies of *Hansard*
(the word-for-word account of
parliament), the government's
white and green papers and plenty
of political literature.

Tate Britain Gift Shops

MAP PAGE 29, POCKET MAP J10
Millbank ⊖ Pimlico. Ⓦ tate.org.uk/visit/
tate-britain/main-shop.
Lots of art posters, from Constable
to Turner Prize nonsense, plus
books – covering history and
culture, as well as art – and arty
accessories.

Café and restaurant

Café in the Crypt

MAP PAGE 26, POCKET MAP G16
St Martin-in-the-Fields, Duncannon St
⊖ Charing Cross. Ⓦ stmartin-in-the-
fields.org/visit/cafe-in-the-crypt.
The tasty home-made comfort
food and convenient, atmospheric
location – below the church in the
crypt – make this an ideal spot
to fill up. Jazz, folk, country, soul
and blues nights Wed from 8pm
(book in advance), and even the
occasional silent disco and cabaret
nights. £

Vincent Rooms

MAP PAGE 29, POCKET MAP H9
76 Vincent Square ⊖ Victoria or St
James's Park. Ⓦ thevincentrooms.co.uk.
Elegant brasserie serving up dishes
cooked by the student chefs of
Westminster Kingsway College,
where Jamie Oliver learnt his
trade. A real bargain, including
a delicious tasting menu in the
Escoffier Room. ££

Red Lion

Pubs

The Chandos

MAP PAGE 26, POCKET MAP G16
29 St Martin's Lane ⊖ Charing Cross.
If you can get one of the booths
downstairs, or the leather sofas
upstairs in the more relaxed Opera
Room Bar, then you'll find it difficult
to leave this Sam Smith's pub.

Red Lion

MAP PAGE 26, POCKET MAP G18
48 Parliament St ⊖ Westminster.
Ⓦ redlionwestminster.co.uk.
Classic old pub with good pies,
convenient for Westminster Abbey
and Parliament. You may spot an
MP or two enjoying a quiet pint.

St Stephen's Tavern

MAP PAGE 29, POCKET MAP H19
10 Bridge St ⊖ Westminster.
Ⓦ ststephenstavern.co.uk.
A beautifully restored and opulent
Victorian pub, built in 1867, wall
to wall with civil servants and MPs.
Good real ales (including seasonal
brews) and traditional pub food;
they even offer breakfast.

St James's

An exclusive little enclave sandwiched between St James's Park and Piccadilly, St James's was laid out in the 1670s close to the royal seat of St James's Palace. Regal and aristocratic residences overlook nearby Green Park and the stately avenue of The Mall, while gentlemen's clubs cluster along Pall Mall and St James's Street, and jacket-and-tie restaurants and expense-account gentlemen's outfitters line Jermyn Street. Hardly surprising, then, that most Londoners rarely stray into this area. Plenty of folk, however, frequent St James's Park, with large numbers heading for the King's chief residence, Buckingham Palace, and the adjacent King's Gallery and Royal Mews.

The Mall

MAP PAGE 35, POCKET MAP G17–E18
⊖ Charing Cross.

The tree-lined sweep of The Mall was laid out in the early twentieth century as a memorial to Queen Victoria. The bombastic **Admiralty Arch** was erected to mark the eastern entrance to The Mall, from Trafalgar Square, while at the other end, in front of Buckingham Palace, stands the ludicrously overblown **Victoria Memorial**, Edward VII's tribute to his mother. The Mall is best visited on a Sunday, when it's closed to traffic.

St James's Park

MAP PAGE 35, POCKET MAP F18
⊖ St James's Park ⓦ royalparks.org.uk.

St James's Park

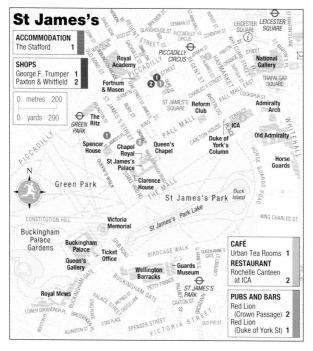

St James's

ACCOMMODATION	
The Stafford	1

SHOPS	
George F. Trumper	1
Paxton & Whitfield	2

0 metres	200
0 yards	200

CAFÉ	
Urban Tea Rooms	1
RESTAURANT	
Rochelle Canteen at ICA	2

PUBS AND BARS	
Red Lion (Crown Passage)	2
Red Lion (Duke of York St)	1

St James's Park is the oldest of London's royal parks, having been enclosed for hunting purposes by Henry VIII and later opened to the public by Charles II. It was landscaped by Nash in the 1820s, and today its tree-lined lake is a favourite picnic spot for Whitehall's civil servants. Pelicans chill out at the eastern end, and there are exotic ducks, swans and geese aplenty. From the bridge across the lake there's also a fine view over to Westminster and the jumble of domes and pinnacles along Whitehall, with the London Eye peeking over it all – even dull Buckingham Palace looks majestic from here.

Guards Museum

MAP PAGE 35, POCKET MAP E19
Birdcage Walk ⊖ St James's Park
Ⓦ theguardsmuseum.com. Charge.
The Neoclassical facade of the **Wellington Barracks**, built in

1833 and fronted by a parade ground, runs along the south side of St James's Park. In a bunker opposite the barracks' modern chapel, the Guards Museum endeavours to explain the complicated evolution of the Household Regiments, and provides a potted military history since the Civil War. Among the exhibits are the guards' glorious scarlet and blue uniforms, a lock of Wellington's hair and a whole load of war booty.

Buckingham Palace

MAP PAGE 35, POCKET MAP D19
Buckingham Gate ⊖ Green Park
Ⓦ royalcollection.org.uk. Charge.
The graceless colossus of Buckingham Palace has served as the monarch's permanent London residence only since Queen Victoria's reign. Bought by George III in 1762, the building was overhauled in the late 1820s,

and again in time for George V's coronation in 1913, producing a Neoclassical monolith that's about as bland as it's possible to be.

For three months of the year, the hallowed portals are grudgingly nudged open to the public; timed tickets can be bought online in advance, or from the box office on the south side of the palace. The interior, however, is a bit of an anticlimax: of the palace's 775 rooms, you're permitted to see nineteen, and there's little sign of life. If the decor is disappointing, at least the art on display is top-notch, with several van Dycks, two Rembrandts, several Canalettos, a de Hooch and a wonderful Vermeer hanging in the Picture Gallery (though works are sometimes moved or loaned).

For the other nine months of the year, the palace is closed to visitors – not that this deters the loitering crowds who gather in some force to watch the Foot Guards' **Changing the Guard** ceremony (⍟householddivision.org.uk). If the King is in, the Royal Standard flies from the roof of the palace and four guards patrol; if not, the Union flag flutters aloft and just two guards stand out front. Though this is the symbolic home of the British monarchy, King Charles III resides at Clarence House whilst extensive renovation work takes place at the Palace itself; he does, however, carry out official business here, including weekly meetings with the Prime Minister.

King's Gallery

MAP PAGE 35, POCKET MAP D19
Buckingham Gate ⊖ Victoria
⍟royalcollection.org.uk. Charge.
The changing exhibitions here are drawn from the **Royal Collection**, the vast array of artworks snapped up by the royal family over the centuries, which is three times larger than that at the National Gallery. Among the thousands of works the curators have to choose from are some incredible masterpieces by Michelangelo, Reynolds, Gainsborough, Vermeer, van Dyck, Rubens, Rembrandt and Canaletto, as well as numerous Fabergé eggs and heaps of Sèvres porcelain.

Buckingham Palace

Royal Mews

MAP PAGE 35, POCKET MAP D19
Buckingham Gate ⊖ Victoria
🕸 royalcollection.org.uk. Charge.

At the Nash-built Royal Mews, you can view the **King's horses** – or at least their backsides – in their luxury stables, along with an exhibition of equine accoutrements, but it's the royal carriages, lined up under a glass canopy in the courtyard, that are the main attraction. The most ornate is the **Gold State Coach**, made for George III in 1762, smothered in 22-carat gilding, panel paintings by Cipriani and weighing four tons, its axles supporting four life-size Tritons blowing conches. Eight horses are needed to pull it and the whole experience apparently made Queen Victoria feel quite sick; since then it has only been used for coronations and jubilees. The mews also house the Royal Family's fleet of Rolls-Royce Phantoms, Daimlers and Bentleys, none of which is obliged to carry number plates.

Gold State Coach

St James's Palace

MAP PAGE 35, POCKET MAP E18
Marlborough Rd ⊖ Green Park 🕸 royal.
gov.uk.

Built by Henry VIII for Anne Boleyn, St James's Palace became the principal royal residence after Whitehall Palace burnt to the ground in 1698, until the court moved down the road to Buckingham Palace under Queen Victoria. The imposing red-brick gate-tower that forms the main entrance, and the **Chapel Royal**, are all that remain of the original Tudor palace. The rambling complex is off-limits to the public, though you can attend services at the Chapel Royal, venue for numerous royal weddings, and at the Neoclassical **Queen's Chapel**.

The gentlemen's clubs

The **gentlemen's clubs** of St James's remain the final bastions of the male chauvinism and public-school snobbery for which England is famous. Their origins lie in the coffee- and chocolate-houses of the eighteenth century, though the majority were founded in the post-Napoleonic peace of the early nineteenth century by those who yearned for the officers' mess; drinking, gambling, and sex work were the major features of early club life. The oldest clubs – like White's, Brooks' and Boodle's – still boast a list of members that includes royals, politicians and the military top brass. The Reform Club, on Pall Mall, from which Phileas Fogg set off in *Jules Verne's Around the World in Eighty Days*, is one of the more "progressive" – it was one of the first to admit women as members.

Clarence House

MAP PAGE 35, POCKET MAP E18
Stable Yard Rd ⊖ Green Park
Ⓦ royalcollection.org.uk. Charge.

Built in the 1820s by John Nash for the future William IV, and used as his principal residence, Clarence House was home to the **Queen Mother**, widow of George VI, until 2002, and is now the official London residence of King Charles III and Queen Camilla. A handful of rooms can be visited over the summer when the royals are in Scotland. Visits must be booked in advance and are by guided tour only, and the rooms are pretty unremarkable, so apart from a peek behind the scenes in a working royal palace, and a few mementoes of the Queen Mum, the main draw is a series of twentieth-century British paintings on display by the likes of Walter Sickert and Augustus John.

Spencer House

MAP PAGE 35, POCKET MAP E18
St James's Place ⊖ Green Park
Ⓦ spencerhouse.co.uk. Charge.

Spencer House

Most of St James's palatial residences are closed to the public, with the exception of this superb Palladian mansion, built between 1756 and 1766. Ancestral home of the late Diana, Princess of Wales, it was last lived in by the family in 1926. Inside, guides take you on an hour-long tour through eight of the state rooms. The **Great Room** features a stunning coved and coffered ceiling in green, white and gold, while the **Painted Room** is a feast of Neoclassicism, decorated with murals in the "Pompeian manner". The most outrageous decor, though, is in **Lord Spencer's Room**, with its gilded palm-tree columns.

Green Park

MAP PAGE 35, POCKET MAP D18
⊖ Green Park Ⓦ royalparks.org.uk.

Laid out on the burial ground of the old lepers' hospital by Henry VIII, Green Park was left more or less flowerless – hence its name (officially "The Green Park") – and, apart from the springtime swathes of daffodils and crocuses, it remains mostly meadow, shaded by graceful London plane trees. A perfect place for a summer picnic. In its time, however, it was a popular place for duels (banned from neighbouring St James's Park), ballooning and fireworks displays. One such display was immortalized by Handel's *Music for the Royal Fireworks*, performed here on April 27, 1749 to celebrate the Peace of Aix-la-Chapelle, which ended the eight-year War of the Austrian Succession – over ten thousand fireworks were let off, setting fire to the custom-built Temple of Peace and causing three fatalities. The music was a great success, however. Along the east side of the park runs the wide path of **Queen's Walk**, laid out for Queen Caroline, wife of George II, who had a little pavilion built nearby.

Shops

George F. Trumper

MAP PAGE 35, POCKET MAP E16
1 Duke of York St ⊖ Piccadilly Circus.
Ⓦ trumpers.com.
Founded in 1875, this impeccably
discreet "gentlemen's perfumer" is
the barber of choice, with a shaving
school that will teach you how to
execute the perfect wet shave.

Paxton & Whitfield

MAP PAGE 35, POCKET MAP E16
93 Jermyn St ⊖ Piccadilly Circus.
Ⓦ paxtonandwhitfield.co.uk.
Quintessentially English, this
two-hundred-year-old cheese shop
offers a very traditional selection
of British and European varieties,
plus a good range of wine and
port.

Café and restaurant

Rochelle Canteen at ICA

MAP PAGE 35, POCKET MAP F17
94 The Mall ⊖ Charing Cross. Ⓦ archive.
ica.art/rochelle-canteen/index.html.
This minimal arts centre
restaurant and bar serves an
inventive menu by Arnold &
Henderson, a team connected to
some of London's most respected
restaurants (the original *Rochelle* is
in east London); expect a mixture
of English dishes (rabbit pie) and
Mediterranean flavours on the
changing menu. ££

Urban Tea Rooms

MAP PAGE 35, POCKET MAP F16
2A St James's Market ⊖ Piccadilly Circus.
The St James's Market development
off Haymarket is a welcome
addition to an area full of tourist
traps, with a couple of classy dining
options. Nestled in among them
is this hip little tea shop and café
serving brunches, home-made
sandwiches, avocado toast, pastries

George F. Trumper

and a good range of teas, plus
drinks and cocktails. £

Pubs and bars

Red Lion

MAP PAGE 35, POCKET MAP E17
23 Crown Passage ⊖ Green Park.
Hidden away in a passageway off
Pall Mall, this is a genuinely warm
and cosy local, with super-friendly
bar staff, well-kept Adnams beer
and good sandwiches.

Red Lion

MAP PAGE 35, POCKET MAP E16
2 Duke of York St ⊖ Piccadilly Circus.
Ⓦ redlionmayfair.co.uk.
Glorious old Victorian gin palace
with elegant etched mirrors and
lots of polished wood. Offers a
commendable range of Fuller's ales,
with seasonal selections that change
every few weeks.

Mayfair and Marylebone

A whiff of exclusivity still pervades the streets of Mayfair, particularly Bond Street and its tributaries, where designer clothes emporia jostle for space with jewellers, bespoke tailors and fine art dealers. Most Londoners, however, stick to the more prosaic pleasures of Regent and Oxford streets, home to the flagship branches of the country's most popular chain stores. It's here that Londoners are referring to when they talk of the West End. Marylebone, to the north of Oxford Street, may not have quite the pedigree and snob value of Mayfair, but it's still a wealthy and aspirational area, and its mesh of smart Georgian streets and squares are a pleasure to wander, especially the chi-chi, village-like quarter around the High Street.

Piccadilly Circus

MAP PAGE 41, POCKET MAP F16
⊖ Piccadilly Circus.

Characterless and congested, Piccadilly Circus is generally unloved by Londoners, who would rather detour through the backstreets of nearby Soho than face the maelstrom of this busy road junction.

Eros, Piccadilly Circus

Originally laid out in 1812 and now a major traffic bottleneck, it's by no means a picturesque place by day. It is best seen at night when the spread of vast illuminated signs (a feature since the Edwardian era) provide a touch of Las Vegas dazzle, and when the human traffic is at its most frenetic. Piccadilly Circus attracts a steady flow of tourists, who come here to sit on the steps of the central fountain, which is topped by an aluminium statue popularly known as **Eros**, designed by Alfred Gilbert and first unveiled in 1893. Despite the bow and arrow, it depicts not the god of love but Anteros, the lesser-known god of requited love, and was erected to commemorate the Earl of Shaftesbury, a Bible-thumping social reformer who campaigned against child labour.

Regent Street

MAP PAGE 41, POCKET MAP D14–E16
⊖ Piccadilly Circus or Oxford Circus.

Drawn up by John Nash in 1812 as both a luxury shopping street and a new, wide triumphal approach to Regent's Park, Regent Street was the city's first real attempt at dealing with traffic congestion.

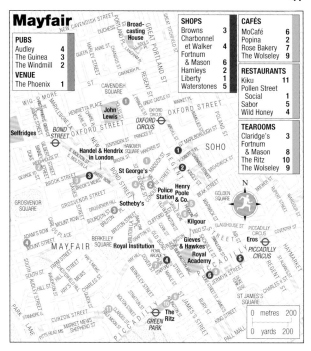

Mayfair

PUBS
Audley 4
The Guinea 3
The Windmill 2
VENUE
The Phoenix 1

SHOPS
Browns 3
Charbonnel
et Walker 4
Fortnum
& Mason 6
Hamleys 2
Liberty 1
Waterstones 5

CAFÉS
MoCafé 6
Popina 2
Rose Bakery 7
The Wolseley 9

RESTAURANTS
Kiku 11
Pollen Street
Social 1
Sabor 5
Wild Honey 4

TEAROOMS
Claridge's 3
Fortnum
& Mason 6
The Ritz 10
The Wolseley 9

At the same time, it helped clear away a large area of slums and create a tangible borderline to shore up fashionable Mayfair against the chaotic maze of Soho. Even today, it's still possible to admire the stately intentions of Nash's plan, particularly evident in the **Quadrant**, the street's partially arcaded section which curves westwards from Piccadilly Circus. During the course of the nineteenth century, however, the increased purchasing power of the city's middle classes brought the tone of the street "down", and heavyweight stores catering for the masses now predominate.

Piccadilly

MAP PAGE 41, POCKET MAP F16–C18
Piccadilly Circus or Green Park.
Piccadilly apparently got its name from the ruffs or "pickadills" worn by the dandies who promenaded along this wide boulevard in the late seventeenth century. Despite its fashionable pedigree, and the presence of **The Ritz** halfway along, it's no place for promenading in its current state, with traffic careering down it nose to tail day and night. Infinitely more pleasant places to window-shop are the various **nineteenth-century arcades** leading off the street, originally built to protect shoppers from the mud and horse-dung on the streets, but now equally useful for escaping exhaust fumes.

Burlington Arcade

MAP PAGE 41, POCKET MAP D16–E16
Piccadilly Green Park.
Lined with mahogany-fronted jewellers and gentlemen's outfitters, the Burlington Arcade is Piccadilly's longest and most expensive nineteenth-century arcade. It was built in 1819 for Lord Cavendish, then owner of neighbouring Burlington House, to prevent

commoners throwing rubbish into his garden. Upholding Regency decorum, it is still illegal to whistle, sing, hum, hurry, carry large packages or open umbrellas on this small stretch – the arcade's beadles (known as Burlington Berties), in their Edwardian frock-coats and gold-braided top hats, take the prevention of such criminality very seriously.

Royal Academy

MAP PAGE 41, POCKET MAP E16
Burlington House, Piccadilly ⊖ Green Park
Ⓦ royalacademy.org.uk. Permanent gallery free; exhibitions charge.

The Royal Academy of Arts (RA) occupies the enormous Burlington House, one of the few survivors of the aristocratic mansions that once lined Piccadilly. The country's first-ever formal art school, the Academy was founded in 1768 by a group of English painters including Thomas Gainsborough and Joshua Reynolds, the first president, whose statue now stands in the main courtyard, palette in hand.

The Academy has recently expanded into a second building – connected via a vaulted underpass, displaying sculpture and works by RA "Academicians" past, followed by a David Chipperfield-designed concrete stairway – with an entrance also on Burlington Gardens. The **Collection Gallery** in the Burlington Gardens building displays highlights from the RA's permanent collection, including a Rembrandtesque self-portrait by Reynolds, an appealing collection of London scenes by Constable and, as a magnificent centrepiece, a marble relief by Michelangelo, known as the *Taddei Tondo*.

The Academy is best known for its large special exhibitions, of which there are usually two or three at any one time, which could cover any genre or period from Old Masters to Ai Weiwei, and can attract large visitor numbers (book tickets in advance for major exhibitions). Its famous **Summer Exhibition** opens in June and runs until mid-August. Anyone can enter paintings in any style, and the lucky winners' works get exhibited and sold. In addition, RA Academicians are allowed to display six of their own works.

Royal Academy

Royal Institution

MAP PAGE 41, POCKET MAP D16
21 Albemarle St ⊖ Green Park Ⓦ rigb.
org. Free.

Founded in 1799 "for teaching by
courses of philosophical lectures
and experiments the application of
science to the common purposes
of life", the Royal Institution is
best known for its six Christmas
Lectures, begun by **Michael
Faraday** and designed to popularize
science among schoolchildren. In
the basement, there's an enjoyable
interactive **museum** aimed at both
kids and adults, where you can
learn about the ten elements that
have been discovered at the RI, and
the famous experiments that have
taken place here: Tyndall's blue sky
tube, Humphry Davy's early lamps
and Faraday's explorations into
electricity and electromagneticism
– there's even a reconstruction of
Faraday's lab from the 1850s.

Bond Street and around

MAP PAGE 41, POCKET MAP C15–D16
⊖ Bond Street or Green Park.

Afternoon tea at The Ritz

While Oxford Street, Regent
Street and Piccadilly are generally
the home of mainstream brands,
Bond Street maintains an air of
exclusivity. It is, in fact, two streets
rolled into one: the southern half,

Afternoon tea

The classic English **afternoon tea** – assorted sandwiches, scones
and cream, cakes and tarts, and, of course, lashings of tea – is
available all over London. The favoured venues for a treat are the
capital's top hotels and most fashionable department stores; a
selection of the best is given below. Leave your jeans and trainers
at home – most hotels will expect "smart casual attire", though
only *The Ritz* insists on jacket and tie. It's essential to book ahead.

CLARIDGE'S
MAP PAGE 41, POCKET MAP C15
49 Brook St ⊖ Bond Street Ⓦ claridges.co.uk.

FORTNUM & MASON
MAP PAGE 41, POCKET MAP E16
181 Piccadilly ⊖ Green Park or Piccadilly Circus Ⓦ fortnumandmason.com.

THE RITZ
MAP PAGE 41, POCKET MAP D17
Palm Court, 150 Piccadilly ⊖ Green Park Ⓦ theritzlondon.com.

THE WOLSELEY
MAP PAGE 41, POCKET MAP D13
160 Piccadilly ⊖ Green Park Ⓦ thewolseley.com.

Henry Poole & Co, Savile Row

laid out in the 1680s, is known as Old Bond Street; its northern extension, which followed less than fifty years later, is New Bond Street. Both are pretty unassuming architecturally, but the shops that line them – and those of neighbouring Conduit Street and South Molton Street – are among the flashiest in London, dominated by **perfumeries**, **jewellers** and **designer clothing** emporia such as Versace, Gucci and Yves Saint-Laurent.

Auction houses

MAP PAGE 41, POCKET MAP D15
⊖ Piccadilly Circus or Green Park.

In addition to fashion, Bond Street is renowned for its auction houses, which you can generally visit – and view their changing exhibits. The oldest is **Sotheby's**, at nos. 34–35, with a gallery at 31 George St. The exhibits (Ⓦsothebys.com) are free and open to the public, as are the auctions themselves.

Christie's, founded in 1766, and now the world's largest auction house, is over in St James's at 8 King St (Ⓦchristies.com).

Savile Row

MAP PAGE 41, POCKET MAP D15–E16
⊖ Green Park.

A classic address in sartorial matters, Savile Row has been *the* place to go for bespoke tailoring since the early nineteenth century. **Gieves & Hawkes**, at no. 1, were the first tailors to establish themselves here, back in 1785, with Nelson and Wellington among their first customers, while modernist **Kilgour**, at no. 5, famously made Fred Astaire's morning coat for *Top Hat*, helping to popularize Savile Row tailoring in the US. **Henry Poole & Co**, who moved to no. 15 in 1846, has cut suits for the likes of Napoleon III, Dickens and Churchill, and invented the short smoking jacket (originally designed for the future Edward VII), later popularized as the tuxedo.

Handel and Hendrix in London

MAP PAGE 41, POCKET MAP C15
25 Brook St ⊖ Bond Street
Ⓦhandelhendrix.org. Charge.

The German-born composer **George Frideric Handel**

(1685–1759) spent the best part of his life in London, producing all his best-known works at what's now the Handel House Museum. The composer used the ground floor of the building as a sort of shop where subscribers could buy scores, while the first floor was employed as a rehearsal room. Although containing few original artefacts, the house has been painstakingly restored, and the exquisite harpsichords are used for rehearsals and regular concerts. By a peculiar quirk of fate, the small third-floor flat of the neighbouring building, no. 23, was for a brief period in 1968–69 home to Jimi Hendrix and his girlfriend Kathy Etchingham. The flat has been re-created, complete with 1960s fabrics they bought from John Lewis and original guitars. There's also an exhibition on Hendrix's time in London.

St George's Church

MAP PAGE 41, POCKET MAP D15
Hanover Square ⊖ Oxford Circus
Ⓦ stgeorgeshanoversquare.org.

The much-copied Corinthian portico of St George's Church was the first of its kind in London when built in the 1720s. The church has long been Mayfair's most fashionable wedding venue, and those who tied the knot here have included the Shelleys, Benjamin Disraeli, George Eliot and Teddy Roosevelt. Handel, a confirmed bachelor, was a church warden for many years and even had his own pew.

Oxford Street

MAP PAGES 41 & 46 POCKET MAP
F14–15, E6–H6
⊖ Marble Arch, Bond Street, Oxford Circus
or Tottenham Court Road.

The old Roman road to Oxford has been London's main **shopping** destination for the last century. Today, despite successive recessions and sky-high rents, this aesthetically unremarkable two-mile hotchpotch of shops is still one of the world's busiest streets. East of Oxford Circus, it forms the northern border of Soho; to the west, the one great landmark is **Selfridges**, a huge Edwardian pile fronted by giant Ionic columns, with the Queen of Time riding the ship of commerce and supporting an Art Deco clock above the main entrance. The store was opened in 1909 by Chicago millionaire Gordon Selfridge, who flaunted its 130 departments under the slogan, "Why not spend a day at Selfridges?"; he was later pensioned off after an altercation with the Inland Revenue.

Wallace Collection

MAP PAGE 46, POCKET MAP B14
Hertford House, Manchester Square
⊖ Bond Street Ⓦ wallacecollection.org.
Free.

Housed in a miniature eighteenth-century French-style chateau, the Wallace Collection is an old-fashioned place, with exhibits piled high in glass cabinets, paintings covering every inch of wall space and a bloody great armoury. The collection is best known for

Wallace Collection

Marylebone

PUB	
Golden Eagle	1
VENUE	
Wigmore Hall	2

ACCOMMODATION	
Central YHA	1
Sumner Hotel	2

SHOPS	
Daunt Books	1
Selfridges	2

RESTAURANTS	
The Ivy Café	4
The Mayfair	
Chippy	7
Phoenix Palace	1

CAFÉS	
Boxcar Baker & Deli	2
Comptoir Libanais	6
Golden Hind	3
Paul Rothe & Son	5

its eighteenth-century French furniture and paintings (especially Watteau); look out, too, for Franz Hals' *Laughing Cavalier*, Titian's *Perseus and Andromeda*, Velázquez's *Lady with a Fan* and Rembrandt's portrait of his teenage son, Titus. Labelling can be pretty terse and paintings occasionally move about, so consider renting an audioguide or join a free tour.

Staircase at RIBA

RIBA

MAP PAGE 46, POCKET MAP C12
66 Portland Place ⊖ Regent's Park
🌐 architecture.com. Free.

With its sleek 1930s Portland-stone facade, the headquarters of the **Royal Institute of British Architects** is easily the finest building on Portland Place. Inside, the main staircase remains a wonderful period piece, with etched glass balustrades, walnut veneer and two large columns of black marble rising up on either side. You can view the interior en route to the institute's often thought-provoking first-floor architectural exhibitions (free) and to its café. The excellent bookshop is also worth a browse.

Madame Tussauds

MAP PAGE 46, POCKET MAP A12
Marylebone Rd ⊖ **Baker Street**
Ⓦ **madametussauds.com. Charge.**
Madame Tussaud's waxworks have been pulling in the crowds ever since the good lady arrived in London from France in 1802 bearing the sculpted heads of guillotined aristocrats. The entrance fee is extortionate, the likenesses occasionally dubious and the automated dummies inept, but you can still rely on finding London's biggest queues here – to avoid joining them, book your ticket online. There are photo opportunities galore throughout the first few sections, which are peppered with contemporary **celebrities** from the BBC to Bollywood. A Sherlock Holmes-themed installation features costumed actors and theatrical sets

that re-create Sherlock's London. The Tussauds finale is a manic five-minute "ride" through the history of London in a miniaturized taxi cab, followed by a thirty-minute, high-tech, Marvel-themed presentation, projected onto the dome of the adjoining Auditorium (formerly the Planetarium).

Sherlock Holmes Museum

MAP PAGE 46, POCKET MAP A12
239 Baker St ⊖ **Baker Street** Ⓦ **sherlock-holmes.co.uk. Charge.**
Sherlock Holmes' fictional address was 221b Baker Street, hence the number on the door of the museum. Unashamedly touristy, the place is stuffed full of Victoriana and life-size models of characters from the books. It's an atmospheric and very competent exercise in period reconstruction – you can even don a deerstalker to have your picture taken by the fireside, looking like the great detective himself.

Sherlock Holmes Museum

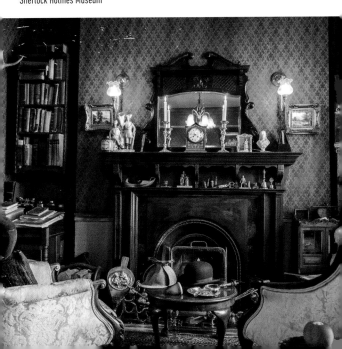

Shops

Browns

MAP PAGE 41, POCKET MAP C15
39 Brook St ⊖ Bond Street
Ⓦ brownsfashion.com.
Huge range of designer wear, with big international names under the same roof as the more cutting-edge, up-and-coming designers.

Charbonnel et Walker

MAP PAGE 41, POCKET MAP D16
1 Royal Arcade, 28 Old Bond St ⊖ Green Park Ⓦ charbonnel.co.uk.
Established in 1875, this is where the late Queen Elizabeth II would stock up on chocolate. The truffles and gift sets are all presented in exquisite packaging.

Daunt Books

MAP PAGE 46, POCKET MAP B13
83 Marylebone High St ⊖ Baker Street
Ⓦ dauntbooks.co.uk.
Wide and inspirational range of travel literature and guidebooks, plus fiction and non-fiction, presented by expert staff in the beautiful, galleried interior of this famous shop.

Selfridges, Oxford Street

Fortnum & Mason

MAP PAGE 41, POCKET MAP E16
181 Piccadilly ⊖ Green Park or Piccadilly Circus Ⓦ fortnumandmason.com.
Beautiful three hundred-year-old department store with heavenly murals, cherubs, chandeliers and fountains as a backdrop to its perfectly English offerings. Justly famous for its fabulous, pricey food, it also specializes in upmarket designer clothes, furniture, luggage and stationery.

Hamleys

MAP PAGE 41, POCKET MAP D15
188–196 Regent St ⊖ Oxford Circus
Ⓦ hamleys.com.
Possibly the world's largest toy shop, and certainly a feast for the eyes of most small children, with lots of gadget demonstrations going on throughout its seven floors of mayhem.

Liberty

MAP PAGE 41, POCKET MAP D15
210–220 Regent St ⊖ Oxford Circus
Ⓦ libertylondon.com.
A fabulous, partly mock-Tudor emporium of luxury. Best known for its fabrics, though it is, in fact, a full-blown department store.

Selfridges

MAP PAGE 46, POCKET MAP B14
400 Oxford St ⊖ Bond Street Ⓦ selfridges.com.
London's first great department store, and still one of its best: a huge, airy palace of luxury clothes and furnishings. There's also a great food hall selling everything from caviar to freshly roasted beans.

Waterstones

MAP PAGE 41, POCKET MAP E16
203–206 Piccadilly ⊖ Piccadilly Circus
Ⓦ waterstones.com.
This flagship bookstore has six well-stocked floors of books and knowledgeable staff. It hosts plenty of bookish events, and the fifth-floor café-bar is pleasant with some intriguing views.

Cafés

Boxcar Baker & Deli

MAP PAGE 46, POCKET MAP E5

7A Wyndham Pl. ⊖ Marylebone ⓦ boxcar.
co.uk.

A great spot for coffee, freshly
baked pastries, salads and
sandwiches, that attracts a hip,
relaxed crowd. The pastries are
the real pull here though; go for a
matcha croissant or a filled savoury
croissant roll. £

Comptoir Libanais

MAP PAGE 46, POCKET MAP B14

65 Wigmore St ⊖ Bond Street
ⓦ comptoirlibanais.com.

Bursting with atmosphere, this is
one of a colourful, kitschy Middle
Eastern deli/café chain; food is
a simple and honest selection of
mezze, wraps and tagines. Try the
home-made lemonades. ££

Golden Hind

MAP PAGE 46, POCKET MAP B13

73 Marylebone Lane ⊖ Bond Street
ⓦ goldenhindrestaurant.com.

Marylebone's heritage fish-and-chip
restaurant, founded in 1914, serves
classic cod and chips, with salmon,
skate and steamed fish options also
available. £

MoCafé

MAP PAGE 41, POCKET MAP E16

25 Heddon St ⊖ Piccadilly Circus.

Serving reasonably priced, tasty
snacks and afternoon tea in a
wonderful Arabic tearoom – part of
Momo restaurant – with a greenery-
entangled terrace screened off from
the restaurant-packed alleyway. £

Paul Rothe & Son

MAP PAGE 46, POCKET MAP B14

35 Marylebone Lane ⊖ Bond Street
ⓦ instagram.com/paulrotheandson.

Traditional deli established in
1900, selling "English & Foreign
Provisions", offering breakfasts,
plus hot food and sandwiches
made to order. Friendly and

Paul Rothe & Son

wonderfully unchanging, with
a few formica tables inside the
shop, which is lined with jars
upon jars of traditional jams and
preserves. £

Popina

MAP PAGE 41, POCKET MAP D16

83 Duke St ⊖ Bond Street ⓦ popina.co.uk.

A cosy deli that's open all day and
best for brunch and lunch; expect
the likes of shakshuka and French
toast, as well as brilliant coffee
options. There's outdoor seating if
the weather plays ball. £

Rose Bakery

MAP PAGE 41, POCKET MAP D16

17–18 Dover St ⊖ Green Park ⓦ london.
doverstreetmarket.com/pages/rose-
bakery.

An offshoot of Paris's favourite
English tearoom, serving simple
home-made lunches and fabulous
cakes in the high-fashion Dover
Street Market designer store. £

Pollen Street Social

The Wolseley

MAP PAGE 41, POCKET MAP D17
160 Piccadilly ⊖ Green Park
Ⓦ thewolseley.com.
The European brasserie food is
good if not that cheap, but the big
draw is the lofty and opulent 1920s
interior (built as the showroom for
Wolseley cars). It's a great place for
breakfast or a cream tea (see page
43) and very popular so book
ahead. £££

Restaurants

The Ivy Café

MAP PAGE 46, POCKET MAP B13
96 Marylebone Lane ⊖ Bond Street
Ⓦ ivycollection.com.
A relaxed, but still glamorous, all-
day brasserie offshoot of the famous
Ivy restaurant, the *Ivy Café* serves
comfort-food classics – fishcakes
or steak, egg and chips – plus an
impressive selection of vegan and
veggie choices. £££

Kiku

MAP PAGE 41, POCKET MAP C17
17 Half Moon St ⊖ Green Park
Ⓦ kikurestaurant.co.uk.
This place has been serving
top-quality sushi and sashimi for
decades. "Kiku" means "pricey",
and although prices do start
at relatively cheap for sushi,
they rapidly rise. Take a seat at
the counter and wonder at the
dexterity of the knife man. £££

Mayfair Chippy

MAP PAGE 46, POCKET MAP D16
14 North Audley St ⊖ Marble Arch
Ⓦ mayfairchippy.com.
It's not easy to find good fish and
chips in London, but Mayfair
Chippy certainly pulls it off; it's
upscale but still traditional. The
oysters and salt and pepper squid
are divine. £££

Phoenix Palace

MAP PAGE 46, POCKET MAP A12
5 Glentworth St ⊖ Baker Street
Ⓦ phoenixpalace.co.uk.
There's plenty to choose from in
this huge, popular restaurant, with
dishes from all over China. Good
dim sum, too, served till 5pm. £££

Pollen Street Social

MAP PAGE 41, POCKET MAP D15
8/10 Pollen St ⊖ Oxford Circus
Ⓦ pollenstreetsocial.com.
Michelin-starred restaurant from
wunderkind chef Jason Atherton,
who produces delicate cuisine with
wit and flair. ££££

Sabor

MAP PAGE 41, POCKET MAP D16
35 Heddon St ⊖ Oxford Circus or Piccadilly
Circus Ⓦ saborrestaurants.co.uk.
Michelin-starred Spanish
restaurant with a fun, lively
atmosphere; impeccable, friendly

service and incredible food including prawn croquettes, fried pig ears and monkfish tempura. ££££

Wild Honey

MAP PAGE 41, POCKET MAP D15
12 St George St ⊖ Oxford Circus or Bond Street ⓦ wildhoneystjames.co.uk.
Very popular, high-end wood-panelled brasserie, serving up a daily-changing menu of slow-cooked, seasonal UK-sourced haute cuisine. £££

Pubs and bars

Audley

MAP PAGE 41, POCKET MAP B16
41 Mount St ⊖ Bond Street or Green Park ⓦ theaudleypublichouse.com.
A grand Mayfair pub, with its original Victorian woodwork, chandeliers and clock.

Golden Eagle

MAP PAGE 46, POCKET MAP B13
59 Marylebone Lane ⊖ Bond Street.
Proper old neighbourhood pub, made up of one single room – they even have regular singalongs on the old "Joanna".

The Guinea

MAP PAGE 41, POCKET MAP C16
30 Bruton Place ⊖ Bond Street or Oxford Circus ⓦ theguinea.co.uk.
Pretty, old-fashioned, flower-strewn back-lane pub, serving good Young's bitter and tasty pies and steak sandwiches. There's a traditional steak restaurant (*The Guinea Grill*) attached.

The Windmill

MAP PAGE 41, POCKET MAP D15
6–8 Mill St ⊖ Oxford Circus ⓦ windmillmayfair.co.uk.
Convivial, well-regarded pub just off Regent Street, a perfect retreat for exhausted shoppers with a summer roof terrace. The Young's beers are top-notch, as are the award-winning pies.

Venues

The Phoenix

MAP PAGE 41, POCKET MAP D14
37 Cavendish Square ⊖ Oxford Circus ⓦ phoenixcavendishsquare.co.uk.
Friendly pub/club with a roster of enjoyable basement club nights from indie via disco to soul, plus good comedy nights.

Wigmore Hall

MAP PAGE 46, POCKET MAP C14
36 Wigmore St ⊖ Bond Street ⓦ wigmore-hall.org.uk.
With its near-perfect acoustics, this intimate classical and chamber music venue – originally a piano showroom – is a favourite with artists and audiences alike. Book ahead.

Golden Eagle

Soho and Covent Garden

Soho is very much the heart of the West End, home to more theatres and cinemas than any other single area in London. As the city's premier red-light district for centuries, it retains an unorthodox and slightly raffish air that's unique in central London. Conventional sights are few and far between, yet it's a great area to wander through – whatever the hour there's always something going on. Soho has long been one of London's LGBTQ+ quarters, focused around Old Compton Street. More sanitized and brazenly commercial, Covent Garden is one of London's chief tourist attractions, thanks to its buskers, pedestrianized piazza and old Victorian market hall. Some three centuries ago the piazza was the great playground of eighteenth-century London. Nowadays, while the market is pretty, but touristy, the streets to the north boast some very fashionable boutiques.

Leicester Square

MAP PAGE 54, POCKET MAP G16

⊖ Leicester Square.

By night, when the big cinemas and nightclubs are doing brisk

Leicester Square

business and the buskers are entertaining passers-by, Leicester Square is one of the most crowded places in London; on a Friday or Saturday night, it can seem as if half the youth of the city's suburbs have congregated here to get drunk, supplemented by a vast number of tourists. As a result, most Londoners avoid the place unless they're heading for one of the cinemas. It wasn't until the mid-nineteenth century that the square began to emerge as an entertainment zone, with accommodation houses (for prostitutes and their clients) and music halls. These included the grandiose **Empire**, now a cinema that's a favourite for big red-carpet premieres, and a couple of blocks east the **Hippodrome** – designed by Frank Matcham in 1900 – which is now the UK's biggest casino. Purpose-built movie houses moved in during the 1930s – a golden age evoked by the sleek black lines of the **Odeon** on the east side – and maintain their grip on the area.

Chinatown

Chinatown

MAP PAGE 54, POCKET MAP F15–G15
⊖ Leicester Square.

A self-contained jumble of shops, cafés and restaurants, Chinatown is one of London's most distinct and popular ethnic enclaves. Centred around **Gerrard Street**, it's a tiny area of no more than three or four blocks, thick with the aromas of Chinese cooking and peppered with ersatz touches. Few of London's sixty thousand Chinese actually live in Chinatown, but it nonetheless remains a focus for the community: a place to do business or the weekly shopping, celebrate a wedding, or just meet up for meals – particularly on Sundays, when the restaurants overflow with Chinese families tucking into dim sum. Most Londoners come to Chinatown simply to eat – easy and inexpensive enough to do. Cantonese cuisine predominates, though the quality is variable.

Charing Cross Road

MAP PAGE 54, POCKET MAP F14–G1
⊖ Leicester Square. 6

Charing Cross Road, which marks Soho's eastern border, boasts the highest concentration of bookshops anywhere in London. One of the first to open here, in 1906, was **Foyles** originally at no. 119 – Éamon de Valera, George Bernard Shaw, Walt Disney and Arthur Conan Doyle were all once regular customers. Now you'll find Foyles in vast premises at no. 107 (see page 60). You'll find more of Charing Cross Road's original character at the string of specialist and secondhand bookshops south of Cambridge Circus. One of the nicest places for specialist and antiquarian book-browsing is **Cecil Court**, the southernmost pedestrianized alleyway between Charing Cross Road and St Martin's Lane. These short, civilized, paved alleys boast specialist bookshops, plus various antiquarian dealers selling modern first editions, old theatre posters, coins and notes, cigarette cards, maps and children's books.

Old Compton Street

MAP PAGE 54, POCKET MAP F15–G15
⊖ Leicester Square.

If Soho has a main drag, it has to be Old Compton Street, which

SOHO AND COVENT GARDEN

Soho and Covent Garden

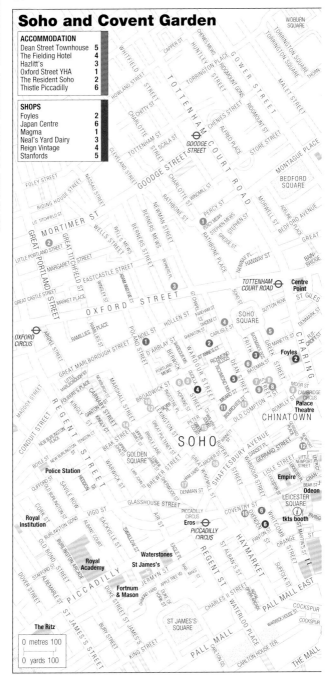

ACCOMMODATION

Dean Street Townhouse	5
The Fielding Hotel	4
Hazlitt's	3
Oxford Street YHA	1
The Resident Soho	2
Thistle Piccadilly	6

SHOPS

Foyles	2
Japan Centre	6
Magma	1
Neal's Yard Dairy	3
Reign Vintage	4
Stanfords	5

0 metres 100

0 yards 100

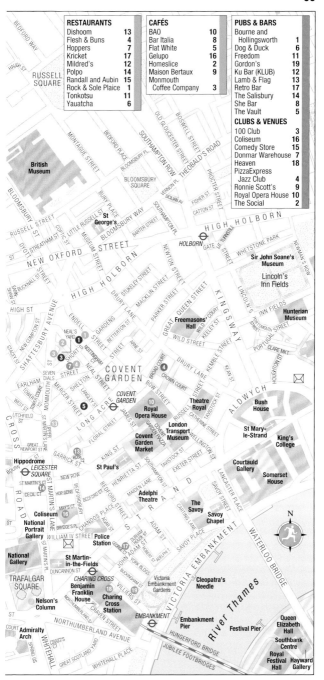

RESTAURANTS

Dishoom	13
Flesh & Buns	4
Hoppers	7
Kricket	17
Mildred's	12
Polpo	14
Randall and Aubin	15
Rock & Sole Plaice	1
Tonkotsu	11
Yauatcha	6

CAFÉS

BAO	10
Bar Italia	8
Flat White	5
Gelupo	16
Homeslice	2
Maison Bertaux	9
Monmouth Coffee Company	3

PUBS & BARS

Bourne and Hollingsworth	1
Dog & Duck	6
Freedom	11
Gordon's	19
Ku Bar (KLUB)	12
Lamb & Flag	13
Retro Bar	17
The Salisbury	14
She Bar	8
The Vault	5

CLUBS & VENUES

100 Club	3
Coliseum	16
Comedy Store	15
Donmar Warehouse	7
Heaven	18
PizzaExpress Jazz Club	4
Ronnie Scott's	9
Royal Opera House	10
The Social	2

Covent Garden Market

runs parallel to Shaftesbury Avenue. The old-school pubs, seedy shops, boutiques, cafés and bars here are typical of the area and a good barometer of the latest Soho fads. The liberal atmosphere of Soho has also made it a permanent fixture on the **gay and queer scene** since the last century, with gay bars, clubs and cafés jostling for position on Old Compton Street. Its cross-streets – Greek, Frith and Dean – feature a tempting mix of old-school Italian cafés, jazz clubs, members' bars and new restaurants.

Carnaby Street

MAP PAGE 54, POCKET MAP E15
⊖ **Oxford Circus.**
Carnaby Street was famous as the fashion focus of London's Swinging Sixties. A victim of its own hype, it quickly declined into an avenue of overpriced tack, and so it remained for several decades. Nowadays, it's pedestrianized and smart again, but dominated by chains – for any sign of contemporary London fashion, you have to go round the corner to **Foubert's Place** and **Newburgh**

Street. Kingsly Court, tucked away just off Carnaby Street, hosts some of the better dining a nd drinking options.

Covent Garden Piazza

MAP PAGE 54, POCKET MAP H15
⊖ **Covent Garden.**
London's oldest planned square, laid out in the 1630s by Inigo Jones, Covent Garden Piazza was initially a great success – its novelty value alone ensured a rich and aristocratic clientele for the surrounding properties. Over the next century, though, the tone of the place fell as the fruit and vegetable **market** expanded, and theatres and coffee houses began to move in. Eventually, a large covered market was constructed in the middle of the square, but when the market closed in 1974, it was very nearly demolished to make way for an office development. Instead, the elegant Victorian market hall and its largely pedestrianized, cobbled piazza were restored to house shops, restaurants and craft stalls.

Cleopatra's Needle

London's oldest monument, **Cleopatra's Needle** (Map page 54, Pocket Map J16) languishes little-noticed on the busy Victoria Embankment, guarded by two Victorian sphinxes (facing the wrong way). The 60ft-high, 180-ton stick of granite actually has nothing to do with Cleopatra – it's one of a pair erected in Heliopolis in 1475 BC (the other one is in New York's Central Park) and taken to Alexandria by Emperor Augustus fifteen years after Cleopatra's suicide. This obelisk was presented to Britain in 1819 by the Turkish viceroy of Egypt, but nearly sixty years passed before it finally made its way to London. It was erected in 1878, above a time capsule containing, among other things, the day's newspapers, a box of hairpins, a railway timetable and pictures of the country's twelve prettiest women.

The piazza is now one of London's major tourist attractions.

St Paul's Church

MAP PAGE 54, POCKET MAP H15
Bedford St ⊖ Covent Garden
ⓦ actorschurch.org. Free.

The proximity of so many theatres has earned this church the nickname of the "**Actors' Church**", and it's filled with memorials to international thespians from Boris Karloff to Gracie Fields. The space in front of the church's Tuscan portico – where Eliza Doolittle was discovered selling violets by Henry Higgins in George Bernard Shaw's *Pygmalion* – is now a legalized venue for the piazza's buskers and street performers, who must audition for a slot months in advance. Round the back, the **churchyard** provides a tranquil respite from the activity outside.

London Transport Museum

MAP PAGE 54, POCKET MAP H15
Covent Garden Piazza ⊖ Covent Garden
ⓦ ltmuseum.co.uk. Charge; kids free.

Housed in the piazza's former flower market, the ever-popular London Transport Museum is a surefire hit for families with kids. To follow the story of London's transport chronologically, head for Level 2, where you'll find a reconstructed 1829 Shillibeer's Horse Omnibus, which provided the city's first regular horse-bus service. Level 1 tells the story of the world's first underground

London Transport Museum

Half-price theatre tickets

The Society of London Theatre (Ⓦ tkts.co.uk) runs the **TKTS booth** in Leicester Square, which sells tickets for all the West End shows for the same day and two days ahead, with discounts of up to fifty percent.

system and contains a lovely 1920s Metropolitan line carriage, fitted out in burgundy and green with pretty, drooping lamps. Down on the ground floor, you can peep inside the first tube train, from the 1890s, whose lack of windows earned it the nickname "the padded cell". Most of the interactive stuff is aimed at kids, but visitors of all ages should check out the tube driver simulator. You can buy reproductions of the Tube's stylish maps and posters, many commissioned from well-known artists, at the shop on the way out.

Royal Opera House

MAP PAGE 54, POCKET MAP H15
Bow St ⊖ Covent Garden Ⓦ roh.org.uk.
In 2018, the arcading in the northeast corner of the piazza was rebuilt as part of the multi-million pound refurbishment of the Royal Opera House; the building's Neoclassical facade, dating from 1811, opens onto Bow Street. The market's spectacular wrought-iron **Floral Hall** now serves as the opera house's impressive first-floor foyer and champagne bar; the next level up is a terrace overlooking the piazza, beyond the *Amphitheatre* bar/restaurant. Excellent **backstage tours** of the opera house (advance booking is recommended) give you a sense of the huge scale of the operation, and depending on the day's schedule, can include a look-in at ballet rehearsals.

Freemasons' Hall

MAP PAGE 54, POCKET MAP H14
60 Great Queen St ⊖ Covent Garden
Ⓦ ugle.org.uk/freemasons-hall. Free.
It's difficult to miss the austere, Pharaonic mass of the Freemasons'

Hall, built as a memorial to all the masons who died in World War I. The interior is worth a peek for the **Grand Temple** alone, whose pompous, bombastic decor is laden with heavy symbolism. To see it, you must sign up for one of the free guided tours. There's a museum of masonic regalia, and a shop, too.

Benjamin Franklin House

MAP PAGE 54, POCKET MAP H16
36 Craven St ⊖ Charing Cross
Ⓦ benjaminfranklinhouse.org. Charge.
From 1757 to 1775, **Benjamin Franklin** (1706–90) lived in London espousing the cause of the British colonies (of which the US was then one), before returning to America to help draft the Declaration of Independence and the US Constitution. Wisely, the curators have left Franklin's house pretty much empty, eschewing any attempt to install period furniture. Instead, aided by a costumed guide and a series of impressionistic audiovisuals, visitors are transported back to the time of Franklin, who lived here with his "housekeeper" in cosy domesticity while his wife and daughter languished in Philadelphia. Note that visits are by guided tour only and should be booked in advance. Shorter tours focusing on the history of the building run on Mondays.

Victoria Embankment

MAP PAGE 54, POCKET MAP J16–H19
⊖ Temple or Embankment.
Built between 1868 and 1874, the Victoria Embankment was the inspiration of civil engineer **Joseph Bazalgette**, whose project

simultaneously relieved congestion along the Strand, provided an extension to the underground railway and sewage systems, and created a new stretch of parkland, now dotted with statues and memorials, and a riverside walk – no longer much fun due to the volume of traffic that barrels along it, though it does afford some good views over the river.

Somerset House

MAP PAGE 54, POCKET MAP J16
Victoria Embankment ⊖ Temple
Ⓦ somersethouse.org.uk. Free.

Sole survivor of the grand edifices which once lined this stretch of the riverfront, Somerset House's four wings enclose an elegant and surprisingly large courtyard. From March to October, a wonderful 55-jet fountain spouts straight from the courtyard's cobbles; in winter, an ice rink is set up in its place. The monumental Palladian building itself was begun in 1776 by William Chambers as a purpose-built governmental office development, but now houses a series of exhibition spaces, and puts on events throughout the year. Various free **guided tours** are available.

In the house's north wing is the **Courtauld Gallery** (charge; Ⓦ courtauld.ac.uk), chiefly known for their dazzling permanent collection of Impressionist and Post-Impressionist paintings. It reopened in 2021 following the most significant modernisation project in its history, providing a transformed home for what some consider to be one of the UK's greatest art collections. Among the most celebrated works are a small-scale version of Manet's nostalgic *Bar at the Folies-Bergère,* Renoir's *La Loge* and Degas' *Two Dancers,* plus a whole heap of Cézanne's canvases, including one of his series of *Card Players.* The Courtauld also boasts a fine selection of works by the likes of Bellini, Brueghel, Rubens, van Dyck, Tiepolo and Cranach the Elder.

Embankment Gardens

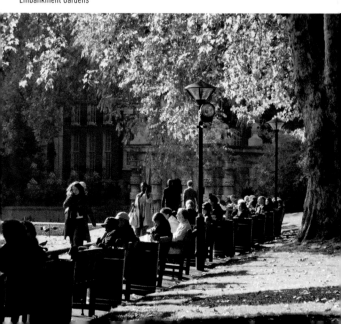

Shops

Foyles

MAP PAGE 54, POCKET MAP G14

107 Charing Cross Rd ⊖ Tottenham Court Road Ⓦ foyles.co.uk.

Long-established, famous and huge bookshop with an excellent selection of titles old and new, plus a jazz music store, a café and a gallery.

Japan Centre

MAP PAGE 54, POCKET MAP F16

35b Panton St ⊖ Piccadilly Circus Ⓦ japancentre.com.

This basement shop and food centre is cram-packed with everything Japanese: *the* place to get every variety of noodle, sushi ingredients, fresh miso, sake and Japanese whiskies. Also has food counters for ramen and other treats.

Neal's Yard Dairy

Magma

MAP PAGE 54, POCKET MAP G14

29 Shorts Gardens ⊖ Covent Garden Ⓦ magma-shop.com.

It's difficult to leave this sleek store empty-handed, filled as it is with beautifully designed, whimsical and affordable gifts, toys, homeware, stationery, books and gizmos.

Neal's Yard Dairy

MAP PAGE 54, POCKET MAP G14

17 Shorts Gardens ⊖ Covent Garden Ⓦ nealsyarddairy.co.uk.

London's finest cheese shop, with a huge selection of quality cheeses from around the British Isles, as well as a few exceptionally good ones from Europe. They're happy for you to taste before you buy.

Reign Vintage

MAP PAGE 54, POCKET MAP F15

12 Berwick St ⊖ Oxford Circus Ⓦ reignvintage.com.

In the heart of rapidly gentrifying Berwick Street, this spruce secondhand shop is a cut above its rivals, sourcing its gear from Europe and helpfully organizing it by colour and style.

Stanfords

MAP PAGE 54, POCKET MAP H15

7 Mercer Walk ⊖ Covent Garden Ⓦ stanfords.co.uk.

The world's largest specialist travel bookshop, stocking pretty much any map of anywhere, plus a huge range of guides, travel literature and gifts.

Cafés

BAO

MAP PAGE 54, POCKET MAP E15

53 Lexington St ⊖ Piccadilly Circus Ⓦ baolondon.com/restaurant/bao-soho.

Minimalist *BAO* is a firm favourite for authentic Taiwanese food. Reservations aren't taken, and queues snake down the road for the moreish, fluffy steamed buns. £

Bar Italia

MAP PAGE 54, POCKET MAP F15
22 Frith St ⊖ Tottenham Court Road
Ⓦ baritaliasoho.co.uk.
This tiny coffee bar is a Soho institution, serving espressos, croissants and sandwiches around the clock (it's open until 4am every day) – as it has been since the 50s. £

Flat White

MAP PAGE 54, POCKET MAP F15
17 Berwick St ⊖ Piccadilly Circus
Ⓦ flatwhitesoho.co.uk.
Famous for introducing the capital to the flat white in 2005 (before it was cool), this is an intimate, kiwi-inspired café that's popular with Londoners and visitors alike. £

Gelupo

MAP PAGE 54, POCKET MAP F15
7 Archer St ⊖ Piccadilly Circus Ⓦ gelupo. com.
The place for artisan gelatos, sorbets and granitas – from roasted plum to burnt caramel and bitter chocolate sorbet (flavours change every day) – and good strong Italian coffee. £

Homeslice

MAP PAGE 54, POCKET MAP G14
13 Neal's Yard ⊖ Covent Garden
Ⓦ homeslicepizza.co.uk.
Buzzing place offering wood-fired thin-crust gourmet pizzas with inventive toppings (think curried minced lamb and tarragon pesto or vegan fennel sausage and lemon pangrattato) plus fizz on tap; you can buy by the slice, or the 20-inch pizza. £

Maison Bertaux

MAP PAGE 54, POCKET MAP G15
28 Greek St ⊖ Leicester Square or Tottenham Court Road Ⓦ maisonbertaux. com.
Long-standing, old-fashioned and wonderfully French patisserie with two floors inside and charming street-side tables. Fabulous cakes,

Maison Bertaux

tarts and croissants in a lively, pretty setting. £

Monmouth Coffee Company

MAP PAGE 54, POCKET MAP G14
27 Monmouth St ⊖ Covent Garden
Ⓦ monmouthcoffee.co.uk.
The marvellous aroma hits you when you walk into this cosy coffee house. Pick your coffee from a fine selection, buy the beans to take home, and grab a pastry to go. £

Restaurants

Dishoom

MAP PAGE 54, POCKET MAP G15
12 Upper St Martin's Lane ⊖ Leicester Square Ⓦ dishoom.com.
Re-creating the atmosphere of the Persian cafés of Old Bombay, this is a buzzy place which serves delicious Indian food; the breakfasts are a hit too. Arrive early, or be prepared to queue. £££

Flesh & Buns

Flesh & Buns

MAP PAGE 54, POCKET MAP G15
41 Earlham St ⊖ Covent Garden
Ⓦ fleshandbuns.com.
Enjoy delicious rice buns with
meat or fish, washed down
with sake, at this loud, friendly,
rock'n'roll *izakaya*-style basement
restaurant; lunch or pre-theatre
set menu. £££

Hoppers

MAP PAGE 54, POCKET MAP F15
49 Frith St ⊖ Leicester Square
Ⓦ hopperslondon.com.
Outstanding, moreish Sri Lankan
food – fiery, unusual curries are
accompanied by "hoppers", bowl-
shaped rice pancakes, or rotis. No
reservations; come early. ££

Kricket

MAP PAGE 54, POCKET MAP E16
12 Denman St ⊖ Piccadilly Circus
Ⓦ kricket.co.uk.
It started life as a pop-up in a
shipping container food market
in South London, but *Kricket* has
now transplanted to Soho, where it

serves sophisticated, gently spiced
cocktails alongside a delicious
menu of small sharing plates of
intriguing Indian dishes. The
menu changes seasonally, but the
samphire pakora and Keralan fried
chicken are firm favourites. £

Mildred's

MAP PAGE 54, POCKET MAP E15
45 Lexington St ⊖ Oxford Circus
Ⓦ mildreds.com.
This cheery veggie restaurant
is a Soho stand-by, serving a
wholesome, delicious and varied
menu of burgers, curries and pies,
as well as wicked but wonderful
puddings. No bookings. ££

Polpo

MAP PAGE 54, POCKET MAP E15
41 Beak St ⊖ Piccadilly Circus Ⓦ polpo.
co.uk.
Fabulous bar-restaurant modelled
on a Venetian *bacaro*. Delicious
small plates – try the crab and
chilli linguine, *pizzette* or any
of the *polpette* (meatballs).
Reservations for lunch; limited
ones for dinner – you may have to
queue. £££

Randall and Aubin

MAP PAGE 54, POCKET MAP F15
16 Brewer St ⊖ Piccadilly Circus
Ⓦ randallandaubin.com.
London's best seafood restaurant
is oh-so chic, darling. With some
seating that faces out onto the
street ideal for people watching
and huge windows that open in
summer, there's a certain European
vibe here; come for a full seafood
dinner or simply to toss back an
oyster or two before you're on your
way. £££

Rock & Sole Plaice

MAP PAGE 54, POCKET MAP H14
47 Endell St ⊖ Covent Garden
Ⓦ rockandsoleplaice.com.
Pricey fish-and-chip shop,
where they do all the staples just
right; you eat in or at one of the
pavement tables. ££

Tonkotsu

MAP PAGE 54, POCKET MAP F15

63 Dean St ⊖ Tottenham Court Road

Ⓦ tonkotsu.co.uk.

Slurpable, silky home-made ramen noodles in rich, savoury stocks, with pork belly, seafood or veggie options – the first in a rapidly expanding franchise. £

Yauatcha

MAP PAGE 54, POCKET MAP E15

15–17 Broadwick St ⊖ Piccadilly Circus

Ⓦ yauatcha.com.

Sleek, contemporary Chinese teahouse-restaurant serving up dim sum and classy patisserie throughout the day. £££

Pubs and bars

Bourne and Hollingsworth

MAP PAGE 54, POCKET MAP F13

28 Rathbone Place ⊖ Goodge Street

Ⓦ bourneandhollingsworth.com.

Prohibition-style vintage cocktail bar in a tucked-away basement, offering a playful, changing cocktail menu.

Dog & Duck

MAP PAGE 54, POCKET MAP F15

18 Bateman St ⊖ Tottenham Court Road.

Tiny Nicholson's pub that retains much of its old character, with beautiful Victorian tiling and mosaics, plus a decent range of real ales.

Freedom

MAP PAGE 54, POCKET MAP F15

66 Wardour St ⊖ Piccadilly Circus

Ⓦ freedombarsoho.com.

Established gay bar, popular with a mixed straight and queer Soho crowd. It's a good spot for evening drinks, and the basement hosts various cabaret and club nights.

Gordon's

MAP PAGE 54, POCKET MAP H17

47 Villiers St ⊖ Embankment

Ⓦ gordonswinebar.com.

Cavernous, shabby, atmospheric wine bar specializing in ports and sherries. The excellent and varied wine list, decent buffet food and genial atmosphere make this a favourite with local office workers, who spill outdoors in the summer.

Ku Bar

MAP PAGE 54, POCKET MAP G15

30 Lisle St ⊖ Leicester Square.

The Lisle Street original, with a downstairs club open late, is one of Soho's largest and best-loved gay bars, serving a scene-conscious yet low-on-attitude clientele. It's joined by a stylish sibling bar on Frith Street.

Lamb & Flag

MAP PAGE 54, POCKET MAP G15

33 Rose St ⊖ Leicester Square or Covent Garden Ⓦ lambandflagcoventgarden.co.uk.

Small, popular historic pub hidden away down an alley between Garrick Street and Floral Street where the Poet Laureate, John Dryden, was beaten up in 1679 by a group of thugs, hired most probably by his rival poet, the Earl of Rochester.

Gordon's

Retro Bar

MAP PAGE 54, POCKET MAP H16
2 George Court, off Strand ⊖ Charing Cross
ⓦ retrobarlondon.co.uk.
Indie/retro gay bar tucked down
a quiet alleyway, playing 1970s
and 80s rock, pop, rockabilly and
alternative sounds, and featuring
regular pub quizzes and DJ
nights.

The Salisbury

MAP PAGE 54, POCKET MAP G16
90 St Martin's Lane ⊖ Leicester Square.
Well-preserved Victorian pub
with cut, etched and engraved
windows, bronze lampstands, Art
Nouveau light fittings and a fine
Lincrusta ceiling.

She Bar

MAP PAGE 54, POCKET MAP F15
23 Old Compton St ⊖ Leicester Square
ⓦ instagram.com/shesohobar.

The Salisbury

Rather swish lesbian bar in the
heart of Soho for queer women,
non-binary folk and their guests,
with regular DJ nights, drag king
shows, and burlesque plus good-
value drinks offers; women-only at
busy times.

The Vault

MAP PAGE 54, POCKET MAP F15
3 Greek Street ⊖ Tottenham Court Road
ⓦ milroysofsoho.com/pages/soho-the-
vault.
A gorgeous underground speakeasy
hidden behind a bookshelf at the
back of Milroy's, which in itself is
a cosy bar specialising in rare malt
whiskeys as well as fine wines and
champagnes. Both are tiny so it's
wise to book.

Clubs and venues

100 Club

MAP PAGE 54, POCKET MAP E14
100 Oxford St ⊖ Tottenham Court Road
ⓦ the100club.co.uk.
Fun venue whose history stretches
back to 1942 and takes in Louis
Armstrong, Glenn Miller and the
Sex Pistols. Now hosts eclectic rock
and indie, with some jazz.

Coliseum

MAP PAGE 54, POCKET MAP G16
St Martin's Lane ⊖ Leicester Square
ⓦ eno.org.
Home to the English National
Opera, which differs from its Royal
Opera House counterpart in that
all its operas are sung in English,
productions tend to be more
experimental, and tickets cost a
lot less.

Comedy Store

MAP PAGE 54, POCKET MAP F16
1a Oxendon St ⊖ Piccadilly Circus
ⓦ thecomedystore.co.uk.
Venerable alternative-comedy
venue, with improv by in-house
comics and a regular stand-up bill.
Weekends are busiest, with two
shows – book ahead.

Royal Opera House

Donmar Warehouse

MAP PAGE 54, POCKET MAP G15
41 Earlham St ⊖ Covent Garden
Ⓦ donmarwarehouse.com.
Excellent theatre noted for its new
plays, top-quality reappraisals of
the classics and star-studded casts.

Heaven

MAP PAGE 54, POCKET MAP H17
Villiers St ⊖ Charing Cross
Ⓦ heavennightclub-london.com.
Wildly popular, iconic gay club
pulling a mixed, up-for-it crowd for
big-name G-A-Y weekend nights
and Popcorn Mondays. Gig listings
too, check website for details.

PizzaExpress Jazz Club

MAP PAGE 54, POCKET MAP F15
10 Dean St ⊖ Tottenham Court Road
Ⓦ pizzaexpresslive.com/venues/soho-
jazz-club.
This branch of the chain restaurant
has a jazz club in the basement.
There's live music seven nights a
week, often from world-class and
internationally-renowned artists –
and you can grab a delicious pizza
or bowl of pasta upstairs before or
after the show.

Ronnie Scott's

MAP PAGE 54, POCKET MAP F15
47 Frith St ⊖ Tottenham Court Road
Ⓦ ronniescotts.co.uk.
The most famous jazz club in
London, this small and atmospheric
place with smart decor is pricey, but
still hosts the best jazz acts in town.

Royal Opera House

MAP PAGE 54, POCKET MAP H15
Bow St ⊖ Covent Garden Ⓦ roh.org.uk.
The ROH can't quite shake
its reputation for elitism, and
certainly its lavish operas are
expensive – though ballet tickets
are a little cheaper. Tickets are best
booked well in advance, though
every Friday at 1pm 49 tickets for
performances for the following
week are released online.

The Social

MAP PAGE 54, POCKET MAP D13
5 Little Portland St ⊖ Oxford Circus
Ⓦ thesocial.com.
Retro club-bar with eclectic live
music and great DJs playing
everything from afro to electronica
to a truly hedonistic, hard-
drinking crowd.

Bloomsbury

Bloomsbury was built in grid-plan style from the 1660s onwards, and the formal, bourgeois Georgian squares laid out then remain the area's main distinguishing feature. In the twentieth century, Bloomsbury acquired a reputation as the city's most learned quarter, dominated by the dual institutions of the British Museum and London's central universities, and home to many of London's chief book publishers, but perhaps best known for its literary inhabitants, among them T.S. Eliot and Virginia Woolf. To its north are the busy main-line train stations of Euston, St Pancras and King's Cross – beyond which, straddling the canal, is one of the city's most dynamic redeveloped quarters.

British Museum

MAP PAGE 68, POCKET MAP G13
Great Russell St ⊖ Tottenham Court Road
ⓦ **britishmuseum.org. Free; exhibitions charge.**

One of the great museums of the world, the BM contains an incredible collection of antiquities, prints, drawings and books. Begun in 1823, the building itself is the grandest of London's Greek Revival edifices, with its central **Great Court** featuring a remarkable curving glass-and-steel roof designed by Norman Foster. At the Court's centre stands the copper-domed former **Round Reading Room** of the British Library, where Karl Marx penned *Das Kapital* (currently closed to the

Great Court, British Museum

public). Enquire at the information desk in the Great Court about free room tours, highlights tours and audioguides.

The BM's collection of **Roman and Greek antiquities** is unparalleled, and is most famous for the Parthenon sculptures, better known as the **Elgin Marbles** after the British aristocrat who walked off with the reliefs in 1801. Elsewhere, the **Egyptian collection** is easily the most significant outside Egypt, ranging from monumental sculptures to the ever-popular mummies and their ornate outer caskets. Also on display is the **Rosetta Stone**, which enabled French professor Champollion to finally unlock the secret of Egyptian hieroglyphs. Other highlights include a splendid series of **Assyrian reliefs** from Nineveh, and several extraordinary artefacts from **Mesopotamia** such as the enigmatic *Ram in the Thicket* (a goat statuette in lapis lazuli and shell) and the remarkable hoard of goldwork known as the Oxus Treasure.

The leathery half-corpse of the 2000-year-old **Lindow Man**, discovered in a Cheshire bog, and the Anglo-Saxon treasure from the **Sutton Hoo** ship burial, by far the richest single archeological find made in Britain, are among the highlights of the **Europe** collection, which ranges from the twelfth-century **Lewis chessmen** carved from walrus ivory to avant-garde Russian ceramics celebrating the 1917 revolution.

The **Enlightenment Gallery**, which once housed the King's Library, directly off the Great Court in the east wing, displays some of the museum's earliest acquisitions and curios, brought back from the far reaches of the British Empire. Just north of the Great Court stands magnificent *Hoa Hakananai'a*, a *moai* stone head sculpture from Easter Island (Rapa Nui). Take the stairs down

Foundling Museum

from here for the museum's superb **African galleries** in the basement. And in the north wing of the museum, closest to the back entrance on Montague Place, there are also fabulous **Asian** treasures including an extraordinary collection of ancient Chinese porcelain.

Foundling Museum

MAP PAGE 68, POCKET MAP J4
40 Brunswick Square ⊖ Russell Square
ⓦ foundlingmuseum.org.uk. Charge.

This museum tells the fascinating story of the **Foundling Hospital**, London's first home for abandoned children founded in 1756 by retired sea captain Thomas Coram. As soon as it was opened, it was besieged, and soon forced to reduce its admissions drastically and introduce a ballot system. Among the most tragic exhibits are the tokens left by the mothers in order to identify the children should they ever be in a position to reclaim them: these range from a heart-rending poem to a simple enamel pot label reading "ale". The museum also boasts an impressive **art collection** including works by Hogarth, Gainsborough and Reynolds, now hung in carefully preserved eighteenth-century interiors of the original hospital.

Charles Dickens Museum

MAP PAGE 68, POCKET MAP K4
48 Doughty St ⊖ Russell Square
ⓦ dickensmuseum.com. Charge.

Dickens moved to this house, now a museum, in 1837 shortly after his marriage to Catherine Hogarth, and they lived here for two years, during which time he wrote *Nicholas Nickleby* and *Oliver Twist*. Catherine gave birth to two of their children in the bedroom here, and her youngest sister, who lived with them, died tragically in Dickens' arms. Much of the house's furniture belonged to Dickens, at one time or another, and there's an early portrait miniature painted by his aunt in 1830. The museum puts on special exhibitions in the adjacent house, no. 49, where you'll also find a café.

Wellcome Collection

MAP PAGE 68, POCKET MAP H4
183 Euston Rd ⊖ Euston or Euston Square
ⓦ wellcomecollection.org. Free.

Excellent temporary exhibitions on topical scientific issues are staged in the ground-floor gallery of the Wellcome Collection, founded by American-born pharmaceutical magnate Henry Wellcome (1853–1936). On the first floor, as part of the permanent collection, **Medicine Man** showcases the weird and wonderful collection of historical and scientific artefacts amassed by Wellcome himself. These range from Florence Nightingale's moccasins to a sign for a Chinese doctor's hung with human teeth, and from erotic figurines to phallic amulets – in other words, this section is an absolute must. Next door, **Medicine Now** focuses on contemporary medical questions, while the top-floor **reading room**

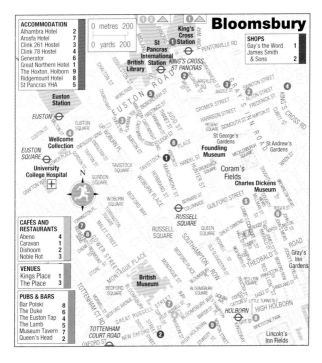

is a quirky, well-designed space for private study and perusing more gruesome exhibits.

British Library

MAP PAGE 68, POCKET MAP H3
96 Euston Rd ⊖ King's Cross St Pancras
🌐 bl.uk. Free.

The red-brick brutalism of the British Library may be horribly out of fashion, but the public exhibition galleries inside are superb. The first place to head for is the dimly lit gallery of **Treasures of the British Library**, where a superlative selection of ancient manuscripts, maps, documents and precious books, including the *Magna Carta*, are displayed. You can also see the Gutenberg Bible, the first to be printed using moveable type; other exhibits, such as Shakespeare first editions, regularly change. The special exhibitions, for which there is sometimes an admission charge, are always excellent.

St Pancras and King's Cross stations

MAP PAGE 68, POCKET MAP J3
Euston Rd.

Completed in 1876, the former Midland Grand Hotel's majestic sweep of Neo-Gothic lancets, dormers and chimney-pots forms the facade of **St Pancras Station**, where Eurostar trains arrive. The adjacent **King's Cross Station**, opened in 1850, is a mere shed in comparison, albeit one with a spectacular semi-circular, glass-roofed concourse on the side. King's Cross is more famous as the station from which **Harry Potter** and his wizarding chums leave for school on the *Hogwarts Express* from platform 9¾. The scenes from the films were shot between platforms 4 and 5, and a station trolley is now embedded in the new concourse wall, providing a perfect photo opportunity for passing Potter fans.

John Betjeman statue, St Pancras Station

King's Cross canal district

MAP PAGE 68, POCKET MAP J2
⊖ King's Cross 🌐 kingscross.co.uk.

To the north of King's Cross, a stretch of Regent's Canal and a cluster of Victorian industrial buildings form focal points for a 67-acre redevelopment project, housing a mixture of high-tech commercial, academic and residential projects. A former granary building, built in 1852 by Lewis Cubitt, architect of King's Cross Station, is home to **Central Saint Martins** school of art, in front of which 1080 fountains jets embedded in the ground dance away in **Granary Square** – irresistible for children on hot days. It's worth exploring the surrounding area of Coal Drops Yard, which has undergone intense redevelopment in the last five years to become an upmarket shopping district and modern public space. There are galleries, restaurants, weekend markets and pleasant green spaces to be found here: some of the area's old **gasholders** have been refurbished, one enclosing a small patch of green, while a footbridge takes you over to **Camley Street Natural Park** (free).

Shops

Gay's the Word

MAP PAGE 68, POCKET MAP J4

66 Marchmont St ⊖ Russell Square

Ⓦ gaystheword.co.uk.

At the UK's oldest LGBTQ+
bookshop, you'll find an extensive
collection of queer classics,
contemporary fiction and non-
fiction, plus cards, calendars and
weekly lesbian discussion groups
and readings.

James Smith & Sons

MAP PAGE 68, POCKET MAP G14

53 New Oxford St ⊖ Tottenham Court Road

Ⓦ james-smith.co.uk.

A survivor from an earlier time
(it was established in 1830), this
beautiful and venerable shop
purveys portable seats and canes,
but its main trade is in umbrellas.

James Smith & Sons

Cafés and restaurants

Abeno

MAP PAGE 68, POCKET MAP H13

47 Museum St ⊖ Tottenham Court Road

Ⓦ abeno.co.uk.

Japanese place that specializes in
okonomiyaki, a stuffed cabbage, egg
and ginger pancake prepared before
your eyes. Noodles and set menus,
too; reservations recommended. ££

Caravan

MAP PAGE 68, POCKET MAP J2

1 Granary Square ⊖ King's Cross St
Pancras Ⓦ caravanandco.com.

A trailblazer on the hip King's
Cross scene – which has since
expanded to eight locations – this
buzzy spot, occupying a huge old
grain store, serves fabulous Modern
European food and coffee to a
lively, in-the-know crowd. £££

Dishoom

MAP PAGE 68, POCKET MAP J2

5 Stable St ⊖ King's Cross St Pancras

Ⓦ dishoom.com.

Dishoom, a mini-chain of gorgeous
Old Bombay-style restaurants, has
nailed sepia-tinted cool and serves
great food. The rich black dhal is a
winner. £££

Noble Rot

MAP PAGE 68, POCKET MAP J12

51 Lamb's Conduit St ⊖ Russel Square

Ⓦ noblerot.co.uk.

A stylish, classic wine bar and
restaurant, known for its extensive
range of wines by the glass. The
restaurant, which serves high-
quality dishes with Mediterranean
influences and impeccable British
ingredients, can be booked, while
bar tables are walk-in only. £££

Pubs and bars

Bar Polski

MAP PAGE 68, POCKET MAP J13

The Lamb greenery

11 Little Turnstile Holborn barpolski.com.
Great Polish bar in an alley near Holborn tube, offering flavoured vodkas and beers, and good, cheap Polish food.

The Duke
MAP PAGE 68, POCKET MAP J12
7 Roger St <N>Russell Square or Holborn.</N>
Cosy neighbourhood pub with lots of interwar design details. Good, simple food, too.

The Euston Tap
MAP PAGE 68, POCKET MAP H4
190 Euston Road <N>Euston</N> <N>eustontap.com.</N>
A huge selection of ales packed into a tiny space – this pub occupies the two original entrance lodges to the old Euston station, and serves a regularly changing selection of cask and craft ales.

The Lamb
MAP PAGE 68, POCKET MAP J12
94 Lamb's Conduit St <N>Russell Square</N> <N>thelamblondon.com.</N>
Marvellously well-preserved Victorian pub of mirrors, polished wood and "snob" screens. The excellent Young's ales round things off splendidly.

Museum Tavern
MAP PAGE 68, POCKET MAP G13
49 Great Russell St <N>Tottenham Court Road.</N>
Large and characterful old pub, opposite the British Museum, and once the drinking hole of Karl Marx. Good range of ales and tasty pub grub.

Queen's Head
MAP PAGE 68, POCKET MAP J4
66 Acton St <N>King's Cross St Pancras.</N>
Laidback little Victorian pub offering craft ales, ciders and a good whisky list, plus simple food (think meat and cheese boards that pair well with pints). Regular live jazz and bar-room piano every Thursday night.

Venues

Kings Place
MAP PAGE 68, POCKET MAP J2
90 York Way <N>King's Cross St Pancras</N> <N>kingsplace.co.uk.</N>
Eclectic venue with several spaces for acoustic and classical music of all stripes, plus spoken word performances and comedy, galleries and other events.

The Place
MAP PAGE 68, POCKET MAP H4
17 Duke's Rd <N>Euston</N> <N>theplace.org.uk.</N>
Excellent small dance theatre presenting the work of new choreographers and student performers, and hosting dance from across the globe, as well as new operas.

The City

The City is where London began, and its boundaries today are only slightly larger than those marked by the Roman walls and their medieval successors. However, you'll find few visible leftovers of London's early days, since four-fifths of it burned down in the Great Fire of 1666. The majority of Londoners lived and worked in or around the City up until the eighteenth century – nowadays, it's primarily one of the world's main financial centres and although three hundred thousand commuters work here, fewer than ten thousand actually live here. The City is only really busy Monday to Friday during the day, so if you're looking for nightlife, you're best off heading for Clerkenwell, which lies on the City's northwest fringe.

Temple

MAP PAGE 74, POCKET MAP K15
⊖ Temple.

Temple is the largest and most complex of the **Inns of Court**, where, since medieval times, every aspiring barrister in England and Wales has had to study in order to qualify for the bar. Despite the fact that only a few very old buildings survive here, the overall atmosphere is like that of an Oxbridge college and the maze of courtyards and passageways is fun to explore – especially after dark, when Temple is gas-lit.

Medieval students ate, attended lectures and slept in the **Middle Temple Hall** (free), still the Inn's main dining room. Constructed in the 1560s, the hall provided the setting for many great

Temple Church

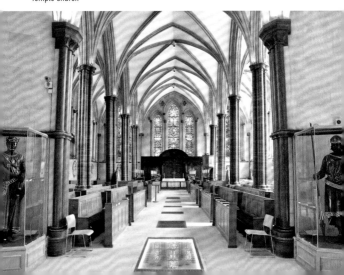

Elizabethan masques and plays – probably including Shakespeare's *Twelfth Night*, which is believed to have been premiered here in 1602. The hall is worth a visit for its fine hammerbeam roof, wooden panelling and decorative Elizabethan screen.

The complex's oldest building, **Temple Church** (£5; Ⓦtemplechurch.com) was built in 1185 by the Knights Templar, the military monks who protected pilgrims heading for the Holy Land. Despite wartime damage, the original round church – modelled on the Holy Sepulchre in Jerusalem – still stands, with its striking Purbeck-marble piers, recumbent marble effigies of knights and tortured grotesques grimacing in the spandrels of the blind arcading. The church features in both the book and the film of *The Da Vinci Code* by Dan Brown.

Fleet Street

MAP PAGE 74, POCKET MAP K6–L6
⊖ Temple.

In the nineteenth century, all the major national and provincial dailies had their offices and **printing presses** in and around Fleet Street. Computer technology rendered the presses here obsolete in the 1980s, however, and within a decade or so all the newspaper headquarters had gone, leaving just a couple of landmarks to testify to five hundred years of printing history. The most remarkable is the city's first glass curtain-wall construction, the former **Daily Express** building at no. 127, with its sleek black Vitrolite facade.

St Bride's

MAP PAGE 74, POCKET MAP L6
Fleet St ⊖ Blackfriars or Temple
Ⓦstbrides.com.

To get a sense of Fleet Street in the days when the press dominated the area, head for the "journalists' and printers' cathedral", St Bride's Church, which boasts Wren's

Lincoln's Inn chapel

tallest and most exquisite spire (said to be the inspiration for the tiered wedding cake). The crypt contains a little museum with a few artefacts dating back to the site's Roman origins.

Lincoln's Inn

MAP PAGE 74, POCKET MAP K14
Lincoln's Inn Fields ⊖ Chancery Lane
Ⓦlincolnsinn.org.uk. Free.

Lincoln's Inn, on the east side of Lincoln's Inn Fields, was the first of the Inns of Court, and in many ways is the prettiest, having miraculously escaped the ravages of the Blitz. Famous alumni include Thomas More, Oliver Cromwell and Margaret Thatcher. The main entrance is the diamond-patterned, red-brick Tudor gateway on Chancery Lane, adjacent to which is the early seventeenth-century **chapel**, with its unusual fan-vaulted open undercroft and, on the first floor, a late Gothic nave, hit by a zeppelin in World War I and much restored since. The Inn's oldest building, the fifteenth-century **Old Hall**, where the lawyers used to live and where Dickens set the case Jarndyce and Jarndyce in *Bleak*

The City

| 0 | metres | 200 |
| 0 | yards | 200 |

ANGEL

City Road Basin

WHITE LION STREET

VINCENT TERR

CITY ROAD

PENTONVILLE ROAD

FINSBURY

GOSWELL ROAD

St Andrew's Gardens

Spa Fields

Postal Museum/Mail Rail

Charles Dickens Museum

Gray's Inn Road

CLERKENWELL

Gray's Inn Gardens

FARRINGDON

CHARTER-HOUSE SQUARE

BARBICAN

CHANCERY LANE

Smithfield Market

St Bartholomew-the-Great

HIGH HOLBORN

St Bartholomew's Hospital

Sir John Soane's Museum

Lincoln's Inn Fields

HOLBORN VIADUCT

Hunterian Museum (closed for redevelopment)

Lincoln's Inn

Dr Johnson's House

City Thameslink Station

Old Bailey (Central Criminal Court)

Royal Courts of Justice

St Clement Danes

St Dunstan-in-the-West

Temple Bar

FLEET STREET

St Bride's

St Paul's Cathedral

Bush House

Temple Church

Inner Temple

St Mary-le-Strand

Middle Temple

King's College

Inner Temple Gardens

BLACKFRIARS

Blackfriars Station

QUEEN VICTORIA

Somerset House

TEMPLE

VICTORIA EMBANKMENT

Blackfriars Millennium Pier

River Thames

N

Festival Pier

National Theatre

THE QUEEN'S WALK

Oxo Tower

Tate Modern

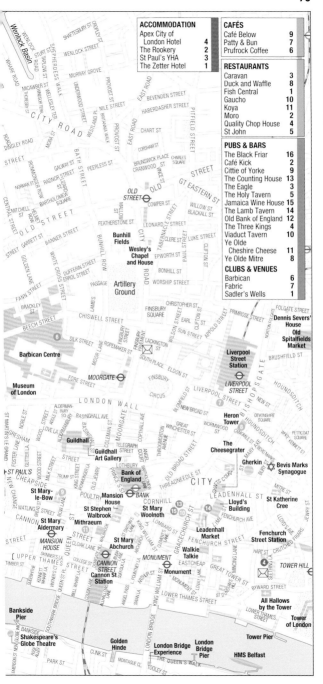

ACCOMMODATION	
Apex City of London Hotel	4
The Rookery	2
St Paul's YHA	3
The Zetter Hotel	1

CAFÉS	
Café Below	9
Patty & Bun	7
Prufrock Coffee	6

RESTAURANTS	
Caravan	3
Duck and Waffle	8
Fish Central	1
Gaucho	10
Koya	11
Moro	2
Quality Chop House	4
St John	5

PUBS & BARS	
The Black Friar	16
Café Kick	2
Cittie of Yorke	9
The Counting House	13
The Eagle	3
The Holy Tavern	5
Jamaica Wine House	15
The Lamb Tavern	14
Old Bank of England	12
The Three Kings	4
Viaduct Tavern	10
Ye Olde Cheshire Cheese	11
Ye Olde Mitre	8

CLUBS & VENUES	
Barbican	6
Fabric	7
Sadler's Wells	1

House, features a fine timber roof, linenfold panelling and an elaborate, early Jacobean screen.

Sir John Soane's Museum

MAP PAGE 74, POCKET MAP J14
12–14 Lincoln's Inn Fields ⊖ Holborn
Ⓦ soane.org. Free.

The chief architect of the Bank of England, **John Soane** (1753–1837) designed this house not only as a home and office but also as a place to stash his large collection of art and antiquities. Arranged much as it was in his lifetime, the ingeniously planned house has an informal, treasure-hunt atmosphere and intriguing spatial tricks, created with Soane's trademark domes, mirrors and skylights. The star exhibits are **Hogarth**'s satirical *Election* series and his merciless morality tale *The Rake's Progress,* as well as the alabaster Egyptian sarcophagus of Seti I rejected by the British Museum. Note that the museum is extremely popular, so you may have to queue – and leave bags in the cloakroom. To see Soane's private apartments, which include a display of his architectural models, you need to join a free tour, or highlights tour (charge).

Dr Johnson's House

MAP PAGE 74, POCKET MAP L6
17 Gough Square ⊖ Blackfriars or Temple
Ⓦ drjohnsonshouse.org. Charge.

Despite appearances, Dr Johnson's House is the only authentic eighteenth-century building on Gough Square. It was here the great savant, writer and lexicographer lived from 1747 to 1759 whilst compiling the 41,000 entries for the first dictionary of the English language. The panelled rooms of the house are peppered with period furniture and lined with portraits and etchings, including one of Johnson's servant Francis Barber. A first-edition of the great *Dictionary* is on display, and you can flick through a reproduction to discover some wonderfully arcane words, such as lucubration (to study by candlelight).

Dr Johnson's House

Old Bailey

MAP PAGE 74, POCKET MAP L6
Newgate St ⊖ St Paul's Ⓦ cityoflondon.
gov.uk. Free.

The **Central Criminal Court** is
more popularly known as the Old
Bailey after the street on which
it stands, which used to form the
outer walls of the medieval city.
It was built on the site of the
notoriously harsh Newgate Prison,
where folk used to come to watch
public hangings. The current,
rather pompous Edwardian
building is distinguished by its
green dome, surmounted by a
gilded statue of Justice, unusually
depicted without blindfold,
holding her sword and scales. The
country's most serious criminal
court cases take place here, and
have included, in the past, the
trials of Lord Haw-Haw, the
Kray twins, and the Guildford
Four and Birmingham Six "IRA
bombers". You can watch the
proceedings from the visitors'
gallery, but large bags, cameras,
mobiles and food and drink are
not allowed in, and there is no
cloakroom.

Statue of Justice on the Old Bailey

Smithfield

MAP PAGE 74, POCKET MAP L5
⊖ Farringdon Ⓦ smithfieldmarket.com.

For more than three centuries
Smithfield was a popular venue for
public executions: the Scottish
hero, William Wallace, was hanged,
disembowelled and beheaded
here in 1305, and the Bishop of
Rochester's cook was boiled alive
in 1531, but the local speciality
was burnings, which reached a
peak in the mid-sixteenth century
during the reign of "Bloody" Mary,
when hundreds of Protestants
were burned at the stake for their
beliefs. These days, Smithfield is
dominated by its historic **meat
market**, housed in a colourful and
ornate Victorian market hall on
Charterhouse Street; try to get here
early – the activity starts around
2am and you should arrive by 7am

to catch the action; monthly tours
are available.

Postal Museum and Mail Rail

MAP PAGE 74, POCKET MAP K4
15–20 Phoenix Place ⊖ King's Cross or
Farringdon. Ⓦ postalmuseum.org. Charge.

Faced with rising city congestion
and an increased demand for
speedy postal delivery, in the early
1900s Royal Mail came up with an
ingenious solution: the **Mail Rail**.
Some 6.5 miles of narrow tunnels
were constructed to run east–west
under the centre of London for
mini-trains to transport the city's
post. It opened in 1927 and
operated until 2003. Now, a mile-
long stretch has been developed as
a tourist attraction – tiny electric
trains whizz you along the tunnels
for 20 minutes, as a former rail
engineer provides the audio tour –
look out for the train "graveyard"
below. It's an intriguing experience,
and the exhibits on the history of
the service are excellent. Just up
the road (and part of the same
operation), the **Postal Museum**
niftily combines a history of the

St Bartholemew-the-Great

postal services with exhibits of vintage vehicles and rare stamps, and hands-on fun – add your own face to a stamp and so on. It's not cheap, but is a good few hours of interest, and very kid-friendly.

St Bartholomew-the-Great

MAP PAGE 74, POCKET MAP L5
Cloth Fair ⊖ Barbican ⓦ greatstbarts. com. Charge.

Begun in 1123, St Bartholomew-the-Great is London's oldest and most atmospheric parish church. Its half-timbered Tudor gatehouse on Little Britain incorporates a thirteenth-century arch that once formed the entrance to the nave; above, a wooden statue of St Bartholomew stands holding the knife with which he was flayed. One side of the medieval cloisters survives to the south, immediately to the right as you enter the church. The rest is a confusion of elements, including portions of the transepts and, most impressively, the chancel, where stout Norman pillars separate the main body of the church from the ambulatory. There are various pre-Fire monuments to admire,

the most prominent being the tomb of Rahere, court jester to Henry I, which shelters under a fifteenth-century canopy north of the main altar.

St Bartholomew's Hospital Museum

MAP PAGE 74, POCKET MAP L5
West Smithfield ⊖ Barbican
ⓦ bartshealth.nhs.uk/bartsmuseum. Free.

Among the medical artefacts, this hospital museum boasts some fearsome amputation instruments, a pair of leather "lunatic restrainers", some great jars with labels such as "poison – for external use only", and a cricket bat autographed by W.G. Grace, who was a student at Bart's in the 1870s. To see the magnificent **Great Hall** you must go on one of the fascinating guided tours, which take in Smithfield and the surrounding area as well; the meeting point is the Henry VIII gate.

Museum of London

MAP PAGE 74, POCKET MAP M5
150 London Wall ⊖ Barbican
ⓦ museumoflondon.org.uk. Free.

Despite London's long pedigree, very few of its ancient structures are still standing. However, numerous Roman, Saxon and Elizabethan remains have been discovered and are now displayed at the Museum of London. The permanent exhibition provides an imaginative and educational trot through London's past from prehistory to the present day. Specific exhibits to look out for include the Bucklersbury Roman mosaic; sculptures from the temple of Mithras, discovered in the City in 1954 (see page 81); a model of Old St Paul's; the Lord Mayor's heavily gilded coach (still used for state occasions); and the cauldron from the 2012 Olympic Games. However th real strength of the museum, though, lies in the excellent temporary exhibitions, lectures, walks and films it organizes throughout the year. There's also a cosey cafe and excellent gift shop on-site.

Guildhall

MAP PAGE 74, POCKET MAP M6
Gresham St ⊖ Bank or Mansion House
ⓦ cityoflondon.gov.uk. Free.

Situated at the geographical centre of the City, Guildhall has been the area's administrative seat for over eight hundred years. It remains the headquarters of the **City of London Corporation**, the City's governing body, and is used for grand civic occasions. Architecturally, however, it's not quite the beauty it once was, having been badly damaged in both the Great Fire and the Blitz, and somewhat scarred by the addition of a grotesque 1970s concrete cloister and wing.

Nonetheless, the **Great Hall**, basically a postwar reconstruction on the fifteenth-century walls, is worth a look if there isn't an event going on. In 1553 the venue for the high-treason trials of Lady Jane Grey and her husband, Lord Dudley, the hall is home

City churches

The City is crowded with churches (ⓦ london-city-churches.org.uk) – well over forty at the last count, the majority of them built or rebuilt by Wren after the Great Fire. Those particularly worth seeking out include **St Dunstan in the West**, its neo-Gothic tower dominating Fleet Street (⊖ Temple; MAP PAGE 74, POCKET MAP K6) and **St Mary Abchurch** (⊖ Cannon Street; MAP PAGE 74, POCKET MAP N6) on Abchurch Lane, unique for an unusual and vast dome fresco painted by a local parishioner and lit by oval lunettes; the superlative lime-wood reredos is by Gibbons. On Lombard Street, **St Mary Woolnoth** (⊖ Bank; MAP PAGE 74, POCKET MAP N6) is a typically idiosyncratic creation of Nicholas Hawksmoor, one of Wren's pupils, featuring an ingenious lantern lit by semicircular clerestory windows and a striking altar canopy held up by barley-sugar columns. **St Mary Aldermary** on Queen Victoria Street (⊖ Mansion House; MAP PAGE 74, POCKET MAP M6) is Wren's most successful stab at Gothic, with fan vaulting in the aisles and a panelled ceiling in the nave, where a café sets up every day. Finally on Walbrook is Wren's most spectacular church interior after St Paul's, **St Stephen Walbrook** (⊖ Bank; MAP PAGE 74, POCKET MAP M6), where sixteen Corinthian columns are arranged in clusters around a central dome, and the dark-wood furnishings are again by Grinling Gibbons.

St Paul's Cathedral

to a handful of vainglorious late eighteenth- and early nineteenth-century monuments, replete with lions, cherubs and ludicrous allegorical figures.

Also worth a visit is the purpose-built **Guildhall Art Gallery**, which contains one or two exceptional works, such as Rossetti's *La Ghirlandata*, plus a massive painting depicting the 1782 Siege of Gibraltar, commissioned by the Corporation. The gallery also hosts regular temporary exhibitions. In the basement, you can view the remains of a **Roman amphitheatre**, dating from around 120 AD, which was discovered during the gallery's construction.

St Paul's Cathedral

MAP PAGE 74, POCKET MAP M6
⊖ St Paul's Ⓦ stpauls.co.uk. Charge.
Designed by **Christopher Wren** and completed in 1710, St Paul's remains a dominating presence in the City despite the encroaching tower blocks. It's topped by an enormous lead-covered dome that's second in size only to St Peter's in Rome, and its showpiece west facade is particularly magnificent.

However, compared to its great rival, Westminster Abbey, St Paul's is a soulless but perfectly calculated architectural set piece, a burial place for captains rather than kings.

The best place to appreciate the building's glory is from beneath the **dome**, adorned (against Wren's wishes) by trompe l'oeil frescoes. The most richly decorated section of the cathedral is the **chancel**, where the late Victorian mosaics of birds, fish, animals and greenery are particularly spectacular. The intricately carved oak and lime-wood choir stalls, and the imposing organ case, are the work of Wren's master carver, Grinling Gibbons.

Beginning in the south aisle, a series of stairs leads to the dome's three galleries, the first of which is the internal **Whispering Gallery**, so called because of its acoustic properties – words whispered to the wall on one side are distinctly audible over one hundred feet away on the other, though you often can't hear much above the hubbub. Of the two exterior galleries, the best views are from the tiny **Golden Gallery**, below the golden ball and cross which top the cathedral.

Although the nave is crammed full of overblown monuments to military types, burials in St Paul's are confined to the **crypt**, reputedly the largest in Europe. The whitewashed walls and bright lighting make this one of London's least atmospheric mausoleums, but **Artists' Corner** here does boast as many painters and architects as Westminster Abbey has poets, including Christopher Wren himself. The star tombs, though, are those of Nelson and Wellington, both occupying centre stage and both with more fanciful monuments upstairs.

It's well worth attending one of the cathedral's **services**, if only to hear the ethereal choir, who perform during most evensongs and on Sundays.

Paternoster Square

MAP PAGE 74, POCKET MAP L6
⊖ St Paul's.

The Blitz destroyed the area immediately to the north of St Paul's, incinerating all the booksellers' shops and around six million books. In their place a modernist pedestrianized piazza was built, only to be torn down in the 1980s and replaced with post-classical office blocks in Portland stone and a Corinthian column topped by a gilded urn. One happy consequence of the square's redevelopment is that **Temple Bar**, the gateway which used to stand at the top of Fleet Street, has found its way back to London after over a hundred years of exile in a park in Hertfordshire. Designed by Wren himself, the triumphal arch, looking weathered but clean, now forms the entrance to Paternoster Square, with the Stuart monarchs, James I and Charles II, and their consorts occupying the niches.

Bank of England

MAP PAGE 74, POCKET MAP M6
Threadneedle St ⊖ Bank
ⓦ bankofengland.co.uk. Free.

Established in 1694 by William III to raise funds for the war against France, the Bank of England stores the official gold reserves of many of the world's central banks. All that remains of the original building, on which John Soane spent the best part of his career (from 1788 onwards), is the windowless outer curtain wall, which wraps itself round the 3.5-acre island site. However, you can view a reconstruction of Soane's Bank Stock Office, with its characteristic domed skylight, in the **museum** (free), which has its entrance on Bartholomew Lane. The permanent exhibition here includes the Bank's original charter and specimens of notes and coins issued by the Bank over the centuries – along with some fakes – plus a gold bar you can feel the weight of. It also attempts to explain the Bank's work in maintaining financial stability through some fairly laboured interactive displays comparing the Bank to a ship's captain in turbulent seas.

Mithraeum (Temple of Mithras)

MAP PAGE 74, POCKET MAP M6
12 Walbrook ⊖ Bank or Cannon Street
ⓦ londonmithraeum.com. Free.

City skyscrapers

Throughout the 1990s, most people's favourite modern building in the City was Richard Rogers' glitzy **Lloyd's Building** – a startling array of glass and blue steel pipes. Lloyd's was eclipsed in the mid-2000s by its near neighbour, Norman Foster's 590ft-high, glass diamond-clad **Gherkin**, which has endeared itself to Londoners thanks to its cheeky shape.

The City skyline continues to sprout yet more skyscrapers, with Richard Rogers' 737ft wedge-shaped office block **The Cheesegrater** (the Leadenhall Building) leading the charge. Close by is the **Scalpel**, a 620ft twisted angular shard of glass, completed in 2018. Still to be finished is the vast, 912ft **22 Bishopsgate**; several even taller constructions are planned, including the 1016ft **1 Undershaft** which will equal the **Shard** in height. More controversial has been Rafael Viñoly's 525ft **Walkie Talkie**, on Fenchurch Street, which features a public "sky garden", as well as bars and restaurants on the top floor (20 Fenchurch St; ⓦ skygarden.london; book free tickets in advance).

In 1954, as the rubble of World War II was being cleared for new developments in the City, archeologists made an extraordinary discovery: the remains of a Roman Temple of Mithras, dedicated to the mysterious all-male cult, and including several sculptures, most famously the head of Mithras – on display at the Museum of London (see page 78). The archeological dig attracted crowds of Londoners, and initially, so as not to disrupt the planned building, the temple remains were reconstructed outside 100m away, where they remained until 2011. In 2017, they were returned to near their original spot, two floors under the new Bloomberg headquarters, and are now presented more accurately, and atmospherically, with sounds and lights used to evoke a sense of cultish mystery. Displayed on the ground floor are some of the numerous archeological finds from the site, including a wooden tablet that is one of the City's earliest financial records, and a tiny amber amulet.

Mansion House

MAP PAGE 74, POCKET MAP M6
Mansion House Place ⊖ Bank
Ⓦ cityoflondon.gov.uk. Access only via group tours.

The Lord Mayor's sumptuous Neoclassical lodgings were designed in 1753. The building's grandest room is the columned **Egyptian Hall** with its barrel-vaulted, coffered ceiling. Also impressive is the vast collection of gold and silver tableware, the mayor's 36-pound gold mace and the pearl sword given by Elizabeth I. Scattered about the rooms are an impressive array of Dutch and Flemish paintings.

Leadenhall Market

MAP PAGE 74, POCKET MAP N6
Leadenhall St ⊖ Monument
Ⓦ leadenhallmarket.co.uk.

Leadenhall Market's picturesque cobbles and graceful Victorian cast-

Bevis Marks Synagogue

Leadenhall Market

ironwork date from 1881. Inside, the traders cater mostly for the lunchtime City crowd.

Bevis Marks Synagogue
MAP PAGE 74, POCKET MAP N6
Bevis Marks ⊖ Aldgate ⓦ sephardi.org.uk/bevis-marks. Charge.

Hidden behind a modern red-brick office block, the Bevis Marks Synagogue was built in 1701 by Sephardic Jews who had fled the Inquisition in Spain and Portugal. It's the country's oldest surviving synagogue, and the roomy, rich interior gives an idea of just how wealthy the worshippers were at the time. The Sephardic community has now dispersed across London and the congregation has dwindled, but the magnificent array of chandeliers ensures that it's a popular venue for candle-lit Jewish weddings. The synagogue was closed at time of writing and due to reopen in 2024.

Monument
MAP PAGE 74, POCKET MAP N6
Monument St ⊖ Monument
ⓦ themonument.org.uk. Charge.

The Monument was designed by Wren to commemorate the **Great Fire of London**, which raged for five days in early September 1666 and destroyed four-fifths of the City. A plain Doric column crowned with spiky gilded flames, it stands 202ft high, making it the tallest isolated stone column in the world; if it were laid out flat it would touch the site of the bakery where the Fire started, east of the Monument. The bas-relief on the base depicts Charles II and the Duke of York in Roman garb conducting the emergency relief operation. The 311 steps to the viewing gallery once guaranteed an incredible view; nowadays it is somewhat dwarfed by the buildings surrounding it.

Cafés

Café Below

MAP PAGE 74, POCKET MAP M6
St Mary-le-Bow, Cheapside ⊖ St Paul's or
Mansion House ⓦ cafebelow.co.uk.
A rare City gem: a café set in a
wonderful Norman church crypt,
serving excellent, good-value bistro-
style food. £

Patty & Bun

MAP PAGE 74, POCKET MAP N5
22 Liverpool St ⊖ Liverpool St
ⓦ pattyandbun.co.uk.
Spawned from a raved-about food
truck, this is dude food incarnate –
succulent burgers on brioche buns,
plus spicy sides – like cheese balls
with hot sauce – and hangover-
busting breakfasts. ££

Prufrock Coffee

MAP PAGE 74, POCKET MAP K5
23–25 Leather Lane ⊖ Chancery Lane or

Farringdon ⓦ prufrockcoffee.com.
Super-hip shrine to the coffee bean,
with a barista school on site. Good
food, too. £

Restaurants

Caravan

MAP PAGE 74, POCKET MAP K4
11–13 Exmouth Market ⊖ Farringdon
ⓦ caravanandco.com.
Creative brunches, modern fusion
food and home-roasted coffee are
on offer at this relaxed, cool all-day
place. £££

Duck and Waffle

MAP PAGE 74, POCKET MAP N5
Heron Tower, 110 Bishopsgate ⊖ Aldgate
ⓦ duckandwaffle.com.
Forty floors up, this smart place
offers amazing City views and
hipster comfort food with creative
flair. The signature dish features
waffles, duck confit, fried duck egg
and mustard maple syrup, while
2am offerings include spiced duck
doughnuts. £££

Fish Central

MAP PAGE 74, POCKET MAP M4
149–155 Central St ⊖ Old Street
ⓦ fishcentral.co.uk.
Sitting on the edge of the Barbican/
City and Clerkenwell's council
estates, this is both a reliable chippy
and a smart fish restaurant. ££

Gaucho

MAP PAGE 74, POCKET MAP M4
1 Bell Inn Yard ⊖ Monument
ⓦ gauchorestaurants.com.
One of 12 London branches,
Gaucho is an Argentinian restaurant
serving delicious juicy steaks (with
corresponding price tags). Not one
for veggies, the interior is low-lit
and cowhide plays a large part in
the décor. ££££

Koya

MAP PAGE 74, POCKET MAP M6
10–12 Bloomberg Arcade ⊖ Bank or
Cannon Street ⓦ koya.co.uk.

Ye Olde Mitre

The huge, swish headquarters of Bloomberg in London has, as well as the Mithraeum (see page 81), an arcade of carefully selected new restaurants, including a branch of *Caravan* (see above), and this small, authentic udon noodle bar, serving delicately flavoured hot and cold noodle dishes. ££

Moro

MAP PAGE 74, POCKET MAP K4
34–36 Exmouth Market ⊖ Angel or Farringdon ⓦ moro.co.uk.
This attractive restaurant is a place of pilgrimage for disciples of the chef's Moorish cookbooks. Food is excellent and reservations recommended. Tapas served all day; mains also available. £££

Quality Chop House

MAP PAGE 74, POCKET MAP K4
88–94 Farringdon Rd ⊖ Farringdon ⓦ thequalitychophouse.com.
Beautiful old dining room, butchers and wine bar with a daily changing menu focusing on the best cuts of British meat and freshest produce. £££

St John

MAP PAGE 74, POCKET MAP L5
26 St John St ⊖ Farringdon ⓦ stjohnrestaurant.com.
Pared-down former smokehouse close to Smithfield meat market that's become famous for serving outstanding British dishes, often involving unfashionable animal parts. £££

Pubs and bars

The Black Friar

MAP PAGE 74, POCKET MAP L6
174 Queen Victoria St ⊖ Blackfriars.
A gorgeous pub, with Art Nouveau marble friezes of boozy monks and a highly decorated alcove – all original, dating from 1905. A lovely fireplace and an unhurried atmosphere make this a relaxing place to drink.

The Black Friar

Café Kick

MAP PAGE 74, POCKET MAP K4
43 Exmouth Market ⊖ Farringdon or Angel ⓦ cafekick.co.uk.
This ramshackle, memorabilia-packed French-style café/bar is great fun, the friendly atmosphere enlivened by its busy table-football games. A daytime menu of sandwiches and hearty soups gives way in the evening to nachos and sharing boards.

Cittie of Yorke

MAP PAGE 74, POCKET MAP K13
22 High Holborn ⊖ Chancery Lane.
A venerable London lawyers' pub now run by Sam Smith's. Head for the vaulted cellar bar or the grand quasi-medieval wine hall at the back with its rows of cosy cubicles.

The Counting House

MAP PAGE 74, POCKET MAP N6
50 Cornhill ⊖ Bank.
An inspired Fuller's bank conversion, the magnificent interior

The Three Kings

featuring high ceilings, marble pillars, mosaic flooring and a large, oval island bar, plus an enormous glass dome.

The Eagle

MAP PAGE 74, POCKET MAP K4
159 Farringdon Rd ⊖ Farringdon
Ⓦ theeaglefarringdon.co.uk.
London's first gastropub continues to produce excellent Mediterranean food from its little open kitchen, but still feels more like a pub than a restaurant, with a refreshingly unpretentious vibe.

The Holy Tavern

MAP PAGE 74, POCKET MAP L5
55 Britton St ⊖ Farringdon
Ⓦ theholytavern.com.
Converted Georgian coffee house – the frontage dates from 1810 – that has retained much of its original character. Better still, the excellent draught beers are from St Peter's Brewery in Suffolk. Something of a gem in these parts.

Jamaica Wine House

MAP PAGE 74, POCKET MAP N6
St Michael's Alley ⊖ Bank
Ⓦ jamaicawinehouse.co.uk.
Located down a narrow alleyway, on the site of London's first coffee house (1652), this old City institution is known locally as the "Jam Pot". Today, it's a Shepherd Neame pub, divided into four large "snugs" by original high wooden-panelled partitions.

The Lamb Tavern

MAP PAGE 74, POCKET MAP N6
10–12 Leadenhall Market ⊖ Monument or Bank Ⓦ lambtavernleadenhall.com.
It's almost exclusively standing room only (both inside and out) at this historic Young's pub situated in the middle of beautiful Leadenhall Market. *Old Tom's Bar* downstairs offers good cheese/sausage platters.

Old Bank of England

MAP PAGE 74, POCKET MAP K14
194 Fleet St ⊖ Temple or Chancery Lane
Ⓦ oldbankofengland.com.
Not the actual Bank of England, but the former Law Courts' branch, this imposing High Victorian banking hall is now a magnificently opulent Fuller's ale-and-pie pub.

The Three Kings

MAP PAGE 74, POCKET MAP L4
7 Clerkenwell Close ⊖ Farringdon.
Tucked away north of Clerkenwell Green, this atmospheric pub has a delightfully eclectic interior and two small rooms upstairs perfect for long occupation. Good craft ales too.

Viaduct Tavern

MAP PAGE 74, POCKET MAP L5
126 Newgate St ⊖ St Paul's
Ⓦ viaducttavern.co.uk.
Fuller's pub situated across from the Old Bailey, with a glorious Victorian interior including walls adorned with oils of faded ladies representing Commerce, Agriculture and the Arts.

Ye Olde Cheshire Cheese

MAP PAGE 74, POCKET MAP L6
Wine Office Court, 145 Fleet St ⊖ **Temple**
Ⓦye-olde-cheshire-cheese.co.uk.
A seventeenth-century watering
hole – famous chiefly because
of patrons such as Dickens and
Dr Johnson – with several snug,
dark-panelled rooms and real fires.
Popular with tourists, but by no
means exclusively so, and serving
keenly priced Sam Smith's brews.

Ye Olde Mitre

MAP PAGE 74, POCKET MAP L5
1 Ely Court, off Hatton Garden
⊖ **Farringdon** Ⓦ yeoldemitreholborn.co.uk.
Hidden down a tiny alleyway off
Ely Place or Hatton Garden, this
wonderfully atmospheric Fuller's
pub dates back to 1546, although
it was actually rebuilt in the
eighteenth century. The real ales are
excellent.

Clubs and venues

Barbican

MAP PAGE 74, POCKET MAP M5
Silk St ⊖ **Barbican** Ⓦ barbican.org.uk.

With the outstanding resident
London Symphony Orchestra,
and top foreign orchestras and big-
name soloists in regular attendance,
the Barbican is one of the city's best
venues for classical music, opera,
theatre, dance and film. You can
also join a 90-minute architecture
tour (charge) of the Brutalist estate.

Fabric

MAP PAGE 74, POCKET MAP L5
77a Charterhouse St ⊖ **Farringdon**
Ⓦ fabriclondon.com.
Despite big queues and a confusing
layout, this 2500-capacity club is
one of the world's finest. Live bands
and lengthy DJ line-ups mean you
can hear a huge variety of acts. ID
essential.

Sadler's Wells

MAP PAGE 74, POCKET MAP L3
Rosebery Ave ⊖ **Angel** Ⓦ sadlerswells.
com.
Home to Britain's best
contemporary dance companies,
and host to the finest international outfits, Sadler's Wells
also puts on theatre pieces and
children's shows.

Performance at Sadler's Wells

The East End

The East End is firmly established as one of the city's most vibrant artistic enclaves, peppered with art galleries and a whole host of cutting-edge bars and clubs. Spitalfields – and in particular Brick Lane – lies at the heart of the old East End, once the first port of call for thousands of immigrants over the centuries, and best known today for hipster cafés, vintage Sunday markets and cheap curries. The scene has now spread north to Shoreditch and Dalston, and east to Bethnal Green and beyond, to the edges of the Olympic Park.

Young V&A

MAP PAGE 90
Cambridge Heath Road ⊖ Bethnal Green
Ⓦ vam.ac.uk/moc. Free.

The newly refurbished Young V&A (previously V&A Museum of Childhood) was originally part of the V&A in South Kensington (see page 125) and was transported here in the 1860s to bring art to the East End. The slightly dowdy interior of the former museum has been reimagined as a bright, tactile house of fun in this new iteration helmed by architects De Matos Ryan (DMR). The Play gallery has interactive displays for babies and toddlers, whilst the new Imagine gallery (aimed at older kids) includes a stage, dressing up boxes and a shadow puppet theatre. The gallery's extensive collection of dolls' houses dating back to 1673 are still on display, however this time you

Museum of the Home

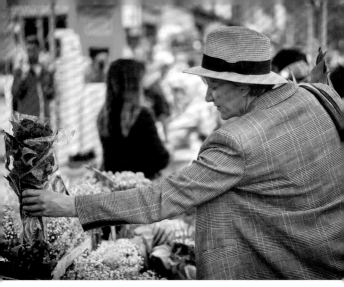

Columbia Road Flower Market

can quite literally walk the "streets" between them. There are regular exhibitions held upstairs and a brand-new café in the main hall.

Museum of the Home

MAP PAGE 90, POCKET MAP O3
136 Kingsland Rd ⊖ Hoxton Overground
ⓦ museumofthehome.org.uk. Free.
Formerly known as the Geffrye Museum, the Museum of the Home reopened in 2021 after an extensive renovation and a rebrand; the new and improved museum boasts double the public space it had previously, and features new galleries and learning spaces as well as a new café. Housed in a grandiose enclave of eighteenth-century ironmongers' almshouses, is essentially a museum of domestic furniture. In 1911, at a time when the East End furniture trade was concentrated in the area, the almshouses were converted into a museum for the "education of craftsmen". The almshouses are rigged out as period living rooms of the urban middle class, ranging from the oak-panelled decor of the seventeenth century to the present. The gardens are beautiful, and

one of the **almshouses** has been restored to its original condition and can be visited by tour.

Columbia Road Flower Market

MAP PAGE 90, POCKET MAP O3
⊖ Shoreditch High Street Overground or Hoxton Overground.
Columbia Road is the city's most popular market (Sun 8am–3pm) for flowers and plants; it's also the liveliest, with the loud and upfront stallholders catering to an increasingly moneyed clientele. As well as seeds, bulbs, potted plants and cut flowers from the stalls, you'll also find every kind of gardening accessory from the chi-chi shops that line the street, and you can keep yourself sustained with bagels, cakes and coffee from the local cafés.

Wesley's Chapel & House

MAP PAGE 90, POCKET MAP N4
49 City Rd ⊖ Old Street ⓦ wesleyschapel.
org.uk & ⓦ wesleysheritage.org.uk. Free.
A place of pilgrimage for Methodists from all over the world, Wesley's Chapel was built in 1777, and heralded the coming of age

THE EAST END

The East End ◁△❶❷❶ & Dalston

SHOPS
Boxpark	4
Freedom Press	6
House of Hackney	1
Labour and Wait	3
Luna & Curious	2
Rough Trade East	5

CLUBS & VENUES
Bethnal Green Working Men's Club	5
Book Club	10
Dalston Superstore	1
The Macbeth	4
Village Underground	13
XOYO	9

CAFÉS
Attendant Coffee Roasters	6
Brick Lane Beigel Bake	7
E. Pellicci	5
Leila's Shop	4

RESTAURANTS
Chez Elles	10
Clove Club	3
Hawksmoor Spitalfields	8
Pidgin	1
St John Bread and Wine	9
Som Saa	12
Tayyab's	11
Viet Hoa Café	2

ACCOMMODATION
The Corner	5
Culpeper	4
Hoxton Hotel	2
One Hundred Shoreditch	1
Shoreditch Rooms	3

PUBS & BARS
The Carpenter's Arms	12
Culpeper	16
Happiness Forgets	14
Mother Kelly's	7
Nightjar	8
The Old Blue Last	11
Railway Tavern	4
Sager + Wilde	13
Ten Bells	15

of the faith founded by **John Wesley** (1703–91). The interior is uncharacteristically ornate, with powder-pink columns of French jasper and a superb, Adam-style gilded plasterwork ceiling. Predictably enough, the **Museum of Methodism** in the basement has only a passing reference to the insanely jealous 40-year-old widow Wesley married, and who eventually left him. Wesley himself spent his last two years in Wesley's House, a delightful Georgian place to the right of the main gates. On display inside are his deathbed and an early shock-therapy machine he was particularly keen on.

Bunhill Fields

MAP PAGE 90, POCKET MAP M4
City Rd ⊖ Old Street.

The main burial ground for Dissenters or Nonconformists (practising Christians who were not members of the Church of England), Bunhill Fields contains three famous graves in the central paved area: the simple tombstone of poet and artist **William Blake** stands next to a replica of writer **Daniel Defoe**'s, while opposite lies the recumbent statue of **John Bunyan**, seventeenth-century author of *The Pilgrim's Progress*.

Whitechapel Art Gallery

MAP PAGE 90, POCKET MAP O5
77–82 Whitechapel High St ⊖ Aldgate East
Ⓦ whitechapelgallery.org. Free.

Founded by one of the East End's Victorian philanthropists, Whitechapel Art Gallery is housed in a beautiful crenellated 1899 Arts and Crafts building, embellished with gilded leaves by sculptor Rachel Whiteread, and a neighbouring building, which was once a library. The gallery has an illustrious history of putting on some of London's most innovative exhibitions of contemporary art, events and talks. The ground floor has a well-stocked art bookshop and a stylish **café/wine bar**. The gallery is a good starting point for finding out more about the east London art scene, particularly on the first Thursday of each month, when it – and some 150 smaller east London galleries – stay open till 9pm and put on events and openings.

Brick Lane

MAP PAGE 90, POCKET MAP 04–05
⊖ Aldgate East or Shoreditch High Street
Overground.

Brick Lane lies at the heart of London's Bengali community, whose inexpensive curry houses dominate the southern end of the street. The red-brick chimney halfway up Brick Lane heralds the **Old Truman Brewery**, founded in 1666 and the largest in the world at the end of the nineteenth century. It ceased operations in 1989 and is now at the centre of a whole series of indoor markets – the Backyard Market, Tea Rooms, the Sunday Upmarket and Boiler House food hall – all of which are buzzing on Sundays, with stalls selling clothes, crafts and food.

The streets north of the brewery and the railway arches are the venue for Brick Lane's **Sunday market**, which extends along Sclater Street and Cheshire Street, with stalls selling everything from household tat to antique furniture.

Christ Church, Spitalfields

MAP PAGE 90, POCKET MAP O5
Commercial St ⊖ Liverpool Street
Ⓦ ccspitalfields.org. Free.

Built between 1714 and 1729 by **Nicholas Hawksmoor**, Christ Church features a huge 225ft-high broach spire and giant Tuscan portico. Inside, there's a forest of columned bays, with a lion and a unicorn playing peekaboo on the top of the chancel beam and London's largest Georgian organ.

Old Spitalfields Market

MAP PAGE 90, POCKET MAP O5
Commercial St ⊖ Liverpool Street.
Ⓦ oldspitalfieldsmarket.com.

Spitalfields Market was the capital's premier wholesale fruit and vegetable market until 1991. The western 1920s half of the market was replaced by a Norman Foster office development, with glass-box

Old Spitalfields Market

The Olympic Park

retail units and food traders built into the old market, although part of the original facade survives on the north side of Brushfield Street. The remaining market now hosts an eclectic and fairly sophisticated selection of shops and stalls selling crafts, clothes and food in the original red-brick and green-gabled 1893 building, to the east. There's a vintage market on Thursdays.

Dennis Severs' House

MAP PAGE 90, POCKET MAP 05
18 Folgate St ⊖ Liverpool Street
ⓦ dennissevershouse.co.uk.

Visiting the former home of the American eccentric Dennis Severs (1948–99) is a bizarre and uncanny theatrical experience, which Severs once described as "passing through a frame into a painting". The house is entirely candlelit and log-fired, and decked out as it would have been over two hundred years ago. Visitors are free to explore the ten rooms unhindered, and are left with the distinct impression that someone has literally just popped out – Severs called it a "still-life drama". The house cat prowls, there's the smell of gravy bubbling, and the sound of horses' hooves on the cobbled street outside. Daytime visits take place on Sundays and Mondays; for the candlelit "Silent Night" visits you must book ahead.

The Olympic Park

The focus of the 2012 Olympics was the **Olympic Park** (ⓦ queenelizabetholympicpark.co.uk), laid out over a series of islands formed by the River Lee and its various tributaries and canals. Since London hosted the Olympics in 2012, the whole area has been replanted with swathes of grass, trees and flowers, and peppered with cafés. This, plus an excellent kids' playground, Tumbling Bay, make it a great park in which to hang out on a sunny day. The centrepiece of the park is the **Olympic Stadium**, now used for large concerts, as well as being home to West Ham United football club. Standing close to the stadium is the **Orbit Tower** (charge; ⓦ arcelormittalorbit.com), a 377ft-high continuous loop of red recycled steel designed by Anish Kapoor, with a tunnel slide by Carsten Höller. But the most eye-catching venue is Zaha Hadid's wave-like **London Aquatics Centre**, four times over budget, but looking very cool and offering very reasonably priced swims. Other venues to look out for are the curvy **Velodrome** with its banked, Siberian pine track and adjacent BMX circuit – part of the **Lee Valley VeloPark** (ⓦ visitleevalley.org.uk) – and the **Copper Box Arena**, now a multi-sports centre. The nearest tube is Stratford.

Shops

Boxpark

MAP PAGE 90, POCKET MAP O4

2-10 Bethnal Green Rd ⊖ Shoreditch High Street Overground ⓦ boxpark.co.uk/shoreditch.

A pop-up shopping mall and food court in old shipping containers. Here you'll find a whole host of independent shops selling everything from homeware, clothes and jewellery to art, records, crystals and trinkets.

Freedom Press

MAP PAGE 90, POCKET MAP O5

Angel Alley, 84b Whitechapel High St ⊖ Aldgate East ⓦ freedompress.org.uk.

Upholding a long East End tradition of radical politics, this small anarchist bookshop is packed with everything from Bakhunin to Chomsky.

House of Hackney

MAP PAGE 90, POCKET MAP N4

131 Shoreditch High St ⊖ Liverpool Street or Shoreditch High Street Overground ⓦ houseofhackney.com.

Whimsical, high-fashion homewares, wallpapers, textiles, clothing and gifts, all designed and made in England.

Labour and Wait

MAP PAGE 90, POCKET MAP O4

85 Redchurch St ⊖ Shoreditch High Street Overground ⓦ labourandwait.co.uk.

The hardware, kitchen gear and cleaning products of your dreams. From enamel kettles to sharpening stones, everything is defined by beautiful design, ingenious functionality and more than a whiff of nostalgia.

Luna & Curious

MAP PAGE 90, POCKET MAP O4

24-26 Calvert Ave ⊖ Shoreditch High Street Overground ⓦ lunaandcurious.com.

A beautiful indie boutique selling a wide variety of clothes, shoes, jewellery, and homeware, as well as toys and books; all the stock is curated by a collective of artisans with exquisite taste.

Rough Trade East

MAP PAGE 90, POCKET MAP O5

Old Truman Brewery, 91 Brick Lane ⊖ Liverpool Street ⓦ roughtrade.com.

It started in west London, but the east London store of this famous purveyor of vinyl has the edge in terms of size. It stocks a huge array of indie, electronica and more, with listening posts, in store recommendations, an interesting selection of books and a small café. It also hosts in-store appearances and special gigs by some impressively high-profile names.

Cafés

Attendant Coffee Roasters

MAP PAGE 90, POCKET MAP O4

74 Great Eastern St ⊖ Shoreditch High Street Overground ⓦ the-attendant.com/

Boxpark

pages/shoreditch.
There's a no-fuss atmosphere at this lovely bright coffee shop full of greenery. Does a brilliant brunch and a perfect flat white. £

Brick Lane Beigel Bake

MAP PAGE 90, POCKET MAP O4
159 Brick Lane ⊖ Shoreditch High Street
Overground Ⓦ bricklanebeigel.co.uk/
london/beigel-bake.
Classic no-frills bagel shop in the heart of the East End – unbelievably cheap, even for fillings such as smoked salmon with cream cheese or salt beef. £

E. Pellicci

MAP PAGE 90
332 Bethnal Green Rd ⊖ Bethnal Green
Ⓦ epellicci.co.uk.
Open since 1900, family-owned caff *Pellicci's* is one of a dying breed in London: original 1940s decor, good-natured banter, giant fry-ups and inexpensive home-made Italian

E. Pellicci

comfort food. A beloved East End institution. £

Leila's Shop

MAP PAGE 90, POCKET MAP O4
17 Calvert Ave ⊖ Shoreditch High Street
Overground Ⓦ leilasshop.co.uk.
Linked to a lovely little deli/ grocer's/farm shop, this simple neighbourhood café serves fresh-made seasonal, Mediterranean food and biodynamic wines. £

Restaurants

Chez Elles

MAP PAGE 90, POCKET MAP O5
45 Brick Lane ⊖ Aldgate East
Ⓦ chezellesbistroquet.co.uk.
Incongruously set on curry-house-lined Brick Lane, this pretty, very French bistro offers rustic Gallic classics – onion soup, duck confit, *moules* – served with charm. ££

Clove Club

MAP PAGE 90, POCKET MAP N4
Shoreditch Town Hall, 380 Old St ⊖ Old
Street Ⓦ thecloveclub.com.
At the vanguard of Shoreditch's foodie scene, offering tasting menu and shorter five-course menus and sharing plates at the bar. Delicious, inventive cooking, if you can stomach the prepaid ticket booking system. ££££

Hawksmoor Spitalfields

MAP PAGE 90, POCKET MAP O5
157a Commercial St ⊖ Liverpool Street or
Shoreditch High Street Ⓦ thehawksmoor.
com.
One for serious meat lovers, the *Hawksmoor* restaurants (there are eight in London; this was the first) serve some of the best steaks in town, as well as seafood and excellent cocktails, all in a sophisticated, leather and mahogany interior. £££

Pidgin

MAP PAGE 90
52 Wilton Way ⊖ Hackney Central

Overground ⓦ pidginlondon.com.
Outstanding food –
contemporary, punchy and
influenced by Asian flavours – on
a weekly changing four-course
menu. Dishes run the gamut
from pigeon pie to aubergine with
Szechuan pepper – the surprise
element simply adds to the
pleasure. ££££

St John Bread and Wine

MAP PAGE 90, POCKET MAP O5
94–96 Commercial St ⊖ Liverpool Street
ⓦ stjohnrestaurant.com.
A more casual, canteen-style
version of Clerkenwell's *St John*
restaurant (see page 85), this
branch also serves traditional and
unusual cuts of meat, so expect
offal and game on the menu –
devilled kidneys, pigeon and
rabbit. ££

Som Saa

MAP PAGE 90, POCKET MAP O5
43a Commercial St ⊖ Aldgate East
ⓦ somsaa.com.
Forget tired green chicken curry
– this Thai food is a cut above
the rest, with fresh, surprising
dishes such as stir-fried clams with
turmeric or Burmese-style pork
belly and shoulder curry. ££

Tayyab's

MAP PAGE 90
83–89 Fieldgate St ⊖ Whitechapel
ⓦ tayyabs.co.uk.
This busy place has been
serving good, freshly cooked,
straightforward Punjabi food
for over forty years. Prices
remain low, booking is essential
and service is speedy and slick.
Unlicensed but you can bring
your own alcohol. £

Viet Hoa Café

MAP PAGE 90, POCKET MAP O3
70–72 Kingsland Rd ⊖ Hoxton Overground
ⓦ viethoa.co.uk.
Simple Vietnamese restaurant
on a street heaving with similar
places. Big portions and lots of

Pidgin

spicy noodle soups to choose
from. ££

Pubs and bars

The Carpenters Arms

MAP PAGE 90
73 Cheshire St ⊖ Bethnal Green
Overground ⓦ thecarpentersarms.net.
Bought by the notorious Reggie
Kray for his beloved mum, this
welcoming pub has cleaned up its
act, offering craft lagers, good food
and a relaxed neighbourhood vibe.

Culpeper

MAP PAGE 90, POCKET MAP O5
40 Commercial St ⊖ Liverpool Street
ⓦ theculpeper.com.
This light-filled, casually stylish
gastropub has a secret: a gorgeous
plant-filled roof terrace where they
serve a simple menu of small plates
that incorporate the plants they
grow. A more substantial menu is
served in the first-floor restaurant
and friendly, ground-floor pub. All
dishes are deftly prepared and the
menu changes regularly.

Mother Kelly's

Happiness Forgets

MAP PAGE 90, POCKET MAP N4
8–9 Hoxton Square ⊖ Old Street
🅦 happinessforgets.com.
This intimate, candlelit basement
bar is a great place to hunker
down and sip on inventive, strong
cocktails, from the "Tokyo Collins"
to the "Perfect Storm".

Mother Kelly's

MAP PAGE 90, POCKET MAP O3
251 Paradise Row ⊖ Bethnal Green
🅦 instagram.com/motherkellys_e2.
One of a number of interesting
ventures occupying a strip of
railway arches in Bethnal Green,
this stripped-back space is a great,
welcoming place for sampling
some of London – and the world's
– most craft beers, with 23 on tap
at any time (served in third-, half-
of full pints), plus huge fridges of
beers to tempt you. Some beers
are very strong hence the third-
and half- pint offerings. Food is
simple sharing boards of meats
and cheeses.

Nightjar

MAP PAGE 90, POCKET MAP O3
129 City Rd ⊖ Old Street 🅦 barnightjar.
com/cocktails.
Speakeasy-style underground bar
serving up inventive cocktails in
brightly-coloured vessels that are
almost as fun to look at as they are
to drink. There's often impressive
live jazz.

The Old Blue Last

MAP PAGE 90, POCKET MAP O3
38 Great Eastern St ⊖ Old Street
🅦 theoldbluelast.com.
A friendly, independent,
refurbished east end boozer,
apparently haunted by the ghost
of Shakespeare. There's a great live
music venue upstairs.

Railway Tavern

MAP PAGE 90, POCKET MAP O3
2 Jude St ⊖ Dalston Kingsland Overground
🅦 railwaytavernn16.co.uk.
Tucked away on a quiet corner
behind Dalston's main drag, this
is a good-looking, feel-good local,
decked out in vintage railway decor,
with well-kept cask ales, tasty Thai
food and live music.

Sager + Wilde

MAP PAGE 90, POCKET MAP O3
193 Hackney Rd ⊖ Hoxton
🅦 sagerandwilde.com.
Gorgeous wine bar in a gussied-
up old East End corner site, with
a fabulous wine selection and
cheese sharing plates and toasties.
Prices can mount, but the quality
is impeccable.

Ten Bells

MAP PAGE 90, POCKET MAP O5
84 Commercial St ⊖ Shoreditch High
Street 🅦 tenbells.com.
Lively historic Spitalfields pub
with beautiful Victorian tiling and
a cocktail bar upstairs. Live music
and DJs at the weekend.

Clubs and venues

Bethnal Green Working Men's Club

MAP PAGE 90
42–44 Pollard Row ⊖ Bethnal Green
Ⓦ workersplaytime.net.

At once hip and friendly, this old-school venue offers cool post-war decor and an impeccable booking policy: burlesque, disco, swing, ska, cabaret, indie, the lot.

Book Club

MAP PAGE 90, POCKET MAP N4
100–106 Leonard St ⊖ Old Street
Ⓦ wearetbc.com.

Enjoy "thinking and drinking" at this eclectic cross-platform basement club. Hip-hop quizzes, drawing classes, stand-up diary reading, rip-roaring DJ nights – there's always something exciting going on.

Dalston Superstore

MAP PAGE 90
117 Kingsland High St ⊖ Dalston
Kingsland Ⓦ dalstonsuperstore.com.

Outrageous, camp and great fun, this Dalston stalwart is nominally a LGBTQ+ bar/club but welcomes all, bringing synth-pop, disco, techno, house, soul and funk to a wild-dancing crowd.

The Macbeth

MAP PAGE 90, POCKET MAP N3
70 Hoxton St ⊖ Old Street Ⓦ the-macbeth.co.uk.

A brilliantly eclectic selection of fun club nights celebrating everything from Bieber to Beyoncé, plus live bands and pop-culture themed events. Check out the roof terrace.

Village Underground

MAP PAGE 90, POCKET MAP N4
54 Holywell Lane ⊖ Shoreditch High Street
Overground Ⓦ villageunderground.co.uk.

Nonprofit, genre-bending arts venue and creative hub (studios include tube carriages and shipping containers and changing street art) with an always intriguing roster of gigs, club nights and theatre. Cool, experimental and progressive (with a crowd to match).

Xoyo

MAP PAGE 90, POCKET MAP N4
32–37 Cowper St ⊖ Old Street Ⓦ xoyo.co.uk.

Huge Shoreditch club whose legendary weekend club nights and regular live gigs pull in the biggest names in everything from dance music to indie rock. Attracts a lively mixed crowd.

Dalston Superstore

The Tower and Docklands

One of the city's main tourist attractions, the Tower of London was the site of some of the goriest events in the nation's history, and is somewhere all visitors should try and get to see. Immediately to the east are the remains of what was the largest enclosed cargo-dock system in the world, built in the nineteenth century to cope with the huge volume of goods shipped in along the Thames from all over the Empire. No one thought the area could be rejuvenated when the docks closed in the 1960s, but since the 1980s, warehouses have been converted into luxury flats, waterside penthouse apartments have been built and the huge high-rise office development of Canary Wharf is now London's second financial centre.

Tower of London

MAP PAGE 100, POCKET MAP O7
⊖ Tower Hill ⓦ hrp.org.uk. Charge.

One of the most perfectly preserved medieval fortresses in the country, the Tower of London sits beside the Thames surrounded by a wide,

Beefeater, Tower of London

dry moat. Begun by William the Conqueror, the Tower is chiefly famous as a place of imprisonment and death, though it has been used variously as a royal residence, armoury, mint, menagerie, observatory and – a function it still serves – a safe-deposit box for the Crown Jewels. Before you set off, join one of the free guided tours, given by the Tower's **Beefeaters** (officially known as Yeoman Warders). As well as giving a good introduction to the history, these ex-servicemen relish hamming up the gory stories.

Visitors today enter the Tower along Water Lane, but in times gone by most prisoners were delivered through **Traitors' Gate**, on the waterfront. The nearby **Bloody Tower** saw the murders of 12-year-old Edward V and his 9-year-old brother, and was used to imprison Walter Raleigh on three separate occasions.

The central **White Tower** is the original "Tower", begun in 1076. Now home to part of the Royal Armouries, and its hands-on "Armouries in Action" displays, it's worth visiting for the beautiful Norman Chapel of St John, on

Tower Bridge

the second floor. To the west of the White Tower is the execution spot on **Tower Green** where seven highly placed but unlucky individuals were beheaded, among them Henry VIII's second and fifth wives.

The **Crown Jewels** are the major reason so many people flock to the Tower, but the moving walkways which take you past the loot are disappointingly swift, allowing you just seconds' viewing during peak periods. The oldest piece of regalia is the twelfth-century Anointing Spoon, but the vast majority of exhibits, including the Imperial State Crown, postdate the Commonwealth (1649–60). Among the jewels are three of the largest cut diamonds in the world, including the legendary Koh-i-Noor, set into the Queen Mother's Crown in 1937.

Tower Bridge

MAP PAGE 100, POCKET MAP O7
⊖ Tower Hill Ⓦ towerbridge.org.uk.
Charge.

Tower Bridge ranks with Big Ben as the most famous of all London landmarks. Completed in 1894, its Neo-Gothic towers are clad in Cornish granite and Portland stone, but conceal a steel frame which, at the time, represented a considerable engineering achievement. The **raising of the bascules** (from the French for "see-saw") remains an impressive sight – check the website to find out when the bridge is opening. It's free to walk across the bridge, but you must pay to gain access to the **elevated walkways**

Docklands Light Railway

The best way to visit Docklands is to take the Docklands Light Railway or **DLR** (Ⓦ tfl.gov.uk/dlr), whose driverless trains run on overhead tracks, and give out great views over the cityscape. DLR trains set off from Bank tube and from Tower Gateway, close to Tower Hill tube and the Tower of London.

THE TOWER AND DOCKLANDS

Tower of London

linking the summits of the towers – closed from 1909 to 1982 due to their popularity with prostitutes and the suicidal. The views are good both out over the river and directly down through the glass floors, and you get to see the giant, defunct, coal-fired boilers in the **Victorian Engine Rooms** on the south side of the bridge.

St Katharine Docks

MAP PAGE 100, POCKET MAP O7
⊖ Tower Hill.

Built in the late 1820s to relieve the congestion on the River Thames, St Katharine Docks were originally surrounded by high walls to protect the warehouses used to store luxury goods – ivory, spices, carpets and cigars – shipped in from all over the Empire. Nowadays, the docks are used as an upmarket marina, and the old warehouses house shops, pubs and restaurants. More interesting, however, are the old

swing bridges over the basins (including one from 1828), the boats themselves – you'll often see beautiful old sailing ships and Dutch barges – and the attractive **Ivory House** warehouse, with its clock tower, at the centre of the three basins. At its peak this warehouse received over 200 tons of ivory annually.

Wapping High Street

MAP PAGE 100
⊖ Wapping Overground.

Once famous for its boatyards and its three dozen riverside pubs, Wapping's Victorian atmosphere has been preserved, and as it lies just a short walk east of the Tower, this is easily the most satisfying part of Docklands to explore. Halfway along Wapping High Street is **Wapping Pier Head**, the former entrance to the London Docks, flanked by grand, curvaceous Regency terraces.

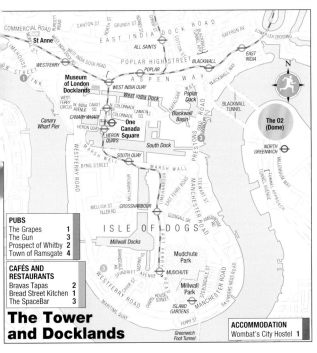

PUBS

The Grapes 1
The Gun 3
Prospect of Whitby 2
Town of Ramsgate 4

CAFÉS AND RESTAURANTS

Bravas Tapas 2
Bread Street Kitchen 1
The SpaceBar 3

The Tower and Docklands

ACCOMMODATION

Wombat's City Hostel 1

Here, you'll find one of the few surviving stairs down to the river beside the **Town of Ramsgate** pub; beneath the pub are the dungeons where convicts were chained before being deported to Australia. It was also at the *Town of Ramsgate* that "Hanging" Judge Jeffreys was captured trying to escape disguised as a collier following the victory of William of Orange in 1688.

St Anne's Church

MAP PAGE 100
5 Newell St ⊖ Westferry DLR.

Designed in 1714 by **Nicholas Hawksmoor**, and dominated by a gargantuan west tower, St Anne's boasts the highest church clock in London. Inside is a superb organ built for the Great Exhibition in 1851. In the graveyard Hawksmoor erected a pyramidal structure carved with masonic symbols, now hopelessly eroded; opposite is a

war memorial with relief panels depicting the horrors of trench warfare.

Canary Wharf

MAP PAGE 100
⊖ Canary Wharf & DLR.

The geographical and ideological heart of the new **Docklands** is Canary Wharf, once a destination for bananas (from the Canary Islands – hence the name). An established business district, this is the one Docklands area that you can happily stroll around, taking in the architecture and having a drink overlooking one of the old wharves – or chill out at Crossrail Roof Garden (daily until sunset), a partially enclosed garden. Canary Wharf's name is, of course, synonymous with Cesar Pelli's landmark tower, officially known as **One Canada Square**. It was Britain's tallest building between 1990 and 2012 (before the Shard).

Museum of London Docklands

MAP PAGE 100
West India Quay ⊖ West India Quay
ⓦ museumoflondon.org.uk/docklands.
Free.

The last surviving Georgian warehouses of the West India Docks lie on the far side of a floodlit floating bridge at **West India Quay**. Amidst the dockside bars and restaurants, you'll find Warehouse No. 1, built in 1803 for storing rum, sugar, molasses, coffee and cotton, and now home to the Museum of London Docklands. Spread over several floors, the museum's exhibits chart the history of London's docks on both sides of the river from Roman times to the present day. Highlights include a model of old London Bridge; an eight-foot long watercolour showing the "legal quays" in the 1790s, just before the enclosed docks eased congestion; and a reconstructed warren of late nineteenthcentury shops and cobbled dockland streets. Those with kids should head for Mudlarks, on the ground floor, where children can learn a bit about pulleys and ballast, drive a DLR train or simply romp around the soft play area.

The O2 (Dome)

MAP PAGE 100
⊖ North Greenwich ⓦ theo2.co.uk.

Clearly visible from the east bank of the Isle of Dogs, the Dome, or **O2**, is a 23,000-seat events arena, designed by Richard Rogers for the millennium celebrations. Over half a mile in circumference, 160ft in height and held up by a dozen, 300ft-tall yellow steel masts, it's the largest of its kind in the world. You can climb the outside of the Dome, though the views are better from the nearby Emirates Airline cable car.

The O2

Cafés and restaurants

Bravas Tapas

MAP PAGE 100, POCKET MAP O7
St Katharine Docks ⊖ Tower Hill
Ⓦ bravastapas.com/
Attractive Spanish restaurant with a sunny dockside terrace, serving tasty tapas (Moorish spiced lamb chops, crispy foie gras-stuffed quail) and Spanish wines. £

Bread Street Kitchen

MAP PAGE 100
44 Narrow St ⊖ Limehouse DLR
Ⓦ gordonramsayrestaurants.com/bread-street-kitchen/on-the-river.
Recently refurbished Gordon Ramsay restaurant with a menu that includes many of his most famous dishes, including wagyu meatballs and beef wellington; also does a great Sunday roast. Ask for a table in the conservatory for river views. ££££

The SpaceBar

MAP PAGE 100
269 Westferry Rd ⊖ Mudchute DLR
Ⓦ space.org.uk/thespacebar.
An oasis in the Docklands desert, this café-bar is in a former church, now arts centre, and does great breakfasts, wraps and hot specials. £

Pubs

The Grapes

MAP PAGE 100
76 Narrow St ⊖ Westferry DLR
Ⓦ thegrapes.co.uk.
A lovely, narrow little pub on a quiet street, with lots of seafaring paraphernalia and a great riverside balcony out back. The ales are good and there's an expensive restaurant upstairs.

The Gun

MAP PAGE 100
27 Coldharbour ⊖ Canary Wharf

Prospect of Whitby

or South Quay or Blackwall DLR
Ⓦ thegundocklands.com.
Legendary dockers' pub, once the haunt of Lord Nelson, and now a classy gastropub. Its cosy back bar has a couple of snugs, and the outside deck offers unrivalled views.

Prospect of Whitby

MAP PAGE 100
57 Wapping Wall ⊖ Wapping Overground
Ⓦ greeneking.co.uk/pubs/greater-london/prospect-of-whitby.
Steeped in history, this is London's most famous riverside pub, with a pewter bar, flagstone floor, ancient timber beams and stacks of maritime memorabilia. Decent beers and terrific views too.

Town of Ramsgate

MAP PAGE 100
62 Wapping High St ⊖ Wapping
Overground Ⓦ townoframsgate.pub.
Dark, narrow, medieval pub located by Wapping Old Stairs, which once led down to Execution Dock. Admiral Bligh and Fletcher Christian were regular drinking partners here in pre-Mutiny days.

South Bank and around

The South Bank has a lot going for it. As well as the massive waterside arts centre, it's home to a host of tourist attractions including the enormously popular London Eye. With most of London's key sights sitting on the north bank of the Thames, the views from here are the best on the river, and thanks to the wide, traffic-free riverside boulevard, the whole area can be happily explored on foot. And a short walk from the South Bank lie one or two lesser-known but nonetheless absorbing sights such as the Imperial War Museum, which contains the country's only permanent exhibition devoted to the Holocaust.

Southbank Centre

MAP PAGE 105, POCKET MAP J17

⊖ Waterloo Ⓦ southbankcentre.co.uk.

The Southbank Centre is home to a whole variety of artistic institutions, the most attractive of which is the **Royal Festival Hall**, built in 1951 for the Festival of Britain and one of London's chief concert venues (see page 104). Their riverside location, the avenue of trees, fluttering banners, buskers and skateboarders, and the weekend food stalls draw in visitors, particularly in summer when weekend festivals, pop-up venues and outside bars are added to the mix. The **Queen Elizabeth Hall** is the complex's second music venue, while the **Hayward Gallery** puts on large modern and contemporary art shows in its spacious, concrete galleries. You'll find secondhand bookstalls outside the nearby **BFI Southbank**, the city's chief arts cinema.

South Bank from Hungerford Bridge

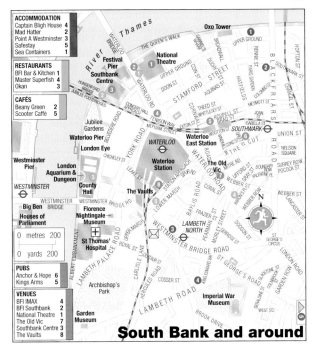

South Bank and around

ACCOMMODATION
Captain Bligh House 4
Mad Hatter 2
Point A Westminster 3
Safestay 5
Sea Containers 1

RESTAURANTS
BFI Bar & Kitchen 1
Master Superfish 4
Okan 3

CAFÉS
Beany Green 2
Scooter Caffè 5

PUBS
Anchor & Hope 6
Kings Arms 5

VENUES
BFI IMAX 4
BFI Southbank 2
National Theatre 1
The Old Vic 7
Southbank Centre 3
The Vaults 8

National Theatre

MAP PAGE 105, POCKET MAP K17
⊖ Waterloo ⓦ nationaltheatre.org.uk.
Looking like a brutalist masterpiece
or a multistorey car park,
depending on whom you ask, the
National Theatre is an institution
first mooted in 1848 but only
realized in 1976. The three
auditoriums within are superb
and can be visited on excellent
backstage tours, for which you
should book online in advance. You
can also peek behind the scenes via
the Sherling Backstage Walkway.

Oxo Tower

MAP PAGE 105, POCKET MAP L7
⊖ Southwark
The Oxo Tower started life as a
Victorian power station before
being converted in the 1930s into
a meat-packing factory for the
company that makes Oxo stock
cubes – the lettering is spelt out
in the windows of the main tower.

The building now contains an
exhibition space on the ground
floor, plus flats for local residents,
sandwiched between a series of
retail workshops for designers on
the first and second floors, and a
swanky restaurant, bar and brasserie
on the top floor. To enjoy the view
without food or drink, visit the
public viewing gallery.

London Eye

MAP PAGE 105, POCKET MAP J18
⊖ Waterloo or Westminster ⓦ londoneye.
com. Charge.
The London Eye is now one of
the city's most famous landmarks.
Standing an impressive 443ft
high, it's the largest **Ferris wheel**
in Europe, weighing over 2000
tonnes, yet as simple and delicate
as a bicycle wheel. It's constantly
in slow motion, which means
a full-circle "flight" in one of
its 32 pods should take around
thirty minutes – that may

seem a long time, but in fact it passes incredibly quickly. Book in advance (and online to save money) as on arrival you'll still have to queue to be loaded on.

London Aquarium

MAP PAGE 105, POCKET MAP J18
County Hall, Riverside Walk ⊖ Waterloo or Westminster Ⓦ sealife.co.uk. Charge.

The most popular attraction in County Hall, the vast former council building by the London Eye, is the London Aquarium, laid out on two subterranean levels. With some super-large tanks, and everything from dog-face puffers and piranhas to the bowmouth guitarfish, this is an attraction that's pretty much guaranteed to please kids. The sea turtles and sharks are always popular. Impressive in scale, the aquarium also has a walk-through underwater tunnel. Ask at the main desk for the times of presentations and feeding times.

London Aquarium

London Dungeon

MAP PAGE 105, POCKET MAP J18
County Hall, Westminster Bridge Rd ⊖ Waterloo or Westminster Ⓦ thedungeons.com. Charge.

Inside the County Hall is the ever-popular horror-fest, the London Dungeon. Young teenagers and the credulous probably get the most out of the life-sized tableaux of folk being hanged, drawn and quartered and tortured, the general hysteria being boosted by actors in period garb. Visitors are led through a series of live-action period scenarios, dwelling on the most gruesome London legends from Sweeney Todd to the inevitable Jack the Ripper section, ending with the "Drop Ride to Doom".

Florence Nightingale Museum

MAP PAGE 105, POCKET MAP J19
Lambeth Palace Rd ⊖ Waterloo or Westminster Ⓦ florence-nightingale.co.uk. Charge.

Hidden among the outbuildings of **St Thomas' Hospital**, the Florence Nightingale Museum celebrates the devout woman who revolutionized the nursing profession by establishing the first school of nursing at St Thomas' in 1860 and publishing her *Notes on Nursing*, which emphasized the importance of hygiene, decorum and discipline. Exhibits include the white lantern that earned her the nickname "The Lady with the Lamp"; Athena, her stuffed pet owl; and a panel on the remarkable **Mary Seacole**, the Jamaican nurse who cared for soldiers in the Crimea itself; a statue of her stands in the hospital grounds.

Garden Museum

MAP PAGE 105, POCKET MAP J9
Lambeth Palace Rd ⊖ Westminster or Lambeth North ⓦ www.gardenmuseum.org.uk. Charge.

Housed in the former church of **St Mary-at-Lambeth**, this museum pays homage to John Tradescant, gardener to James I and Charles I, whose sarcophagus is located in the **graveyard** garden (another belongs to Captain Bligh, the commander of the *Bounty*). Tradescant amassed an "Ark" – a cabinet of curiosities – a few items of which are displayed in the museum, along with all sorts of gardening memorabilia, horticultural artworks and interactive displays. It's a charming hotch-potch of stuff, and you can also climb the 131 steps of the church tower for unsurpassed views across to the Houses of Parliament. There's a good café-restaurant on-site.

Imperial War Museum

MAP PAGE 105, POCKET MAP L9
Lambeth Rd ⊖ Lambeth North ⓦ iwm.org.uk. Free.

Housed in a domed building that was, until 1930, the central portion of the infamous "Bedlam" lunatic asylum, the Imperial War Museum holds by far the best collection

Imperial War Museum

of militaria in the capital. The treatment of the subject matter is impressively wide-ranging and fairly sober, with the main hall's display of guns, rockets, tanks and fighter planes shown alongside such objects as a car destroyed by a suicide bomb in Baghdad in 2007, installed by artist Jeremy Deller. There's a large, extremely thorough series of galleries on **World War I** which includes a walk-through **trench**, and a section telling the story of family life during the Blitz. The museum's **art galleries** on the third floor are well worth a visit for their superb exhibitions of war artists, official and unofficial. Entered from the fourth floor, the harrowing **Holocaust Exhibition** (not recommended for children under 14) pulls few punches, and has made a valiant attempt to avoid depicting the victims of the Holocaust as nameless masses by focusing on individual cases, interspersing the archive footage with eyewitness accounts from contemporary survivors.

Cafés

Beany Green

MAP PAGE 105, POCKET MAP K19
Under Hungerford Bridge ⊖ Waterloo
ⓦ southbankcentre.co.uk/visit/cafes-restaurants-bars/beany-green.
A colourful café-bar located in a converted shipping container. Good coffee and cakes (especially the banana bread), as well as cocktails and craft beer. The outdoor seating is a great place to people watch if the weather is good. £

Scooter Caffè

MAP PAGE 105, POCKET MAP K19
132 Lower Marsh ⊖ Waterloo
ⓦ scootercaffe.com.
This quirky café-bar is charmingly boho, all vintage memorabilia and mismatched furniture. Coffee, wine and snacks served with a smile. £

Anchor & Hope

Restaurants

BFI Bar & Kitchen

MAP PAGE 105, POCKET MAP K17
BFI Southbank ⊖ Waterloo ⓦ benugo.com/sites/cafes/bfi-bar.
This smart, buzzy restaurant/bar (to the side of the BFI, rather than the busier riverfront one), convenient for a pre- or post-movie supper, is the best of the South Bank chains – it's run by Benugo. Portions are small for the price, but the Modern British food has some creative flashes. ££

Masters Superfish

MAP PAGE 105, POCKET MAP L8
191 Waterloo Rd ⊖ Waterloo
ⓦ masterssuperfish.has.restaurant.
An old-fashioned, unpretentious fish-and-chip restaurant, which serves up huge portions with all the trimmings: gherkins, pickled onions and a few complimentary prawns. ££

Okan

MAP PAGE 105, POCKET MAP J18
County Hall, Belvedere Road ⊖ Waterloo
ⓦ okanlondon.com.
Be instantly transported to Osaka at this authentic Japanese restaurant serving experimental tapas-style dishes. ££

Pubs

Anchor & Hope

MAP PAGE 105, POCKET MAP L8
36 The Cut ⊖ Southwark
ⓦ anchorandhopepub.co.uk.
Gastropub that dishes up truly excellent, yet simple grub: Modern European and creative, with mouthwatering puds. You can't book a table, except for Sunday lunch.

Kings Arms

MAP PAGE 105, POCKET MAP K7
25 Roupell St ⊖ Waterloo
ⓦ thekingsarmslondon.co.uk.

Terrific local on a quiet Victorian terraced street: the front part is a traditional drinking area, while the tastefully cluttered rear is a glass and wood conservatory-style space where they serve good-value and tasty Thai food.

Venues

BFI IMAX

MAP PAGE 105, POCKET MAP K17
1 Charlie Chaplin Walk ⊖ Waterloo Ⓦ bfi. org.uk.
Remarkable glazed drum housing Britain's largest screen, showing 2D and 3D films – mostly superhero franchises, action movies and family entertainment – in a vertiginous auditorium.

BFI Southbank

MAP PAGE 105, POCKET MAP K17
South Bank ⊖ Waterloo Ⓦ bfi.org.uk.
Known for its attentive audiences and an exhaustive, eclectic programme that includes directors' seasons, talks and themed series. Around eight films daily are shown in the vast NFT1 and three smaller screens.

National Theatre

MAP PAGE 105, POCKET MAP K17
South Bank ⊖ Waterloo Ⓦ nationaltheatre. org.uk.
The NT consists of three separate theatres – the 1150-seater Olivier, the proscenium-arched Lyttelton and the experimental Dorfman – and puts on a programme ranging from Greek tragedies to Broadway musicals. Some productions sell out months in advance, and prices aren't low, though the Travelex ticket scheme releases hundreds of seats at £15 for each show.

The Old Vic

MAP PAGE 105, POCKET MAP K8
The Cut, South Bank ⊖ Waterloo Ⓦ oldvictheatre.com.
This elegant old theatre was founded in 1818 and shows a

National Theatre

mixture of high-profile new plays and imaginative stagings of classic works, drawing big-name actors.

Southbank Centre

MAP PAGE 105, POCKET MAP J17
South Bank ⊖ Waterloo Ⓦ southbankcentre.co.uk.
The SBC has three concert venues. The 2500-seat Royal Festival Hall (RFH) is tailor-made for large-scale choral and orchestral works, and is home to the Philharmonia and the London Philharmonic. The lugubrious Queen Elizabeth Hall (QEH) is used for chamber concerts, solo recitals and contemporary work, while the Purcell Room is the most intimate venue.

The Vaults

MAP PAGE 105, POCKET MAP K18
Leake Street ⊖ Waterloo Ⓦ thevaults. london.
Just off Lower Marsh, you'll find Leake Street, a graffiti-covered tunnel which has attracted the city's street artists for a decade. It's an area to watch, with bars and restaurants opening up in the arcades along here, but long-time residents are The Vaults, a warren of theatre spaces and bars, known for immersive theatre and other inventive shows.

Bankside and Borough

In Tudor and Stuart London, the chief reason for crossing the Thames to Southwark was to visit the then disreputable Bankside entertainment district around the south end of London Bridge. Four hundred years on, Londoners have rediscovered the area, thanks to wholesale regeneration that has engendered a wealth of new attractions along the riverside – with the charge led by the mighty Tate Modern. And with a traffic-free, riverside path connecting most of the sights, plus the magnificent, gourmet Borough Market to tempt you (see page 116), this is easily one of the most enjoyable areas of London in which to hang out.

Millennium Bridge

MAP PAGE 112, POCKET MAP L6–L7

⊖ Southwark.

The first new bridge to be built across the Thames since Tower Bridge opened in 1894, the sleek, stainless-steel Millennium Bridge is London's sole pedestrian-only river crossing. A suspension bridge of innovative design, it famously bounced up and down when it first opened and had to be closed immediately for two years for repairs. It still wobbles a bit, but most people are too busy enjoying the spectacular views across to St Paul's Cathedral and Tate Modern to notice.

Millennium Bridge

Tate Modern

MAP PAGE 112, POCKET MAP L7
Bankside ⊖ Southwark ⓦ tate.org.uk.
Free; charge for special exhibitions.

Bankside is dominated by the austere power station transformed by the Swiss duo Herzog & de Meuron into Tate Modern, where the Tate shows off its vast collection of international modern art. Opened in 2000 as the world's largest modern art gallery, astonishingly it has since doubled in size, with a brick-clad, twisting eleven-storey extension by the same architects. This is the **Blavatnik Building**; the original power station is the **Boiler House**. Linking the two is the stupendously large **Turbine Hall**, normally used to display one huge installation. You can enter from the riverside – which brings you to the bridge spanning the Turbine Hall – the west side, with a ramp sloping down to level 0 of the Turbine Hall; or via the piazza on the south side. Level 0 of the Blavatnik Building, directly off the Turbine Hall, is the power station's original **Tanks** – roughly finished, large circular spaces for performance art, film and large installations. Levels 2, 3 and 4 of both wings are the main gallery spaces (level 3 of the Boiler House is dedicated to temporary exhibitions). The curators have eschewed the usual chronological approach and gone instead for hanging works according to themes and ideas, so you'll find works by the likes of Picasso, Brancusi, Lichtenstein, Riley and Hepworth alongside newer names as befits the particular exhibit. Increasingly Tate also displays works by artists from across the globe. They also regularly rehang the galleries, so expect things to change between

Extension at Tate Modern

visits. Given the size – there are around eight hundred works on show – you need to devote the best part of a day to do it justice, or be very selective. It's worth picking up a plan or multimedia guide. If you're not sure where to begin, take the escalator to level 2 of the Boiler House for the small **Start Display**, which features a few of Tate's most famous works, including Matisse's *The Snail* (1953), as an introduction to the collection. Also on level 2, you'll find rooms dedicated to Joseph Beuys – at the centre of the Artists and Society exhibition that links politics, social movements and art – and Mark Rothko, whose abstract Seagram Murals have their own shrine-like room. Finally, take the time to enjoy the magnificent views – out over the river from the restaurant on level 6 of the main building,

Tate to Tate

The **Tate Boat** shuttles between Tate Britain and Tate Modern every twenty to thirty minutes; journey time is twenty minutes.

Bankside and Borough

or from the spectacular viewing level at the top of the Blavatnik Building.

Shakespeare's Globe Theatre

MAP PAGE 112, POCKET MAP M7
21 New Globe Walk ⊖ Southwark or London Bridge 🌐 shakespearesglobe.com. Charge for exhibition.

Dwarfed by the Tate Modern, but equally remarkable in its own way, Shakespeare's Globe Theatre is an open-air reconstruction of the polygonal playhouse where most of the Bard's later works were first performed. Sporting the first new thatched roof in central London since the 1666 Great Fire, the theatre puts on plays by Shakespeare and his contemporaries, both outside and in the indoor candlelit theatre (see page 117). To find out more about Shakespeare and Bankside, visit the Globe's stylish **exhibition**, whose imaginative hands-on displays really hit the spot. Visitors also get taken on an informative half-hour **guided tour** round the theatre itself, except in the afternoons during the summer season, when you can only visit the exhibition. Tours of Shakespeare's Southwark and the Sam Wanamaker Playhouse are on offer too.

Golden Hinde

MAP PAGE 112, POCKET MAP M7
St Mary Overie Dock, Cathedral St ⊖ London Bridge 🌐 goldenhinde.com. Charge.

An exact replica of the galleon in which **Francis Drake** sailed around the world from 1577 to 1580, this modern version of the *Golden Hinde* circumnavigated the globe for some twenty years before eventually settling permanently in Southwark. The ship is surprisingly small, and its original crew of eighty-plus must

ACCOMMODATION	
Ibis Styles London	1
Thameside YHA	2

MARKETS	
Borough Market	1
Maltby Street Food Market	2

VENUES	
Sam Wanamaker Playhouse	1
Shakespeare's Globe Theatre	1

PUBS	
George Inn	3
Market Porter	2
The Miller	4
Royal Oak	5

RESTAURANTS	
40 Maltby Street	2
Bala Baya	1
Pizarro	3

have been cramped to say the least. They put on lots of activities for kids – such as all-important pirate training – and host evening gigs for grown-ups.

Clink Prison Museum

MAP PAGE 112, POCKET MAP N7
1 Clink St ⊖ London Bridge Ⓦ clink.co.uk. Charge.

Housed in the suitably dismal confines of an old cellar, this museum explores the history of the former **Clink Prison**, which once stood close by. The prison began as a medieval dungeon for disobedient clerics under the Bishop of Winchester's Palace – the **rose window** of the Great Hall has survived just east of the museum – and later became a dumping ground for Bankside lowlife, before being burnt to the ground by rioters in 1780. The exhibition features a handful of prison-life tableaux and plenty of graphic descriptions of the torture and horror experienced by the prisoners.

Southwark Cathedral

MAP PAGE 112, POCKET MAP M7
Cathedral St ⊖ London Bridge
Ⓦ southwarkcathedral.org.uk. Free.

Of the original thirteenth-century Augustinian priory church of St Mary Overie, only the choir and retrochoir now remain, separated by a tall and beautiful stone Tudor screen; they're thought to be the oldest Gothic structures left in London. The nave was rebuilt in the nineteenth century, but the cathedral contains numerous interesting monuments, from a thirteenth-century oak effigy of a knight to an early twentieth-century memorial to Shakespeare (his brother is buried here). Above the memorial is a stained-glass window featuring a whole cast of characters from the plays.

HMS Belfast

Old Operating Theatre and Herb Garret

MAP PAGE 112, POCKET MAP N7
9a St Thomas St ⊖ London Bridge
ⓦ oldoperatingtheatre.com. Charge.

By far the most educational – and strangest – of Southwark's museums is the Old Operating Theatre. Visitors must climb up to the attic of a former church tower, which houses an old hospital **apothecary**, with displays explaining the painful truth about pre-anaesthetic operations. These took place in the adjacent women's **operating theatre**, designed in 1821 "in the round", literally like a theatre, so that students (and members of high society) could view the proceedings. There's an informative tour too (charge).

The Shard

MAP PAGE 112, POCKET MAP N7
32 London Bridge ⊖ London Bridge
ⓦ theviewfromtheshard.com. Charge.

London's – and the country's – tallest building, Renzo Piano's 1016ft-high, tapered, glass-clad skyscraper **The Shard**, once seen as hubristic, has become part of the cityscape since it topped out in 2012. It houses a mixture of flats, restaurants, a hotel and expensive top-floor viewing platforms (the uppermost open to the sky). The views are sublime, making everything else in London look small, from the unicycle of the London Eye to the tiny box that is St Paul's Cathedral, while the model railway of London Bridge is played out below you.

HMS Belfast

MAP PAGE 112, POCKET MAP N7
The Queen's Walk ⊖ London Bridge
ⓦ iwm.org.uk/visits/hms-belfast. Charge.

An 11,550-ton **Royal Navy cruiser**, HMS *Belfast* saw action both in World War II and in the Korean War, and has been permanently moored on the Thames since 1971. The most enjoyable aspect of a visit is exploring the maze of cabins and scrambling up and down the vertiginous ladders. Be sure to check out the top Flag Deck for the views and the claustrophobic lowest levels, the Boiler and Engine rooms.

City Hall

MAP PAGE 112, POCKET MAP N7
The Queen's Walk ⊖ London Bridge or
Tower Hill Ⓤ london.gov.uk. Free.
Bearing a striking resemblance
to a giant car headlight, Norman
Foster's startling glass-encased
City Hall previously served as
the headquarters for the **Greater
London Authority** and the Mayor
of London. Visitors are welcome to
stroll up the helical walkway, visit
the café and watch proceedings
from the second floor. The outside
amphitheatre, "the Scoop", is a
venue for free events in summer.

Bermondsey Street

MAP PAGE 112, POCKET MAP N8
⊖ London Bridge.
Bermondsey, the area east of
London Bridge, was once famous
for its wharves, tanneries and
factories. The wharves along
the river underwent extensive
redevelopment in the 1980s,
particularly east of Tower Bridge
around Butler's Wharf, while the
area's old high street has been
transformed over the last decade

or so into an appealing stretch
of cafés, pubs, art galleries and
restaurants; you'll also find small
breweries and street food stalls
at weekends at nearby Maltby
Street, and gourmet delights
at Borough Market (see page
116). For contemporary art, the
biggest player around is the White
Cube gallery at nos. 144–152
(Ⓦ whitecube.com; free). On
Bermondsey Square, the venerable
Bermondsey antique market takes
place early on Friday mornings.

Fashion & Textile Museum

MAP PAGE 112, POCKET MAP N8
83 Bermondsey St ⊖ London Bridge or
Borough Ⓦ fashiontextilemuseum.org.
Charge.
Lifelong dream of Zandra Rhodes,
fashion's *grande dame extraordinaire*,
the FTM is an arresting sight –
daubed in yellow, pink and orange.
The museum's exhibitions are
wide-ranging – from vintage frocks
to specialist textile shows. Items
on display draw from her own vast
collection and beyond, and are
exhibited with care and flair.

City Hall

Markets

Borough Market

MAP PAGE 112, POCKET MAP M7

8 Southwark St ⊖ London Bridge
ⓦ boroughmarket.org.uk.

Fine-food heaven, Borough has long been *the* London institution for gourmets, and attracts suppliers from all over the UK who converge to sell organic and artisan goodies from around the world. There's also a global array of street food vendors most days of the week, and cooking displays in the glass foyer. The Victorian market hall, with its slender wrought-iron columns, is lovely. Prices are high and Saturdays can be a crush; arrive early.

Maltby Street Food Market

MAP PAGE 112, POCKET MAP O8

Maltby St ⊖ Tower Bridge
ⓦ maltbystreetmarket.co.uk.

Near Borough Market, this street food hot spot huddles under the railway arches near Tower Bridge. Most action is on the lively Ropewalk, with its pop-up bars, cafés and snack stalls – plus tap rooms for several of the microbreweries that cluster here.

Maltby Street Food Market

Restaurants

40 Maltby Street

MAP PAGE 112, POCKET MAP O8

40 Maltby St ⊖ Bermondsey
ⓦ 40maltbystreet.com.

Hunker down in this market wine bar for exceptional, gutsy food and natural wines. No reservations. ££

Bala Baya

MAP PAGE 112, POCKET MAP L8

Arch 25, Old Union Yard Arches, 229 Union St ⊖ Borough or Southwark ⓦ balabaya. co.uk.

Nestled under the railway arches, among a clutch of new restaurants, this minimal place draws on the style and flavours of Tel Aviv. Grab a pitta for lunch – with braised beef and tahini, or salmon and pomegranate molasses – or linger over small plates and cocktails come evening. ££

Pizarro

MAP PAGE 112, POCKET MAP N8

194 Bermondsey St ⊖ London Bridge
ⓦ josepizarro.com/venues/pizarro-restaurant-bermondsey.

Smart restaurant run by José Pizarro, one of London's finest Spanish chefs – his sherry/tapas bar, *José*, nearby at no. 104, is also terrific. With its short menu of unfussy, beautifully executed food, Spanish wines and sherries, it's at the heart of Bermondsey's foodie scene. Tapas, coffee and pastries served all day. £££

Pubs

George Inn

MAP PAGE 112, POCKET MAP M7

77 Borough High St ⊖ London Bridge.
London's only surviving galleried coaching inn, dating from the seventeenth century, and now owned by the National Trust. Expect lots of wonky flooring, half-timbering, a good range of real ales and a fair smattering of tourists.

Globe Theatre

Market Porter

MAP PAGE 112, POCKET MAP M7
9 Stoney St ⊖ London Bridge
Ⓦ themarketporter.co.uk.
Handsome corner pub by Borough
Market, with an interesting range
of real ales and decent food.
Outrageously popular, as evidenced
by the masses that spill out onto
the surrounding pavements.

The Miller

MAP PAGE 112, POCKET MAP N8
96 Snowsfields ⊖ London Bridge
Ⓦ themiller.co.uk.
A big, fun – sometimes raucous
– and slightly studenty pub, the
Miller has lots of outdoor space,
an impressive craft beer and cider
selection, ping-pong table, pool
and table football.

Royal Oak

MAP PAGE 112, POCKET MAP M8
44 Tabard St ⊖ Borough
Ⓦ royaloaklondon.co.uk.
Lovingly unchanging Victorian
pub that has the air of a village
local, and opts simply for serving a
superb stock of real ales (mild, pale
and old) from Harveys Brewery in
Sussex. Good old-fashioned pub
grub and excellent Sunday roasts.

Venues

Sam Wanamaker Playhouse

MAP PAGE 112, POCKET MAP M7
21 New Globe Walk ⊖ Southwark or
London Bridge Ⓦ shakespearesglobe.
com.
Attached to Shakespeare's Globe
theatre, this Jacobean-style indoor
venue presents an intriguing
programme of Shakespeare, early
theatre and music events – all
in an intimate and atmospheric,
candlelit space.

Shakespeare's Globe Theatre

MAP PAGE 112, POCKET MAP M7
21 New Globe Walk ⊖ Southwark or
London Bridge Ⓦ shakespearesglobe.com.
This thatch-roofed replica of the
famous Elizabethan theatre (see
page 112) uses natural light
and the minimum of scenery,
and puts on fun, historically
authentic and critically acclaimed
plays by Shakespeare and his
contemporaries – though they do
experiment with new stagings –
with Yard tickets (standing-room
only) for £5.

Kensington and Chelsea

London's wealthiest district, the Royal Borough of Kensington and Chelsea is particularly well-to-do in the area south of Hyde Park. The moneyed feel here is evident in the flash shops and swanky bars as well as the plush houses and apartments. The most popular area for tourists, meanwhile, is South Kensington, where three of London's top museums stand side by side. Further south, Chelsea has a slightly more bohemian pedigree, although these days, it's really just another wealthy west London suburb. To the north, Notting Hill is rammed solid with trendy – but wealthy – media folk, yet retains a strong Moroccan and Portuguese presence, as well as vestiges of the African-Caribbean community who initiated – and still run – Carnival, the city's largest street party.

Wellington Arch

MAP PAGE 120, POCKET MAP B18
Hyde Park Corner ⊖ Hyde Park Corner
Ⓦ english-heritage.org.uk. Charge.
Standing in the midst of one of London's busiest traffic interchanges, Wellington Arch was erected in 1828 to commemorate Wellington's victories in the Napoleonic Wars. In 1846, it was topped by an equestrian statue of the Duke himself, which was later replaced by Peace driving a four-horse chariot. Inside, you can view an informative exhibition on the arch and temporary exhibitions and take a lift to the top of the monument, where the exterior balconies offer a bird's-eye view of the surrounding area.

Wellington Arch

Apsley House

MAP PAGE 120, POCKET MAP B18
Hyde Park Corner ⊖ Hyde Park Corner
Ⓦ english-heritage.org.uk. Charge.
The former London residence of the "Iron Duke", Apsley House contains a plethora of Wellington memorabilia and gifts he received, though the highlight here is the **art collection**, much of which used to belong to the King of Spain. Among the best pieces, displayed in the Waterloo Gallery on the first floor, are works by de Hooch, van Dyck, Velázquez, Goya, Rubens and Murillo. The famous, more than twice life-size, nude statue of Napoleon by

The Serpentine in Hyde Park

Antonio Canova stands at the foot of the main staircase. It was disliked by the sitter, not least for the figure of Victory in the emperor's hand, which appears to be trying to fly away.

Hyde Park

MAP PAGE 120, POCKET MAP E7
Ⓦ royalparks.org.uk.
Seized from the Church by Henry VIII to satisfy his desire for yet more hunting grounds, Hyde Park was first opened to the public by James I, when refreshments available included "milk from a red cow". Hangings, muggings and duels, the **1851 Great Exhibition** and numerous public events have all taken place here – and it's still a popular gathering point or destination for political demonstrations. For the most part, however, Hyde Park is simply a leisure ground – a wonderful open space that allows you to lose all sight of the city beyond a few persistent tower blocks.

At the treeless northeastern corner is **Marble Arch**, erected in 1828 as a triumphal entry to Buckingham Palace but now stranded on a ferociously busy traffic island at the west end of Oxford Street. This is the most historically charged spot in Hyde Park, as it marks the site of Tyburn gallows, the city's main location for public executions until 1783, when the action moved to Newgate. It's also the location of **Speakers' Corner**, a peculiarly English Sunday tradition, featuring an assembly of soap-box orators, religious extremists and hecklers.

At the centre of the park is the curvaceous lake of the **Serpentine**. Rowing boats and pedalos can be rented from the boathouse on the north bank, while the lake's popular **Lido** is situated on the south bank. Nearby is the **Diana Memorial Fountain**, less of a fountain, and more of a giant oval-shaped mini-moat, in which kids can dip their feet.

Kensington and Chelsea

ACCOMMODATION	
Aster House	12
B+B Belgravia	11
Caring Hotel	4
Columbia Hotel	6
Garden Court Hotel	2
The Halkin	9
Kensington House Hotel	8
The Main House	3
Meininger	10
The Resident	13
Safestay Holland Park	7
Sonder Chelsea Green	14
St David's Hotels	1
Vancouver Studios	5

CLUBS & VENUES	
Ciné Lumière	11
Electric Cinema	2
Notting Hill Arts Club	4
Royal Albert Hall	7
Royal Court	12

PUBS & BARS	
Chelsea Potter	14
Churchill Arms	5
Coopers Arms	15
The Cow	1
Fox and Hounds	13
Grenadier	9
Nag's Head	8
The Queen's Arms	10
Victoria	3
Windsor Castle	6

Kensington Gardens

MAP PAGE 120, POCKET MAP C7
⊖ Queensway, Lancaster Gate or High Street Kensington ⊛ royalparks.org.uk.

The more tranquil, leafier half of Hyde Park, Kensington Gardens is home to **Long Water**, the pretty upper section of the Serpentine and the **Italian Gardens**, a group of five fountains laid out symmetrically in front of an Italianate loggia.

One of the park's best-loved monuments is **Peter Pan**, the fictional character who enters London along the Serpentine in the eponymous tale. The book's author, J.M. Barrie, used to walk his dog in Kensington Gardens, and it was here that he met the five pretty, upper-class Llewelyn Davies boys, who wore "blue blouses and bright red tam o'shanters". They were the inspiration for the book's "Lost Boys", and he eventually became their guardian. Barrie himself paid for the statue, which was erected in secret during the night in 1912. More fun for kids (and also inspired by Peter Pan), is the nearby excellent **Diana Memorial Playground**.

To the south of Peter Pan is the **Serpentine Gallery** (⊛ serpentinegalleries.org; free), which has a reputation for lively and often controversial contemporary art exhibitions. Their second building, the **Serpentine North Gallery**, is in a converted gunpowder store with Zaha-Hadid-designed restaurant extension, on the other side of Long Water. The gallery also commissions a leading architect each year to design a summer **pavilion**.

The park's most impressive monument by far, however, is the **Albert Memorial**, erected in 1876. It's as much a hymn to the glorious achievements of the British Empire as to its subject, Queen Victoria's husband, whose gilded image sits under its central canopy, clutching a catalogue for the 1851 Great Exhibition. If you want to learn more about the 169 life-sized depictions of long-gone artists (all men) around the pediment, join

Diana Memorial Playground

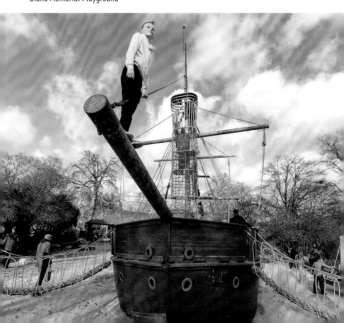

one of the monthly guided tours (45min; charge).

Kensington Palace

MAP PAGE 120, POCKET MAP B8
Kensington Gardens ⊖ Queensway or High Street Kensington Ⓦ hrp.org.uk. Charge.
Bought by William and Mary in 1689, the modestly proportioned Jacobean brick mansion of Kensington Palace was the chief royal residence for the next fifty years. KP, as it's fondly known in royal circles, is best known today as the place where **Princess Diana** lived from her marriage until her death in 1997. Today, it's the official residence of a number of royals including Prince William and Kate Middleton.

The palace is home to the **Royal Ceremonial Dress Collection**, which means you usually get to see a few of the frocks worn by Diana, as well as several of the late Queen's dresses. The highlights of the **King's State Apartments** are the trompe-l'oeil ceiling paintings by William Kent, particularly those in the Cupola Room, and the paintings in the King's Gallery by, among others, Tintoretto. Also of interest in the King's Gallery is the wind dial above the fireplace, connected to the palace weather vane, which was built for William III and is still fully functioning. The **Queen's State Apartments** are more modest.

Exhibits also cover the life – and jewels – of **Queen Victoria**, who spent an unhappy childhood under the steely gaze of her strict German mother. According to her diary, her best friends were the palace's numerous "black beetles".

Brompton Oratory

MAP PAGE 120, POCKET MAP D9
Brompton Rd ⊖ South Kensington Ⓦ bromptonoratory.co.uk. Free.
London's most flamboyant Roman Catholic church, Brompton Oratory was completed in 1886 and modelled on the Gesù church

Brompton Oratory

in Rome. The ornate Italianate interior is filled with gilded mosaics and stuffed with sculpture, much of it genuine Italian Baroque, while the pulpit is a superb piece of Neo-Baroque from the 1930s; note the high cherub count on the tester. And true to its architecture, the church practises "smells and bells" Catholicism, with daily Mass in Latin.

Natural History Museum

MAP PAGE 120, POCKET MAP D9
Cromwell Rd ⊖ South Kensington Ⓦ nhm. ac.uk. Free.
With its 675ft terracotta facade, Alfred Waterhouse's purpose-built mock-Romanesque 1881 colossus ensures the Natural History Museum's status as London's most handsome museum. The collections are as much an important resource for serious zoologists as they are a popular attraction.

The main entrance leads to the vast central **Hintze Hall**, dominated by a huge blue whale

Natural History Museum

skeleton suspended from the ceiling in a dramatic diving pose. To one side, you'll find the **Dinosaur** gallery, where the highlight for many kids is the grisly life-sized animatronic dinosaur tableau. Other child-friendly sections include the **Creepy-Crawlies** room, which features a live colony of leaf-cutter ants and the old-fashioned **Mammals** gallery.

For a visually exciting romp through evolution, head for the **Red Zone** (once the Geology Museum); popular sections include the slightly tasteless Kobe earthquake simulator, and the spectacular display of gems and crystals in the Earth's Treasury.

Little visited compared to the rest of the museum, the **Orange Zone** is dominated by the Cocoon, a giant concrete egg encased within the Darwin Centre's atrium, and home to over 20-million specimens. On the top floors visitors can learn more about the scientific research and specimen collections, and, in the nearby Zoology spirit building, view a small selection of bits and bobs pickled in glass jars (behind

the scenes tours available). From here you can exit via the wildlife garden.

Science Museum

MAP PAGE 120, POCKET MAP D9
Exhibition Rd ⊖ South Kensington
ⓦ sciencemuseum.org.uk. Free.
The Science Museum is undeniably impressive, filling its large, multi-level spaces with items from every conceivable area of science, including space travel, telecommunications, time, mathematics, chemistry and medicine. First off, ask at the information desk for details of the day's events and demonstrations. By the entrance is the Energy Hall – dominated by large pumping engines from the days of steam – the ground floor continues on to Exploring Space, with some impressive rockets and space craft, then Making the Modern World, a display of iconic inventions. Beyond here is the Wellcome Wing, with its interactive galleries and IMAX cinema. Kids will love the third floor for its hands-on experimentation and whizz-bang science shows at the Wonderlab

Interactive gallery, while an endearingly vintage museum feel is retained up in the hangar-like Flight Gallery on the third floor, with some wonderful old flying machines.

Victoria and Albert Museum

MAP PAGE 120, POCKET MAP D9
Entrances on Cromwell & Exhibition roads
⊖ South Kensington Ⓦ vam.ac.uk. Free.

In terms of sheer variety and scale, the **V&A** is the greatest museum of applied arts in the world. Beautifully but haphazardly displayed across a seven-mile, four-storey maze of halls and corridors, the V&A's treasures are impossible to survey in a single visit.

The most celebrated of the V&A's exhibits are the **Raphael Cartoons**, seven vast biblical paintings that served as designs for a set of tapestries destined for the Sistine Chapel. Close by, you can view highlights from the UK's largest dress collection and the world's biggest collection of Indian art outside India. In addition, there are extensive Chinese, Islamic and Japanese galleries; a gallery of twentieth-century **objets d'art** to rival the Design Museum; and more Constable **paintings** than Tate Britain. And the V&A's temporary shows – for which you have to pay – are among the best in Britain, some housed in the new subterranean exhibition spaces near the elegant Exhibition Road entrance, where the original Portland stone screen has been opened up to give access onto the gleaming white Sackler Courtyard.

Wading through the huge collection of European sculpture, you come to the surreal **plaster casts** gallery, filled with copies of European art's greatest hits, from Michelangelo's *David* to Trajan's Column from the forum in Rome (sawn in half to make it fit). The chronologically displayed British and European galleries are superb, with a number of complete period interiors displayed. Before you leave, make sure you check out the museum's beautifully decorated trio of original refreshment rooms, the **Morris, Gamble & Poynter Rooms**, at the back of the main galleries.

Holy Trinity Church

MAP PAGE 120, POCKET MAP F9
Sloane Square ⊖ Sloane Square
Ⓦ holytrinitysloanesquare.co.uk. Free.

An architectural masterpiece created in 1890, Holy Trinity is probably the finest **Arts and Crafts** church in London. The east window is the most glorious of the furnishings, a vast, 48-panel extravaganza designed by Edward Burne-Jones, and the largest ever made by Morris & Co. Holy Trinity is very High Church, filled with the smell of incense, statues of the Virgin Mary and confessionals.

Victoria and Albert Museum

Saatchi Gallery

MAP PAGE 120, POCKET MAP E10
King's Rd ⊖ Sloane Square
ⓦ saatchigallery.com. Free for most exhibitions.

On the south side of King's Road, a short stroll from Sloane Square, are the former **Duke of York's Barracks**, now housing upmarket shops and cafés. The main building, erected in 1801 and fronted by a solid-looking Tuscan portico, is home to the privately run Saatchi Gallery. Its fifteen whitewashed rooms – "a study in blandness" according to one art critic – host changing exhibitions of contemporary art.

Royal Hospital Chelsea

MAP PAGE 120, POCKET MAP F10
Royal Hospital Rd ⊖ Sloane Square
ⓦ chelsea-pensioners.co.uk. Free.

Founded as a retirement home for army veterans by Charles II in 1682 and still going strong, the Wren-designed Royal Hospital is worth a visit for the vast, barrel-vaulted **chapel**, with its colourful apse fresco, and the equally grand, wood-panelled **dining hall**, opposite, with its allegorical mural of Charles II and his hospital. In the Secretary's Office, on the east side of the hospital, there's a small **museum**, displaying Pensioners' uniforms, medals and two German bombs.

National Army Museum

MAP PAGE 120, POCKET MAP E11
Royal Hospital Rd ⊖ Sloane Square
ⓦ nam.ac.uk. Free.

Appropriately housed in a sort of concrete bunker, the National Army Museum has recently been completely remodelled. Beyond the array of historical artefacts, uniforms, medals and artworks – including the skeleton of Napoleon's horse – it re-examines military life and the role of the British Army as an instrument of empire through five themed exhibition areas, including lots of hands-on stuff for kids, and an "assault course" play centre.

Portobello Road

Chelsea Physic Garden

MAP PAGE 120, POCKET MAP E11
Royal Hospital Rd ⊖ Sloane Square
Ⓦ chelseaphysicgarden.co.uk. Charge.
Hidden from the road by a high
wall, Chelsea Physic Garden is a
charming little inner-city escape.
Founded in 1673, it's the second
oldest botanic garden in the
country. Unfortunately, it's also
rather small, and a little too close
to Chelsea Embankment to be a
peaceful oasis, but keen botanists
will enjoy it nevertheless. There's
also a café, which serves home-
made cakes.

Portobello Road Market

MAP PAGE 120, POCKET MAP A6
⊖ Notting Hill Gate or Ladbroke Grove
Ⓦ visitportobello.com.
Situated in one of the wealthiest
parts of town, Portobello Road
Market is always a great spot for
a browse and a bargain. Things
kick off, at the intersection with
Chepstow Villas, with junky
antique stalls and classier, pricier
antique shops. After a brief
switch to fruit and veg around
the 1910 **Electric Cinema**, the
market gets a lot more fun at
Portobello Green, where the
emphasis switches to retro clothes
and jewellery, records and books.
Further up again, the secondhand
material becomes pure boot-sale,
laid out on rugs on the road.
Beyond, **Golborne Road market**
(same times as Portobello) is
cheaper and less crowded, with
attractive antique and retro
furniture.

Museum of Brands, Packaging and Advertising

MAP PAGE 120, POCKET MAP A5
111–117 Lancaster Rd ⊖ Ladbroke Grove
Ⓦ museumofbrands.com. Charge.
Despite its rather unwieldy title,
it's definitely worth popping into
this museum, which is based on
the private collection of Robert
Opie, a Scot whose compulsive
collecting has left him with ten

Museum of Brands

thousand yoghurt pots alone.
From Victorian ceramic pots of
anchovy paste to the alcopops of
the 1990s, the displays provide a
fascinating social commentary on
the times.

Design Museum

MAP PAGE 120, POCKET MAP A8
224–238 Kensington High St ⊖ High
St Kensington Ⓦ designmuseum.org.
Permanent collection free; charge for
special exhibitions.
One of the most striking 1960s
buildings in London, a concrete-
framed structure with a hyperbolic
paraboloid roof and the former
home of the Commonwealth
Institute, has been taken over
by the Design Museum. The
permanent exhibition, **Designer
Maker User**, features highlights
from the museum's collection of
design classics and everyday objects,
while temporary exhibitions cover
fashion, industrial design, graphics,
materials and more.

Leighton House

MAP PAGE 120, POCKET MAP A9
12 Holland Park Rd ⊖ High Street
Kensington ⓦ rbkc.gov.uk/museums.
Charge.

Leighton House was built by the architect George Aitchison for Frederic Leighton, President of the Royal Academy and the only artist ever to be made a peer (albeit on his deathbed). "It will be opulence, it will be sincerity", the artist opined before construction commenced in the 1860s. The big attraction is its domed **Arab Hall**. Based on the banqueting hall of a Moorish palace in Palermo, it has a central black marble fountain, and is decorated with Saracen tiles, gilded mosaics and latticework drawn from all over the Islamic world. The other rooms are less spectacular but in compensation are hung with excellent paintings by Lord Leighton and his Pre-Raphaelite friends Edward Burne-Jones, Lawrence Alma-Tadema and John Everett Millais.

Holland Park

MAP PAGE 120, POCKET MAP A8
⊖ Holland Park or High Street Kensington.

Holland Park is laid out in the former grounds of the Jacobean mansion of Holland House – sadly only the east wing survived the war, but it's enough to give an idea of what the place looked like. Several formal gardens are laid out before the house, drifting down in terraces to a café, a restaurant (the former Garden Ballroom) and an art gallery. The most unusual of the gardens is the **Kyoto Garden**, a Japanese-style sanctuary to the northwest of the house, peppered with modern sculpture and complete with koi carp and peacocks.

Holland Park Kyoto Garden

Kensal Green Cemetery

MAP PAGE 120
Harrow Rd ⊖ Kensal Green
ⓦ kensalgreencemetery.com &
ⓦ kensalgreen.co.uk. Free.

Opened in 1833, Kensal Green Cemetery was the first of the city's commercial graveyards, and contains some of London's most extravagant Gothic tombs. The cemetery is vast, so it makes sense to join one of the **guided tours** (extra charge). Graves of the more famous incumbents – Thackeray, Trollope, Siemens and the Brunels – are less interesting architecturally than those on either side of the **Centre Avenue**, which leads from the eastern entrance on Harrow Road. Worth looking out for are Major-General Casement's bier, held up by four grim-looking turbaned Indians; circus manager Andrew Ducrow's conglomeration of beehive, sphinx and angels; and artist William Mulready's neo-Renaissance extravaganza.

Shops

Harrods

MAP PAGE 120, POCKET MAP E8
87–135 Brompton Rd ⊖ Knightsbridge
Ⓦ harrods.com.
London's most famous department
store is an enduring landmark of
quirks and pretensions – not least
its dress code (no clothing revealing
intimate parts of the body). It's
notable for its Art Nouveau tiled
food hall, the huge toy department
and its range of designer labels.

Harvey Nichols

MAP PAGE 120, POCKET MAP A19
109–125 Knightsbridge ⊖ Knightsbridge
Ⓦ harveynichols.com.
Absolutely fabulous, darling, with
eight floors of the latest designer
collections and more casual
clothing. The gorgeous cosmetics
department is frequented by A- and
Z-listers alike, while the fifth-floor
food hall offers frivolous goodies at
high prices.

Lutyens & Rubinstein

MAP PAGE 120
21 Kensington Park Rd ⊖ Ladbroke Grove
Ⓦ landrbookshop.co.uk.
Classy bookshop with a hand-
selected array of classics, titles in
translation, poetry, art books and
literary gifts. A bibliophiles' dream.

Rigby & Peller

MAP PAGE 120, POCKET MAP E10
13 King's Rd ⊖ Sloane Square
Ⓦ rigbyandpeller.com.
Once corsetières to the late
Queen, if that can be counted as a
recommendation, this store stocks a
wide range of beautiful lingerie and
swimwear, with designer names as
well as its own range, for all shapes
and sizes. The personal fitting service
is deemed to be London's best.

Rough Trade

MAP PAGE 120, POCKET MAP A6
130 Talbot Rd ⊖ Ladbroke Grove
Ⓦ roughtrade.com.

Harvey Nichols

Legendary indie music specialist
shop, first opened in 1976 at the
height of punk/new wave, with
knowledgeable, friendly staff and a
dizzying array of genres from indie-
pop and electronica to country and
beyond. There is a sister store across
town on Brick Lane (see page 93).

Worlds End

MAP PAGE 120, POCKET MAP D11
430 King's Rd ⊖ Sloane Square
Ⓦ viviennewestwood.com/en-gb/
sustainability/craftsmanship-and-
heritage/worlds-end-collection.
Iconic Vivienne Westwood outlet,
on the far end of the King's Road,
selling classics, new pieces and
samples, some of them recycled. In
a previous incarnation, when it was
co-owned by Malcolm McLaren, it
sold proto-punk fetishist gear, and
became a magnet for the young
punks who went on to form the
Sex Pistols.

Cafés

Books for Cooks

MAP PAGE 120
4 Blenheim Crescent ⊖ Ladbroke Grove
Ⓦ booksforcooks.com.

Pasteis de nata at Lisboa Patisserie

Tiny "test kitchen" within London's top cookery bookshop. It's cramped but friendly; this is an experience not to be missed, with tasty dishes at low prices. Make sure you get there in time to grab a table for the set-menu lunch (check their X (formerly Twitter) account for the day's menu). £

Capote y Toros

MAP PAGE 120, POCKET MAP C10
157 Old Brompton Rd ⊖ Gloucester Road or South Kensington ⓦ cambiodeterciogroup.co.uk/capote-y-toros.
Sunny bar with emphasis on sherries (more than 125 available, dozens by the glass), and interesting tapas. ££

Hagen Espresso Bar

MAP PAGE 120
151 King's Road ⊖ South Kensington ⓦ thehagenproject.com.

Tiny Danish specialty coffee with an emphasis on sustainability. Tiny with limited seating options, and very chic. Delicious cinnamon buns – as you might expect. £

Lisboa Patisserie

MAP PAGE 120
57 Golborne Rd ⊖ Ladbroke Grove ⓦ lisboapatisserie.co.uk.
Authentic Portuguese *pastelaria*, with the best *pasteis de nata* (custard tarts) this side of Lisbon – also coffee, cakes and a friendly atmosphere. £

Orée

MAP PAGE 120, POCKET MAP E10
65 King's Road ⊖ Sloane Square ⓦ oree.co.uk.
Bakery-patisserie specializing in delicious classic French pastries – immaculate eclairs and Paris-Brest – and a few contemporary flavours (yuzu lemon tart). It also serves open sandwiches, brunch and gluten-free options. Not cheap – but this is the King's Road – and they also have eleven other branches. ££

Restaurants

Al Waha

MAP PAGE 120, POCKET MAP B6
75 Westbourne Grove ⊖ Bayswater or Queensway ⓣ 020 7229 0806.
Arguably London's most authentic Lebanese restaurant; courteous service and delicious meze, but also mouthwatering main course dishes involving various permutations of grilled chicken and lamb. ££

Dinner by Heston Blumenthal

MAP PAGE 120, POCKET MAP A19
Mandarin Oriental Hotel, 66 Knightsbridge ⊖ Knightsbridge ⓦ dinnerbyheston.co.uk.
Heston doesn't actually cook here, but one of his former *Fat Duck* chefs serves wildly imaginative

food, using old English recipes that give you a once-in-a-lifetime experience. £££

Hereford Road
MAP PAGE 120, POCKET MAP B6
3 Hereford Rd ⊖ Bayswater or Notting Hill Gate ⓦ herefordroad.org.
Highly accomplished English cooking focusing on simple, old-fashioned excellence and seasonal produce. ££

Hunan
MAP PAGE 120, POCKET MAP F10
51 Pimlico Rd ⊖ Sloane Square
ⓦ hunanlondon.com.
Despite the name, this serves Taiwanese/Chinese fusion food. There's no menu: tell them how spicy you like things, and they will bring you a vast array of small dishes. ££££

The Ledbury
MAP PAGE 120, POCKET MAP A6
127 Ledbury Rd ⊖ Westbourne Park
ⓦ theledbury.com.
Aussie chef Brett Graham's modern food – elegant, confident and delicate – well deserves its two Michelin stars. ££££

Medlar
MAP PAGE 120, POCKET MAP D11
438 King's Rd ⊖ Fulham Broadway
ⓦ medlarrestaurant.co.uk.
A lovely, upscale place offering French-influenced Modern British food in a welcoming dining room. It's all prix fixe, and excellent value. £££

Pubs

Chelsea Potter
MAP PAGE 120, POCKET MAP B&
119 King's Road ⊖ South Kensington
ⓦ greeneking.co.uk/pubs/greater-london/chelsea-potter.
Once a favourite of Jimi Hendrix and The Rolling Stones, this traditional corner pub is now a Greene King – but still serves

reliably good pub food and cask ales.

Churchill Arms
MAP PAGE 120, POCKET MAP B7
119 Kensington Church St ⊖ Notting Hill Gate ⓦ churchillarmskensington.co.uk.
Very cosy, quirky, flower-festooned pub serving Fuller's beers, Guinness and good Thai food.

Coopers Arms
MAP PAGE 120, POCKET MAP E11
87 Flood St ⊖ Sloane Square
ⓦ coopersarms.co.uk.
Popular, easy-going neighbourhood pub, offering first-rate Young's beer and British pub grub. The gussied-up interior features lots of vintage styling.

The Cow
MAP PAGE 120, POCKET MAP B5
89 Westbourne Park Rd ⊖ Westbourne Park or Royal Oak ⓦ thecowlondon.com.
Owned by Tom Conran, son of gastro-magnate Terence, this boho pub pulls a lively crowd, due in

Dinner by Heston Blumenthal

part to its food, served in the bar and dining room, which includes a daily supply of fresh oysters.

Fox and Hounds

MAP PAGE 120, POCKET MAP F10

29 Passmore St ⊖ Sloane Square ⓦ foxandhoundssw1.co.uk.

On a quiet street near Sloane Square, this tiny Young's pub provides a perfect winter retreat. With its piano, faux books, oil paintings and relaxed, neighbourhood feel, it's a world away from the glitzier options in these parts.

Grenadier

MAP PAGE 120, POCKET MAP B19

18 Wilton Row ⊖ Hyde Park Corner or Knightsbridge ⓦ grenadierbelgravia.com.

Located in a cobbled mews, this quaint little pub was Wellington's local (his horse mounting block survives outside) and his officers' mess; the original pewter bar survives and the wood-panelled interior is cosy. Serves real ales and pricey food.

Grenadier

Nag's Head

MAP PAGE 120, POCKET MAP A19

53 Kinnerton St ⊖ Hyde Park Corner or Knightsbridge.

A convivial, quirky and raffish little pub in a posh mews, with dark wood-panelling, a mobile phone ban and a wealth of tatty nostalgic bric-a-brac attesting to its bohemian credentials. The sunken backroom has a flagstone floor.

The Queen's Arms

MAP PAGE 120, POCKET MAP C9

30 Queens Gate Mews ⊖ Gloucester Road or South Kensington ⓦ thequeensarmskensington.co.uk.

Tucked away in a charming mews just a short walk from both the Royal Albert Hall and South Ken's museums, the *Queen's Arm's* is a very welcome, relaxed neighbourhood pub in this area.

Victoria

MAP PAGE 120, POCKET MAP D6

10a Strathearn Place ⊖ Lancaster Gate or Paddington ⓦ victoriapaddington.co.uk.

Fabulously ornate corner pub, with two open fires, much Victorian brass and tilework, and gold-trimmed mirrors. The Fuller's beer here is excellent, too.

Windsor Castle

MAP PAGE 120, POCKET MAP A7

114 Campden Hill Rd ⊖ Notting Hill Gate ⓦ thewindsorcastlekensington.co.uk.

Popular, pretty, early Victorian wood-panelled pub with a large courtyard. Good ales, craft beers and classy pub grub – it's a welcoming spot to come across, tucked away in the backstreets of one of London's poshest residential neighbourhoods.

Clubs and venues

Ciné Lumière

MAP PAGE 120, POCKET MAP D9

17 Queensberry Place ⊖ South Kensington ⓦ institut-francais.org.uk.

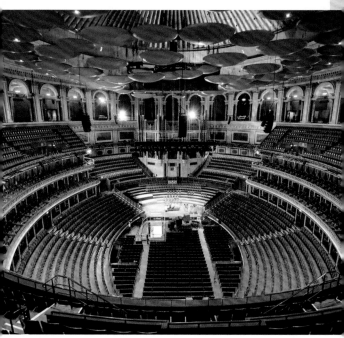

Royal Albert Hall

Predominantly, but by no means exclusively, French films, both old and new (sometimes with subtitles), put on by the Institut Français.

Electric Cinema

MAP PAGE 120
191 Portobello Rd ⊖ Ladbroke Grove
Ⓦ electriccinema.co.uk.
One of the oldest cinemas in the country (opened 1911), the Electric is a stunner, with luxury leather armchairs, footstools, two-seater sofas and an excellent bar.

Notting Hill Arts Club

MAP PAGE 120, POCKET MAP B7
21 Notting Hill Gate ⊖ Notting Hill Gate
Ⓦ nottinghillartsclub.com.
Arty basement club that's popular for everything from Latin-inspired funk, jazz and disco through to soul, house and indie.

Royal Albert Hall

MAP PAGE 120, POCKET MAP C8
Kensington Gore ⊖ South Kensington or High Street Kensington Ⓦ royalalberthall. com.
Splendid red-brick, terracotta and marble concert hall built in 1871 that serves as the main venue for the annual BBC Proms summer festival of classical music (Ⓦ www.bbc.co.uk/proms), and also the place for a whole range of popular shows from opera to pop concerts. Guided tours of the opulent building itself include architectural and behind the scenes options.

Royal Court

MAP PAGE 120, POCKET MAP F10
Sloane Square ⊖ Sloane Square
Ⓦ royalcourttheatre.com.
One of the best places in London to catch radical new writing, either in the proscenium arch downstairs theatre or the smaller-scale studio space; the café-bar buzzes pre- and post-performance. There's also a bookshop on-site.

Regent's Park and Camden

Framed by dazzling Nash-designed, magnolia-stuccoed terraces, and home to London Zoo, Regent's Park is a very civilized and well-maintained spot. Nearby Camden, by contrast, has a scruffy feel to it, despite its many well-to-do residential streets. This is partly due to the chaos and fall-out from the area's perennially popular weekend market, centred around Camden Lock on the Regent's Canal. A warren of stalls with an alternative past still manifest in its quirky wares, street fashion, books, records and street food stalls, the market remains one of the city's best-known off-beat attractions.

Regent's Park

MAP PAGE 135, POCKET MAP E4–F4
🚇 Regent's Park, Great Portland Street or Baker Street 🌐 royalparks.org.uk.

It was under the Prince Regent (later George IV) that Regent's Park began to take its current form – hence its official title – and the public weren't allowed in until 1845 (and even then for just two days of the week). According to John Nash's 1811 masterplan, the park was to be girded by a continuous belt of terraces, and sprinkled with a total of 56 villas, including a magnificent pleasure palace for the prince himself. The plan was never fully realized, but enough was built to create something of the idealized garden city that Nash and the Prince Regent envisaged. Pristine,

Regent's Park

mostly Neoclassical terraces form a near-unbroken horseshoe around the Outer Circle, which marks the park's perimeter along with a handful of handsome villas.

By far the prettiest section of the park is **Queen Mary's Gardens**, within the central Inner Circle. As well as a pond replete with exotic ducks, and a handsomely landscaped giant rockery, a large slice of the gardens is taken up with a glorious **rose garden**, featuring some four hundred varieties surrounded by a ring of ramblers. Along the eastern edge of the park, the tree-lined **Broad Walk** forms a stately approach (much appreciated by rollerbladers) to the park's most popular attraction, London Zoo.

London Central Mosque

MAP PAGE 135, POCKET MAP E4
146 Park Rd, Regent's Park ⊖ St John's Wood or Marylebone ⓦ iccuk.org.

Prominent on the Regent's Park skyline is the shiny copper dome and minaret of the London Central Mosque, an entirely appropriate addition to the park given the Prince Regent's taste for the Orient. Non-Muslim visitors are welcome to look in at the Islam Gallery.

Regent's Canal

MAP PAGE 135, POCKET MAP J2–A4
⊖ Warwick Avenue or Camden Town.
The Regent's Canal, completed in 1820, was constructed as part of a direct link from Birmingham to the newly built London Docks. After an initial period of heavy usage it was overtaken by the railway, and never really paid its way as its investors had hoped. By some miracle, however, it survived, and its nine miles, 42 bridges, twelve locks and two tunnels stand as a reminder of another age. The lock-less stretch of the canal between **Little Venice**

Regent's Canal by boat

Three companies run daily boat services on the Regent's Canal between Camden and Little Venice, passing through the Maida Hill tunnel. The narrowboat **Jenny Wren** (Ⓦwalkersquay.com) starts off at Camden, goes through a canal lock and heads for Little Venice and then back again; while **Jason's** narrowboats (Ⓦjasons.co.uk) start off at Little Venice (though you can get on at Camden). The **London Waterbus Company** (Ⓦlondonwaterbus.com) calls in at London Zoo en route; journey time is 45 minutes one-way.

and Camden Town is the busiest, most attractive section, tunnelling through to Lisson Grove, skirting Regent's Park, offering views of London Zoo, and passing straight through the heart of Camden Market. It's also the one section that's served by scheduled narrow-boats. Alternatively, you can cycle, walk or jog along the towpath.

London Zoo

MAP PAGE 135, POCKET MAP F3
Outer Circle, Regent's Park ⊖ **Camden Town** Ⓦzsl.org/zsl-london-zoo. **Charge.**

London Zoo

The northeastern corner of Regent's Park is occupied by London Zoo. Founded in 1826 with the remnants of the royal menagerie, the enclosures here are as humane as any inner-city zoo could make them, and kids usually enjoy themselves. In particular they love **Animal Adventure**, the children's zoo (and playground) where they can actually handle the animals, and the regular "Animals in Action" live shows. Highlights include the invertebrate house, the **Gorilla Kingdom**, the walk-through **Rainforest Life** where you might get close-up to a sloth, and **Land of the Lions**, designed to look like India's Sasan Gir National Park. The zoo boasts some striking architectural features, too, such as the 1930s modernist, spiral-ramped concrete former **penguin pool** (where Penguin Books' original colophon was sketched but now unused), designed by the Tecton partnership led by Berthold Lubetkin, who also made the zoo's Round House. The **Giraffe House**, by contrast, was designed in Neoclassical style by Decimus Burton. Other landmark features are the mountainous **Mappin Terraces**, from just before World War I, and the colossal tetrahedral aluminium-framed tent of Lord Snowdon's modern **aviary**.

Camden Market

MAP PAGE 135, POCKET MAP F1–G2
⊖ **Camden Town** Ⓦcamdenlock.net.

The Kerb in Camden market

For all the tourist hordes, Camden Market (in actual fact, a conglomeration of markets) remains a genuinely offbeat place. The tiny crafts market, which began in the 1970s in the cobbled courtyard by **Camden Lock**, has since mushroomed out of all proportion, with everyone trying to grab a piece of the action in the warren-like stretch along Camden High Street and Chalk Farm Road. Encroaching developments and several damaging fires haven't dampened its popularity, and it can be quite a crush at weekends.

Many stalls stay open all week long, alongside a crop of shops, cafés and bars. **Stables Market** (the old horse hospital), on Chalk Farm Road, is good for vintage and antiques, and the vast 90s throwback clubwear emporium Cyberdog. And there are plenty of takeaway food outlets ready to fuel hungry shoppers. Though the quality is mixed, some better stalls have opened up in the Stables, and there's a tempting variety at **Kerb Camden** in West Yard (ⓦ kerbfood.com), which hosts some of London's favourite

street food outlets. There's also a brand-new development, **Hawley Wharf**, which boasts more chi-chi eateries, bars and shops, as well as a yoga studio, beauty salon, boxing club and even an underground fairground. Predictably it's had a mixed reception; some love it, but others feel that it only serves to further gentrify the area.

Jewish Museum

MAP PAGE 135, POCKET MAP G2
129 Albert St ⊖ Camden Town
ⓦ jewishmuseum.org.uk. Charge.
Camden is home to London's purpose-built Jewish Museum. On the first floor, there's an engaging exhibition explaining Jewish practices, illustrated by cabinets of Judaica. On the second floor, there's a special Holocaust gallery, which tells the story of Leon Greenman (1920–2008), one of only two British Jews who suffered and survived Auschwitz. The museum also puts on a lively programme of special exhibitions, discussions and concerts, and has a café on the ground floor.

Namaaste Kitchen

Shops

Cyberdog
MAP PAGE 135, POCKET MAP G2
The Stables Market ⊖ Camden Town
Ⓦ cyberdog.net.
An absolute marvel, this mostly underground store is instantly recognizable by the huge silver statues that guard the doors, towering over the hordes of people that flock in and out. Inside, expect techno music, dancing staff members, futuristic clubwear and lots and lots of glow-in-the-dark garments.

Sounds That Swing
MAP PAGE 135, POCKET MAP G2
88 Parkway ⊖ Camden Town
Ⓦ nohitrecords.co.uk.
The bricks-and-mortar store of No Hit Records offers an impeccable selection of retro rockabilly, blues, gospel, ska and the like on vinyl.

Cafés

Greenberry
MAP PAGE 135, POCKET MAP E1
101 Regents Park Rd ⊖ Chalk Farm
Ⓦ greenberrycafe.co.uk.

This buzzy neighbourhood bistro serves fresh, creative food with global influences, weekend brunches, plus home-made ice cream. £

Mamasons Dirty Ice Cream
MAP PAGE 135, POCKET MAP G1
91 Kentish Town Rd ⊖ Kentish Town
Ⓦ dirtyicecream.co.uk.
Touted as London's first Filipino ice cream parlour, these guys are famous for their ube ice cream, a purple yam that gives the ice cream its attractive lilac colour. £

The Regent's Bar & Kitchen
MAP PAGE 135, POCKET MAP F4
Inner Circle, Regent's Park ⊖ Baker Street.
Busy park café with lots of outdoor seating. It's run by the Benugo group and serves wood-fired pizza and Modern European café food. £

Restaurants

Casa Tua
MAP PAGE 135, POCKET MAP G2
176 Royal College St ⊖ Chalk Farm
Ⓦ casatualondon.com/location/camden.
Tiny, brilliant, authentic Italian restaurant with very friendly staff, serving fresh pasta, cocktails, cannoli, and fantastic coffee – naturally. ££

Manna
MAP PAGE 135, POCKET MAP E1
4 Erskine Rd ⊖ Chalk Farm
Ⓦ mannalondon.co.uk.
Long-established restaurant serving large portions of very good vegan food from around the world – with jackfruit burgers, raw lasagne and other vegan inventiveness. ££

Namaaste Kitchen
MAP PAGE 135, POCKET MAP G2
64 Parkway ⊖ Camden Town
Ⓦ namaastekitchen.co.uk.
Superb modern Indian restaurant presenting unusual dishes such as

venison kebab, or splash out on lobster in Kerala spices, along with familiar favourites like chicken tikka masala. ££

Pubs

Edinboro Castle

MAP PAGE 135, POCKET MAP G2
57 Mornington Terrace ⊖ Camden Town
Ⓦ edinborocastlepub.co.uk.
A huge pub with a standard menu, good beer selection and a large, leafy beer garden. Very popular on hot summer days.

Lock Tavern

MAP PAGE 135, POCKET MAP F1
35 Chalk Farm Rd ⊖ Chalk Farm Ⓦ lock-tavern.com.
Rambling pub with comfy sofas, a leafy terrace and beer garden. There's hipster pub grub and DJs/live bands playing anything from punk, funk and electro to avant-country.

Princess of Wales

MAP PAGE 135, POCKET MAP F2
22 Chalcot Rd ⊖ Chalk Farm
Ⓦ lovetheprincess.com.
Smart, popular gastropub with excellent food. You can eat in the pub, the dining room, or the stylish beer garden with its own Banksy-style mural.

Clubs and venues

Electric Ballroom

MAP PAGE 135, POCKET MAP G2
184 Camden High St ⊖ Camden Town
Ⓦ electricballroom.co.uk.
Long-running, grungy venue that hosts rock, metal and indie gigs, plus disco and pop club nights.

Green Note

MAP PAGE 135, POCKET MAP G2
106 Parkway ⊖ Camden Town
Ⓦ greennote.co.uk.
Intimate music venue that punches way above its weight with its

excellent roots, folk and world music. Good veggie snacks, too.

Jazz Café

MAP PAGE 135, POCKET MAP G2
5 Parkway ⊖ Camden Town
Ⓦ thejazzcafelondon.com.
Buzzing venue whose classy music policy explores world music, funk and r'n'b, as well as jazz. If you fancy a sit-down book a seat at one of the restaurant tables.

Open Air Theatre

MAP PAGE 135, POCKET MAP F4
Regent's Park, Inner Circle ⊖ Baker Street
Ⓦ openairtheatre.com.
This beautiful space in Regent's Park hosts a tourist-friendly summer programme of Shakespeare, musicals, contemporary theatre and concerts; perfect when the weather's good.

Roundhouse

MAP PAGE 135, POCKET MAP F1
Chalk Farm Rd ⊖ Chalk Farm
Ⓦ roundhouse.org.uk.
Camden's barn-like former engine shed puts on a variety of theatrical spectacles, circus performances and excellent live gigs.

Open Air Theatre, Regents Park

Hampstead and Highgate

The high points of north London, both geographically and aesthetically, the elegant, largely eighteenth-century developments of Hampstead and Highgate have managed to cling on to their village origins. Of the two, Highgate is slightly sleepier and more aloof, Hampstead busier and buzzier, with high-profile intelligentsia and discerning pop stars among its residents. Both benefit from direct access to one of London's wildest patches of greenery, Hampstead Heath, where you can enjoy stupendous views over London, as well as outdoor concerts and high art in and around the country mansion of Kenwood House.

Hampstead Heath

MAP PAGE 142
Gospel Oak or Hampstead Heath Overground, or ⊖ Hampstead or Golders Green.

Hampstead Heath is the city's most enjoyable public park, with a wonderful variety of bucolic scenery across its 800 acres. At the park's southern end are the rolling green pastures of **Parliament Hill**, north London's premier spot for kite-flying. On either side are numerous **ponds**, three of which – one for men, one for women and one mixed – you can swim in (Ⓦhampsteadheath. net/swimming-ponds; charge). The thickest woodland is to be found in the West Heath, also the

Hampstead Heath

site of the most formal section, **Hill Garden**, a secretive and romantic little gem with eccentric balustraded terraces and a ruined pergola. Beyond lies **Golders Hill Park**, where you can gaze at pygmy goats and fallow deer, and inspect the impeccably maintained aviaries, home to flamingos, cranes and other exotic birds.

Kenwood House

MAP PAGE 142
⊖ Highgate or Golders Green. Ⓦ english-heritage.org.uk. Free.

The Heath's most celebrated sight is the whitewashed Neoclassical mansion of **Kenwood House**, set in its own magnificently landscaped grounds at the high point of the Heath. The house is home to a superlative collection of seventeenth- and eighteenth-century art, including masterpieces by Vermeer, Rembrandt, Boucher, Gainsborough and Reynolds. Of the period interiors, the most spectacular is Robert Adam's sky-blue and gold library.

Keats House

MAP PAGE 142
Keats Grove ⊖ ⊕ Hampstead or Hampstead Heath Overground Ⓦ cityoflondon.gov.uk. Charge.

An elegant, whitewashed Regency double villa, Keats House is a shrine to Hampstead's most lustrous figure. Inspired by the tranquillity of the area and by his passion for girl-next-door Fanny Brawne (whose house is also part of the museum), Keats wrote some of his most famous works here before leaving for Rome, where he died of consumption in 1821 aged just 25. The neat, rather staid interior contains books and letters, and the four-poster bed in which the poet first coughed up blood.

2 Willow Road

MAP PAGE 142
⊖ ⊕ Hampstead or Hampstead Heath Overground Ⓦ nationaltrust.org.uk. Charge.

Kenwood House

An unassuming red-brick terraced house built in the 1930s by the Hungarian-born architect **Ernö Goldfinger** (1902–87), 2 Willow Road gives a fascinating insight into the modernist mindset. This was a state-of-the-art pad when Goldfinger moved in, and as he changed little during the following fifty years, what you see today is a 1930s avant-garde dwelling preserved in aspic, a house at once both modern and old-fashioned. An added bonus is that the rooms are packed with **works of art** by the likes of Henry Moore and Man Ray. Before 3pm, visits are by hour-long guided tour only; after 3pm the public has unguided, unrestricted access.

Fenton House

MAP PAGE 142
Windmill Hill ⊖ Hampstead Ⓦ nationaltrust.org.uk. Charge.

Decorated in the eighteenth-century taste, grand Fenton House is home to a collection of European and Oriental ceramics, as well as a superb collection of **early musical instruments**. Experienced keyboard players are let loose on some of the instruments most weeks (Wed 2.30pm) and you can book tickets for one of the

Hampstead and Highgate

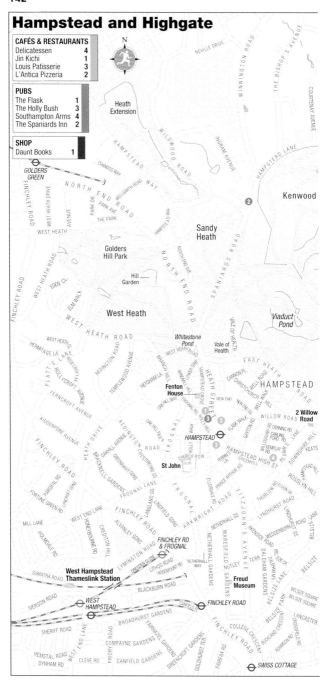

CAFÉS & RESTAURANTS	
Delicatessen	4
Jin Kichi	1
Louis Patisserie	3
L'Antica Pizzeria	2

PUBS	
The Flask	1
The Holly Bush	3
Southampton Arms	4
The Spaniards Inn	2

SHOP	
Daunt Books	1

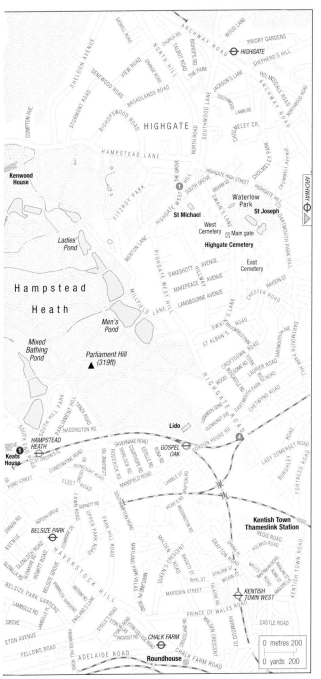

GASKELL ROAD
ARCHWAY ROAD
WOOD LANE
PRIORY GARDENS
CHURCH RD
TALBOT ROAD
BISHOPS RD
HIGHGATE
SHEPHERD'S HILL
HOLMESDALE ROAD
NORTHWOOD ROAD
SHELDON AVENUE
VIEW ROAD
NORTH HILL
GRANGE ROAD
THE PARK
JACKSON'S LANE
ARCHWAY ROAD
DENEWOOD ROAD
SOUTHWOOD LANE
LAWN RD
STORMONT ROAD
BROADLANDS ROAD
CHOLMELEY CR.
COMPTON AVE
BISHOPSWOOD ROAD
HIGHGATE
CHOLMELEY PARK
CROMWELL AVENUE
HAMPSTEAD LANE
NORTH ROAD
SOUTHWOOD LANE
HIGHGATE HILL
FITZROY PARK
THE GROVE
HIGHGATE HIGH STREET
DARTMOUTH PARK HILL

Kenwood House

HIGHGATE WEST HILL
SOUTH GROVE
BISHAM GDS
St Michael
Waterlow Park
St Joseph

Ladies' Pond

MERTON LANE
SWAIN'S LANE
West Cemetery
Main gate
Highgate Cemetery

Hampstead
Heath

HIGHGATE WEST HILL
OAKESHOTT AVENUE
HILLWAY
MAKEPEACE AVENUE
LANGBOURNE AVENUE
East Cemetery
CHESTER ROAD
RAYDON ST

MILLFIELD LANE
SWAIN'S LANE
BROOKFIELD PARK
ST ALBAN'S ROAD
DARTMOUTH PARK HILL

Men's Pond
CROFTDOWN ROAD
WOOD
BOSCASTLE RD
YORK
LAURIER ROAD
DARTMOUTH PARK AVE
DARTMOUTH PARK ROAD

Mixed Bathing Pond
Parliament Hill
▲ (319ft)
HIGHGATE ROAD
VOSSOKEN GDNS
GLENHURST AVE
DARTMOUTH PARK ROAD
CHETWYND ROAD

SOUTH HILL PARK
PARLIAMENT HILL
TANZA ROAD
NASSINGTON RD
Lido
SAVERNAKE ROAD
GORDON HOUSE RD
LADY SOMERSET ROAD
BURGHLEY ROAD
FORTESS ROAD

GROVE
HAMPSTEAD HEATH
ST CRISPIN'S CL.
SOUTH END RD
GOSPEL OAK
ESTELLE RD
ROAD
Keats House
POND STREET
CONSTANTINE ROAD
AGINCOURT ROAD
INKERMAN RD
COURTHOPE RD
RODERICK RD
SHIRLOCK RD
MANSFIELD ROAD
LAMBLE ST
GRAFTON RD

FLEET ROAD
GARNETT RD
SOUTHAMPTON ROAD
VICAR'S RD
WEEDINGTON RD

ORNAN RD
LAWN ROAD
UPPER PARK ROAD
PARK HILL ROAD
Kentish Town Thameslink Station
REGIS ROAD
HOLMES ROAD

ASPERN GROVE
BELSIZE PARK
DOWNSIDE CR
MAITLAND PARK VILLAS
MALDEN ROAD
QUEEN'S CRESCENT
BASSETT ST
ATHLONE ST
WILKIN ST
SPRING PL
GRAFTON ROAD
WILLES
WEEKMAN ROAD
RAGLAN ST
ANGLERS LA
KENTISH TOWN ROAD

AVENUE
GLENLOCH ROAD
HOWITT ROAD
GLENMORE RD
BELSIZE GROVE
HAVERSTOCK HILL
MAITLAND PK ROAD
RHYL ST
FALKLAND RD
KENTISH TOWN WEST

GLENILLA RD
BELSIZE PARK GARDENS
ANTRIM RD
ENGLAND'S LANE
MARSDEN STREET
PRINCE OF WALES ROAD

LAMBOLLE RD
LAMBOLLE PL
PRIMROSE GARDENS
MALDEN CRESCENT
HARMOOD ST
CASTLE ROAD

GROVE
ETON AVENUE
ELSWORTHY RD
STEELE'S RD
ETON VILLAS
ETON RD
ETON COLLEGE RD
PROVOST RD
CROGSLAND RD
CHALK FARM

FELLOWS ROAD
PRIMROSE HILL ROAD
ADELAIDE ROAD
CHALK FARM ROAD
Roundhouse

0 metres 200
0 yards 200

Highgate Cemetery

occasional **concerts**. Tickets for the house also allow you to take a stroll in the beautiful orchard, kitchen garden and formal **garden**, which features some top-class topiary and herbaceous borders.

Freud Museum

MAP PAGE 142
20 Maresfield Gardens ⊖ Finchley Road.
ⓦ freud.org.uk. Charge.
Hidden away in the leafy streets of south Hampstead, the Freud Museum is one of the most poignant of London's museums. Having lived in Vienna for his entire adult life, **Sigmund Freud** was forced to flee the Nazis, and arrived in London during the summer of 1938 as a semi-invalid (he died within a year). The ground-floor study and library look exactly as they did when Freud lived here – the collection of erotic antiquities and the famous couch, sumptuously draped in Persian carpets, were all brought here from Vienna. Upstairs, home movies of family life in Vienna are shown continually, and a small room is dedicated to his daughter, Anna, herself an influential child analyst, who lived in the house until her death in 1982.

Highgate Cemetery

MAP PAGE 142
Swain's Lane ⊖ Archway
ⓦ highgatecemetery.org.
Receiving far more visitors than Highgate itself, Highgate Cemetery is London's most famous graveyard. The most illustrious incumbent of the **East Cemetery** (charge) is **Karl Marx**. Erected by the Communist movement in 1954, his vulgar bronze bust surmounting a granite plinth is a far cry from the unfussy memorial he had requested; close by lies the much simpler grave of the author George Eliot. The East Cemetery's lack of atmosphere is in part compensated for by the fact that you can wander at will through its maze of circuitous paths.

On the other side of Swain's Lane, the overgrown **West Cemetery**, with its spooky Egyptian Avenue and terraced catacombs, is the ultimate Hammer Horror graveyard, and one of the city's most impressive sights. Visitors can only enter by way of a **guided tour** (charge also includes East Cemetery; no under 8s). Among the prominent graves usually visited are those of artist Dante Gabriel Rossetti, and of lesbian novelist Radclyffe Hall.

Shop

Daunt Books

MAP PAGE 142

51 South End Rd ⊖ Hampstead Heath
Ⓦ dauntbooks.co.uk.
Hampstead branch of this
excellent bookshop, which is
strong on guidebooks, travel
writing and fiction, and has a
good kids' section.

Cafés and restaurants

Delicatessen

MAP PAGE 142

46 Rosslyn Hill ⊖ Hampstead
Ⓦ delicatessen.company/mobile-
restaurant.
The name is misleading – this
is no deli, but a small, buzzing
and distinctly high-end kosher
restaurant. Its delicious and
inventive menu takes inspiration
from across the southern
Mediterranean and Middle East,
so expect flavours of tahini, sumac
and preserved lemons, and dishes
like Turkish pizza and *ras el hanout*
lamb chops. It's all designed for
sharing. £££

Jin Kichi

MAP PAGE 142

73 Heath St ⊖ Hampstead Ⓦ jinkichi.com.
Cramped, homely and very busy
(so book ahead), *Jin Kichi* offers
almost every Japanese dish, though
it specializes in grilled skewers of
meat. ££

Louis Patisserie

MAP PAGE 142

32 Heath St ⊖ Hampstead Ⓦ louis-
patisserie.com.
This tiny, understated, old-
fashioned Hungarian tearoom/
patisserie has long been serving
sticky cakes, tea and coffee to a
mixed crowd. Also serves cooked
breakfasts. £

L'Antica Pizzeria

MAP PAGE 142

66 Heath St ⊖ Hampstead
Ⓦ anticapizzeria.co.uk/hampstead.
Slinging arguably one of the best
Neapolitan pizzas in London, this
cosey spot gets very busy so go early
to secure a spot. ££

Pubs

The Flask

MAP PAGE 142

77 Highgate West Hill. Bus #210, #270
from ⊖ Archway Ⓦ theflaskhighgate.com.
Ideally situated at the heart of
Highgate village green, this Fuller's
pub has a rambling, low-ceilinged
interior and a roomy summer
terrace – as a result, it's very, very
popular at weekends.

The Holly Bush

MAP PAGE 142

22 Holly Mount ⊖ Hampstead
Ⓦ hollybushhampstead.co.uk.
A lovely old Fuller's pub, with
a cosy real fire in winter and a
charming wooden interior, tucked
away in the steep backstreets of
Hampstead village. Some guest ales
on offer, as well as decent food.

Southampton Arms

MAP PAGE 142

139 Highgate Rd ⊖ Gospel Oak
Ⓦ thesouthamptonarms.co.uk.
You'll find an excellent choice of
ales and ciders, from small British
producers at this friendly boozer,
with proper sausages, scotch eggs
and cheese plates to fill up on.
Cash only.

The Spaniards Inn

MAP PAGE 142

Spaniards Rd ⊖ Hampstead
Ⓦ thespaniardshampstead.co.uk.
Curl up in this creaky sixteenth-
century inn, featured in *The
Pickwick Papers*. Perfect for a lazy
Sunday afternoon after a walk on
the Heath. The large pub garden is
packed on sunny days.

Greenwich

Greenwich is one of London's most beguiling spots. Its nautical associations are trumpeted by the likes of the magnificent *Cutty Sark* tea clipper and the National Maritime Museum; its architecture, especially the Old Royal Naval College and the Queen's House, is some of the finest on the river; and its Observatory is renowned throughout the world. With the added attractions of riverside pubs and walks, a large and well-maintained park with superb views across the river and to the Docklands, plus a popular arts and crafts market, you can see why Greenwich is the one place in southeast London that draws large numbers of visitors.

Old Royal Naval College

MAP PAGE 148
Romney Rd ⊖ Cutty Sark DLR Ⓦ ornc.
org. Free.

It's entirely appropriate that the Old Royal Naval College is the one London building that makes the most of its riverbank location. Initially intended as a royal palace, Wren's beautifully symmetrical Baroque ensemble was eventually converted into a hospital for disabled seamen in the eighteenth century. From 1873 until 1998 it was home to the Royal Naval College, but now houses the University of Greenwich and the Trinity Laban's college of music.

Old Royal Naval College chapel

The two grandest rooms, situated underneath Wren's twin domes, are magnificently opulent and well worth visiting. The **Chapel**'s exquisite pastel-shaded plasterwork and spectacular decorative ceiling detail were designed by James "Athenian" Stuart, after a fire in 1799 destroyed the original interior. The magnificent **Painted Hall** features trompe-l'oeil fluted pilasters, and James Thornhill's gargantuan allegorical ceiling painting depicting William and Mary handing down Peace and Liberty to Europe, with a vanquished Louis XIV clutching a broken sword below them.

National Maritime Museum

National Maritime Museum and Queen's House

MAP PAGE 148
Romney Rd ⊖ Cutty Sark DLR Ⓦ rmg. co.uk. Free.

The excellent **National Maritime Museum** houses a vast collection of boats and nauticalia, imaginatively displayed in modern, interactive galleries designed to appeal to visitors of all ages; you'll find several hands-on sections for kids throughout the museum. The glass-roofed central courtyard is home to the museum's largest artefacts, among them the splendid 63ft-long gilded **Royal Barge**, designed in Rococo style for Prince Frederick, the much unloved eldest son of George II.

Nearby is a room dedicated to Turner's *Battle of Trafalgar*. On the second floor, a large exhibition on Nelson includes the coat he wore at Trafalgar.

A bright white Palladian villa flanked by colonnades, the **Queen's House** is the focal point of Greenwich's riverside architectural ensemble and an integral part of the Maritime Museum. Inside, one or two features survive from Stuart times, most notably the cuboid Great Hall, the beautiful cantilevered Tulip Staircase and Queen's Presence Chamber, which retains its rich ceiling decoration from the 1630s. The rooms provide a permanent home for the museum's vast maritime **art collection**, while the lavishly restored King's Presence Chamber displays Gentileschi's *Joseph and*

Visiting Greenwich

The most scenic and leisurely way to reach Greenwich is to take a **boat** from one of the piers in central London (every 15–30min peak times). Greenwich can also be reached by **train** from London Bridge (every 10–20min), or by **Docklands Light Railway** (DLR) from Bank or Tower Gateway direct to Cutty Sark. For the best view of the Wren buildings, get out at Island Gardens station to admire the view across the river, and then take the Greenwich Foot Tunnel under the Thames.

Greenwich

ISLE OF DOGS

SHOP
Greenwich
Market 1

Greenwich Foot Tunnel

River Thames

Greenwich Pier

ACCOMMODATION
Number 16 1

Tunnel entrance
Cutty
Sark

Old
Royal Naval
College

Trinity
Hospital

HORSEFERRY PL
CREEK ROAD
BARDSLEY LANE
CUTTY
SARK

THAMES ST
COLLEGE APP
CREENWICH CHURCH ST

Painted Hall
Greenwich
Market
Great
Hall

Chapel

BALLAST QUAY
HOSKINS STREET
LASSELL STREET

EASTNEY ST
OLD WOOLWICH ROAD

St Alfege

KING WILLIAM WALK
NELSON RD
ROMNEY ROAD
PARK ROW

GREENWICH STREET
ROAD

TRAFALGAR

Maze Hill
Station

RANDALL PL
STRAIGHTSMOUTH
GREENWICH HIGH ROAD
STOCKWELL ST

National
Maritime
Museum

Queen's
House

PARK VISTA

FEATHERS PL

MAZE HILL

BURNEY STREET
Fan
Museum
GLOUCESTER

CROOM'S HILL

Playground

CIRCUS ST
CIRCUS

G r e e n w i c h

ROYAL HILL
KING GEORGE STREET

P a r k

THE AVENUE

HYDE VALE
DIAMOND TERRACE

Royal Observatory
Planetarium
Astronomy Centre

BLACKHEATH AVENUE

WEST GROVE

GREAT CROSS AVENUE

CADE ROAD

CHESTERFIELD WALK

GENERAL WOLFE ROAD

Flower
Gardens

WAT TYLER RD

Ranger's House

Rose Garden

BOWER AVENUE

The Wilderness

HARE AND BILLET ROAD

S H O O T E R S   H I L L

C H A R L T O N   W A Y

MOUNTS POND ROAD

LONG POND ROAD
HILL ROAD

N

ELIOT VALE
ORCHARD RD

GOFFERS ROAD

TALBOT PLACE

Black Heath

PRINCE CHARLES ROAD

HEATH LANE
ELIOT PLACE

DUKE HUMPHREY ROAD

BAIZDON ROAD

TRANQUIL VALE
CAMDEN ROW

MONTPELIER VALE
ROYAL PARADE
ALL SAINTS DRIVE
MONTPELIER ROW

PRINCE OF WALES ROAD
SOUTH ROW

PARAGON PLACE
RYCULFF
SQUARE
POND ROAD
WEMYSS ROAD

PUBS
Cutty Sark 1
The Prince of Greenwich 3
Trafalgar Tavern 2

CAFÉ & RESTAURANT
Champagne + Fromage 1
Sticks'n'Sushi 2

B L A C K H E A T H

Blackheath
Station

LAWN TERRACE
LEE ROAD
BENNETT PARK

- - - Prime Meridian

0   metres   400

0   yards   400

Greenwich train station

Potiphar's Wife, one of the house's original artworks.

Cutty Sark

MAP PAGE 148

King William Walk ⊖ Cutty Sark DLR ⓦ rmg.co.uk. Charge.

Wedged in a dry dock by the Greenwich Foot Tunnel is the majestic *Cutty Sark*, the world's last surviving **tea clipper**. Launched from the Clydeside shipyards in 1869, the *Cutty Sark* was more famous in its day as a wool clipper, returning from Australia in just 72 days. The vessel's name comes from Robert Burns' *Tam O'Shanter*, in which Tam, a drunken farmer, is chased by Nannie, an angry witch in a short Paisley linen dress, or "cutty sark"; the clipper's figurehead shows her clutching the hair from the tail of Tam's horse. After a devastating fire in 2007, the ship has been beautifully restored from the bunkhouses on deck, to the ship's brass-lined keel. A collection of more than eighty ships' figureheads are lined up beneath the ship's prow.

Greenwich Park

MAP PAGE 148

⊖ Cutty Sark DLR ⓦ royalparks.org.uk.

A welcome escape from the traffic and crowds, Greenwich Park is a great place to have a picnic or collapse under the shade of one of the giant plane trees. The chief delight, though, is the superb view from the steep hill crowned by the Royal Observatory (see page 149), from which Canary Wharf looms large over Docklands and the Dome. The park is also celebrated for its rare and ancient trees, its royal deer enclosure in "The Wilderness" and its semicircular rose garden.

Fan Museum

MAP PAGE 148

12 Crooms Hill ⊖ Greenwich DLR ⓦ thefanmuseum.org.uk. Charge.

The Fan Museum is a fascinating little place (and an extremely beautiful house) to the west of Greenwich Park, revealing the importance of the fan as a social and political document. The permanent exhibition on the ground floor traces the history of the fan and the materials employed, from peacock feathers to straw, while the temporary exhibitions on the first floor draw from the museum's extensive collection.

Royal Observatory

MAP PAGE 148

Greenwich Park ⊖ Cutty Sark DLR ⓦ rmg.co.uk. Charge.

Established in 1675 by Charles II to house the first Astronomer Royal, John Flamsteed, the Royal Observatory perches on the crest of Greenwich Park's highest hill. The oldest part of the complex is the rather dinky Wren-built red-brick building, whose northeastern turret sports a bright-red time-ball that climbs the mast at 12.58pm and drops at 1pm GMT precisely; it

Cutty Sark

was added in 1833 to allow ships on the Thames to set their clocks. On the house's balcony overlooking the Thames, you can take a look at a **Camera Obscura**, of the kind which Flamsteed used to make safe observations of the sun.

Flamsteed's chief task was to study the night sky in order to discover an astronomical method of finding the **longitude** of a ship at sea, the lack of which was causing enormous problems for the emerging British Empire. Greenwich's greatest claim to fame, nowadays, is as the home of **Greenwich Mean Time** (GMT) and the Prime Meridian. Since 1884, Greenwich has occupied zero longitude – hence the world sets its clocks by GMT.

The old observatory is now a very popular **museum**. First off, you can see Flamsteed's restored apartments and the Octagon Room, where the king used to show off to his guests. The Time galleries beyond display four of the fabulous marine clocks designed by **John Harrison**, including "H4", which helped him win the Longitude Prize in 1763. In the Meridian Building, you get to see several meridians, including the present-day Greenwich Meridian fixed by the cross hairs in Airy's "Transit Circle", the astronomical instrument that dominates the last room. Reached via the shop (and free to enter), is the Great Equatorial Telescope from 1893.

Astronomers continued to work here until the postwar smog forced them to decamp; in 2018 they returned, as new technology allowed them to circumvent light pollution. The **Annie Maunder Astrographic Telescope** was subsequently installed in the Altazimuth Pavilion; it's not accessible to the public, but its images will be posted online and shown at the Planetarium (see below).

In the **Astronomy Centre**, housed in the fanciful, domed terracotta South Building, the high-tech galleries give a brief rundown of the Big Bang theory of the universe. You can also watch one of the thirty-minute presentations in the **Planetarium**, introduced by a Royal Observatory astronomer.

The Royal Observatory

Shop

Greenwich Market

MAP PAGE 148
Greenwich Church St ⊖ Cutty Sark or
Greenwich DLR & Greenwich train station
Ⓦ greenwichmarket.london.
An attractive historic covered market
in the centre of Greenwich, the stalls
here change every day, with arts,
crafts and plenty of food stalls always
on offer; antiques and vintage on
Tues, Thurs & Sun. Independent
shops nearby offer further treasures,
while on weekends flea markets
spread further afield.

Café and restaurant

Champagne + Fromage

MAP PAGE 148
34 Church St ⊖ Cutty Sark DLR
Ⓦ champagneplusfromage.co.uk.
This cool little place gets the
balance just right with champagne
from small producers, plus
artisanal French cheeses, pâtés and
charcuterie to nibble on. Baked
cheeses, raclette and champagne
afternoon teas, too. One of three
branches in London. £££

Sticks 'n' sushi

MAP PAGE 148
1 Nelson Road ⊖ Cutty Sark DLR
Ⓦ sticksnsushi.com.
Very good Japanese restaurant
serving top-notch small plates and
platters. On the pricier side, but
worth every penny; the standard
of food and service along with the
cool Danish décor make it hard to
believe it's a chain. £££

Pubs

Cutty Sark

MAP PAGE 148
Ballast Quay, off Lassell St ⊖ Cutty Sark
DLR Ⓦ cuttysarkse10.co.uk.

Greenwich Market

This Georgian pub is the best one
along Greenwich's riverside, a few
paces away from the main tourist
drag, with a good range of Young's
and guest ales.

The Prince of Greenwich

MAP PAGE 148
72 Royal Hill ⊖ Cutty Sark DLR
Ⓦ theprinceofgreenwichpub.com.
A quirky Victorian pub that
refers to itself as a "museum pub"
due to its historical location
and interesting décor. There's a
welcoming and homely vibe, as
well as great Italian food.

Trafalgar Tavern

MAP PAGE 148
5 Park Row ⊖ Cutty Sark DLR
Ⓦ trafalgartavern.co.uk.
Frequented by the likes of
Dickens (and mentioned in
Our Mutual Friend), William
Thackeray and Wilkie Collins,
this Regency-style inn is a firm
tourist favourite. It has a great
riverside position and serves good
meals and snacks.

Kew and Richmond

The wealthy suburbs of Kew and Richmond like to think of themselves as apart from the rest of London, and in many ways they are. Both have a distinctly rural feel: Kew, thanks to its outstanding botanic gardens; Richmond, owing to its picturesque riverside setting and its gigantic park. Taking the leafy towpath from Richmond Bridge to one of the nearby stately homes, or soaking in the view from Richmond Park, you'd be forgiven for thinking you were in the countryside. Both Kew and Richmond are an easy tube ride from the centre, but the most pleasant way to reach them is to take one of the boats that plough up the Thames from Westminster.

Syon Park

MAP PAGE 154
Twickenham Rd. Syon Lane train station from Waterloo Ⓦ syonpark.co.uk. Charge.
From its rather plain, castellated exterior, you'd never guess that **Syon House** boasts London's

Treetop Walkway, Kew Gardens

most opulent eighteenth-century interior. The splendour of Robert Adam's refurbishment is immediately revealed in the pristine Great Hall, an apsed double cube with a screen of Doric columns at one end and classical statuary dotted around the edges. There are several more Adam-designed rooms to admire, and a smattering of works by van Dyck, Lely, Gainsborough and Reynolds adorn the walls. While Adam beautified Syon House, Capability Brown laid out its **gardens** around an artificial lake, surrounding the water with oaks, beeches, limes and cedars. The gardens' real highlight, however, is the crescent-shaped Great Conservatory.

Kew Gardens

MAP PAGE 154
⊖ Kew Gardens Ⓦ kew.org. Charge.
Established in 1759, Kew's **Royal Botanic Gardens** have grown from their original eight acres into a 300-acre site in which more than 33,000 species are grown in plantations and glasshouses. The display attracts nearly two million visitors every year, who come to enjoy the beautiful, landscaped parkland and steamy palmhouses.

Great Conservatory, Syon Park

There's always something to see, whatever the season, but to get the most out of the place, come sometime between spring and autumn, bring a picnic and stay for the day.

The majority of people arrive at Kew Gardens tube and train station, a few minutes' walk east of the Victoria Gate. Immediately opposite the Victoria Gate, the **Palm House** is by far the most celebrated of the glasshouses, a curvaceous mound of glass and wrought-iron designed by Decimus Burton in the 1840s. Its drippingly humid atmosphere nurtures most of the known palm species, while there's a small but excellent tropical aquarium in the basement. South of here is the largest of the glasshouses, the **Temperate House**, which contains over 1500 plant specimens from every continent. Nearby is the **Treetop Walkway**, which lifts you 60ft off the ground, and gives you a novel view of the tree canopy.

Elsewhere in the park, Kew's origins as an eighteenth-century royal pleasure garden are evident in the diminutive royal residence, **Kew Palace**, bought by George II as a nursery for his umpteen children. There are numerous follies dotted about the gardens, the most conspicuous of which is the ten-storey, 163ft-high **Pagoda**, visible to the south of

River transport

From April to October, **Westminster Passenger Services** (🅦 wpsa.co.uk) runs a scheduled service from Westminster Pier to Kew, Richmond and Hampton Court. The full trip takes three hours one-way. In addition, **Turks** (🅦 turks.co.uk) runs a regular service from Richmond to Hampton Court. For the latest on boat services on the Thames, see 🅦 tfl.gov.uk.

Kew and Richmond

Kew Bridge Station

Brentford Station

M4

WINDMILL RD

BOSTON MANOR ROAD

HALF ACRE ST

EALING ROAD

KEW BRIDGE ROAD

BRENTFORD

HIGH STREET

LONDON ROAD

River Thames

Kew Palace

Kew Green

KEW

MORTLAKE RD

SCHOOL ROAD

KEW ROAD

Royal Botanic Gardens

Palm House

Victoria Gate

KEW GARDENS RD

BROOMFIELD RD

LICHFIELD RD

KEW GARDENS

Syon House

Syon Park

PARK ROAD

Queen Charlotte's Cottage

Treetop Walkway

Temperate House

Pagoda

Lion Gate

ENNERDALE ROAD

SANDYCOMBE ROAD

KEW ROAD

MANOR ROAD

Old Deer Park

Towpath

LOWER MORTLAKE ROAD

North Sheen Station

TWICKENHAM ROAD

RICHMOND

Richmond Station

SHEEN ROAD

RICHMOND

ST MARGARET'S ROAD

Richmond Lock

RAILSHEAD DRIVE

ST PETER'S ROAD

TWICKENHAM BR

OLD PALACE LA

Richmond Green

THE GREEN

KING ST

GEORGE ST

SHEEN RD

PARADISE RD

RED LION ST

MOUNT ARARAT ROAD

CHURCH ROAD

KINGS ROAD

THE AVENUE

Richmond Riverside

RICHMOND BR

WATER LA

HILL ST

THE VINEYARD

RICHMOND HILL

FRIARS STILE ROAD

QUEEN'S ROAD

St Margarets Station

JARVIS RD

ST MARGARETS ROAD

CROWN RD

TWICKENHAM

RICHMOND ROAD

ORLEANS ROAD

PETERSHAM ROAD

Terrace Gardens

Marble Hill House

LEBANON PARK

RIVERSIDE

Hammerton's Ferry

Towpath

Petersham Meadows

Royal Star & Garter Home

Richmond Gate

SAWYER'S HILL

STAR & GARTER HILL

Richmond Park

River Thames

HAM

Ham House

HAM STREET

RIVERSIDE DRIVE

SANDY LANE

PETERSHAM ROAD

King Henry VIII's Mound

Pembroke Lodge

N

0 metres 400
0 yards 400

ACCOMMODATION
The Old Stables 1

PUBS
The Greyhound 1
Stein's 3
Tap Tavern 2
White Swan 4

CAFÉS & RESTAURANTS
Chez Lindsay 2
The Glasshouse 1
Hollyhock 3
Petersham Nurseries 4

the Temperate House. A sure way to lose the crowds is to head for the thickly wooded, southwestern section of the park around **Queen Charlotte's Cottage**, a tiny thatched summerhouse built in the 1770s as a royal picnic spot for George III's queen.

Richmond

MAP PAGE 154

⊖ Richmond & Richmond train station.
Pedestrianized, terraced and redeveloped in the 1980s, Richmond's **riverside** is a neo-Georgian pastiche for the most part, and a popular one at that. The real joy of the waterfront, though, is **Richmond Bridge**, an elegant span of five arches made from Purbeck stone in 1777 and cleverly widened in the 1930s, thus preserving what is London's oldest extant Thames bridge. From April to October you can rent rowing boats from the nearby jetties, or take a boat trip to Hampton Court or Westminster. Alternatively, simply head south down the towpath, past the terraced gardens which give out great views over the river. On either side are the wooded banks of the Thames: to the left cows graze on Petersham Meadows; beyond lies Ham House.

Ham House

MAP PAGE 154

Ham St. Bus #371 or #65 from ⊖ Richmond & Richmond train station Ⓦ nationaltrust.org.uk/hamhouse. Charge.
Expensively furnished in the seventeenth century but little altered since then, Ham House boasts one of the finest Stuart interiors in the country, from the stupendously ornate Great Staircase to the Long Gallery, featuring six "Court Beauties" by Peter Lely. Elsewhere, there are several fine Verrio ceiling paintings, some exquisite parquet flooring, lavish plasterwork and

Paddle boarding, Richmond

silverwork, and paintings by van Dyck and Reynolds. A bonus is the formal **gardens**, especially the Cherry Garden, with a lavender parterre surrounded by yew hedges and pleached hornbeam arbours. The Orangery, overlooking the original kitchen garden, serves as a tearoom.

Marble Hill House

MAP PAGE 154

Marble Hill Park, Richmond Rd. St Margarets train station from Waterloo Ⓦ english-heritage.org.uk. Charge.
This stuccoed Palladian villa, set in rolling green parkland, was built in 1729 for the **Countess of Suffolk**, mistress of George II for some twenty years and, conveniently, also a lady-in-waiting to his wife, Queen Caroline. She was renowned for her wit and intelligence and she entertained the Twickenham Club of Pope, Gay and Horace Walpole. The few original furnishings are enhanced with

reproductions, giving the place something of the feel of an eighteenth-century villa. **The Great Room**, on the piano nobile, is a perfect cube whose coved ceiling carries on up into the top-floor apartments. Copies of van Dycks decorate the walls as they did in Lady Suffolk's day, but the highlight is **Lady Suffolk's Bedchamber**, with its Ionic columned recess – a classic Palladian device – where she died in 1767 at the age of 79. In the grounds, there are occasional **open-air concerts** on summer evenings.

Richmond Park

MAP PAGE 154
Bus #371 or #65 from ⊖ Richmond
ⓦ royalparks.org.uk. Free.
Richmond's greatest attraction is its enormous park, at the top of Richmond Hill – 2500 acres of undulating grassland and bracken, dotted with coppiced ancient woodland. Eight miles across at its widest point, this is Europe's largest city park, famed for its red and fallow deer, which roam freely, and for its venerable oaks. For the most part untamed, the park does have a couple of deliberately landscaped areas. The most popular spot is **Isabella Plantation**, a carefully landscaped woodland park, with a little rivulet running through it, two small artificial ponds, and spectacular rhododendrons and azaleas in the spring. For refreshment, head for **Pembroke Lodge**, once the childhood home of the philosopher Bertrand Russell, and now a teahouse at the park's highest point, affording wonderful views up the Thames valley. Tradition has it that Henry VIII waited here for the flare that signalled the execution of his second wife, Anne Boleyn.

Richmond Park

Cafés and restaurants

Chez Lindsay

MAP PAGE 154
11 Hill Rise ⊖ Richmond ⊛ chez-lindsay.
co.uk.
There's a wide choice of galettes or
more formal French main courses,
including lots of fresh fish and
shellfish, at this bright, authentic
Breton *creperie*. ££

The Glasshouse

MAP PAGE 154
14 Station Parade ⊖ Kew Gardens
⊛ sevenrooms.com/reservations/
theglasshouse/ig
A swish restaurant for a swish
neighbourhood, serving delicate,
accomplished French/Modern
British dishes. ££££

Hollyhock

MAP PAGE 154
Terrace Gardens ⊖ Richmond
⊛ tidetablescafe.co.uk/hollyhock-café.
Laidback, fair-trade veggie café,
perfect for tea and cakes on the
terrace overlooking the gardens and
the river. £

Petersham Nurseries

MAP PAGE 154
Off Petersham Rd. Bus #371 or #65 from
Richmond ⊛ petershamnurseries.com.
Expect fresh, organic, expensive
food at this lovely restaurant,
hidden away in a posh garden
centre. There's a cheaper self-service
tearoom too. £££

Pubs

The Greyhound

MAP PAGE 154
82 Kew Green ⊖ Kew Gardens
⊛ thegreyhoundkew.co.uk.
One of a handful of options on
and around Kew Green, this light,
contemporary pub offers real ales
and a long food menu.

Petersham Nurseries

Stein's

MAP PAGE 154
Richmond Towpath ⊖ Richmond ⊕ 020
8948 8189.
An authentic Bavarian beer garden,
serving up wurst and sauerkraut
washed down with *echt* beers (no
beer without food). Outdoor
seating only; the place is closed in
wet weather.

Tap Tavern

MAP PAGE 154
Princes Street ⊖ Richmond ⊛ taptavern.
co.uk.
Just off Richmond's High Street,
the Tap ticks all the boxes for
current drinks trends: dozens of
local and international craft beers,
a dedicated artisan gin menu and
comfort food bar snacks to soak up
the booze, making this a tempting
place to linger.

White Swan

MAP PAGE 154
Riverside. Twickenham train station from
Waterloo ⊛ whiteswantwickenham.co.uk.
Filling pub food, draught beer and
a quiet riverside location – except
on rugby match days – make this a
good halt on any towpath ramble.
The riverside terrace is a big draw.

Hampton Court

Hampton Court Palace is the finest of England's royal abodes and well worth the trip out from central London. A wonderfully imposing, sprawling red-brick ensemble on the banks of the Thames, it was built in 1516 by the upwardly mobile Cardinal Wolsey, Henry VIII's Lord Chancellor, only to be purloined by Henry himself after Wolsey fell from favour. Charles II laid out the gardens, inspired by what he had seen at Versailles, while King William III and Queen Mary II had large sections of the palace remodelled by Wren. With so much to see, both inside and outside the palace, you're best off devoting the best part of a day to the place, taking a picnic with you to have in the grounds.

State Apartments

MAP PAGE 159

Ⓦ hrp.org.uk. Charge.

The palace's Tudor west front may no longer be moated but it positively prickles with turrets, castellations, chimneypots and pinnacles. Its impressive **Great Gatehouse** would have been five storeys high in its day. King Henry lavished more money on Hampton Court than any other palace, yet the only major survival from Tudor times in **Henry VIII's Apartments** is his Great Hall, which features a glorious double hammerbeam ceiling. The **Haunted Gallery** is home to the ghost of Henry's fifth wife, 19-year-old Catherine Howard, who ran down the gallery

Hampton Court Palace

Hampton Court

to plead for the king's mercy – only to be dragged kicking and screaming back to her chambers. Another highlight is the superbly ornate **Chapel Royal**, one of the most memorable sights in the whole palace, with its colourful plasterwork vaulting, heavy with pendants of gilded music-making cherubs.

The **Cumberland Art Gallery**, housed in the Georgian part of the palace, shows some truly remarkable paintings from the royal collection. Artemisia Gentileschi's *Self-portrait as the Allegory of Painting* from 1638–9 is a uniquely powerful depiction of the female artist as worker, and is shown alongside works by Caravaggio, who she was influenced by, Rembrandt and Holbein. **William III's Apartments** are extremely grand, particularly the militaristic trompe-l'oeil paintings on the King's Staircase and the King's

Great Bedchamber, which boasts a superb vertical Gibbons frieze and ceiling paintings by Verrio.

Several early Tudor rooms, with striking linenfold panelling and gilded strapwork ceilings, are now used to display **Young Henry VIII's Story**. This is a worthy attempt by the palace to portray Henry in his virile youth, during his happy, twenty-year marriage to his first wife, Catherine of Aragon. Last, but not least, are the earthy and evocative **Henry VIII's Kitchens**, large sections of which have survived to this day and have been restored and embellished with historical reconstructions.

The Gardens and the Maze

MAP PAGE 159
Charge.

If you're coming from the State Apartments, you'll probably emerge onto the magnificent Broad Walk, which runs along Wren's austere

Getting to and around the palace

Trains from Waterloo take around half an hour to reach Hampton Court train station, which is just across the river from the palace; in summer you can also take the boat from Westminster, Richmond or Kew (see page 152).

Hampton Court is a huge complex – the most rewarding sections are Henry VIII's Apartments, the Cumberland Gallery, William III's Apartments and Henry VIII's Kitchens. And be sure not to miss out on the splendid Maze.

You can pick up **audioguides** (included in ticket price) from the information centre off Base Court. **Historical scenes and tours** take place throughout the State Apartments in summer; all are led by period-costumed historians, who do a fine job of bringing the place to life; ask at the information centre what's on that day when you arrive.

east front and is lined with superbly maintained herbaceous borders. Halfway along is the indoor **Royal Tennis Court**, established here by Henry VIII – if you're lucky, you might catch a game of this arcane precursor of modern tennis (summer only).

Interior of Hampton Court Palace

Fanning out from the Broad Walk is the **Fountain Garden**, a grand, semicircular parterre featuring conical, overgrown dwarf yew trees. To the south of the palace is the more formal **Privy Garden**, which features magnificent wrought-iron riverside railings by Jean Tijou. The **Pond Gardens**, originally constructed as ornamental fish ponds stocked with freshwater fish for the kitchens, feature some of the gardens' most spectacularly colourful flowerbeds. Further along, protected by glass, is the palace's celebrated **Great Vine**, grown from a cutting in 1768 by Capability Brown and averaging about seven hundred pounds of Black Hamburg grapes per year (sold at the palace in September).

Close by stands the Wren-built **Lower Orangery**, now home to Andrea Mantegna's luminous richly coloured masterpiece, *The Triumphs of Caesar*, painted around 1486 for the Ducal Palace in Mantua and characterized by an accomplished use of perspective and archeological and historical accuracy.

The most famous feature of the palace gardens, however, is the deceptively tricky trapezoidal yew hedge **Maze**, planted in the 1690s. Mazes, or labyrinths as they were called at the time, were originally

Formal Gardens

designed for pilgrims, who used to crawl along on hands and knees reciting prayers as penance for not making a pilgrimage to the Holy Land. They were all the rage among the eighteenth-century nobility, who used them primarily for amusement, secret conversations and flirtation. The maze was originally planted with hornbeam, but with the onset of the tourist boom in the 1960s, the hornbeam took quite a battering and had to be replaced with yew. Nearby, in Henry VIII's former tiltyard, the **Magic Garden** is an imaginative adventure playground, designed around such fairy-tale themes as dragons, beasts and battlements.

Bushy Park

MAP PAGE 159

Ⓦ royalparks.org.uk. Free.

Beyond the Lion Gates to the north of the Maze and across Hampton Court Road lies **Bushy Park**, the palace's semi-wild enclosure of over a thousand acres, which sustains copious herds of fallow and red deer. Wren's mile-long royal road, **Chestnut Avenue**, cuts through the park, and is at its best in May when the trees are in blossom. The park's main architectural feature is the **Diana Fountain**, situated a third of the way along to help break the monotony. The statue – which, in fact, depicts Arethusa – was commissioned by Charles II from Francesco Fanelli and originally graced the Privy Garden; stranded in the centre of a vast pond, she looks ill-proportioned and a bit forlorn.

Off to the west, a little further up the avenue, you'll come upon the **Waterhouse Woodland Gardens**, which are at their most colourful each spring when the rhododendrons, azaleas and camellias are in bloom. The crowds are fairly thin even here, but if you really want to escape the visitors make for the park's wilder western section, which is home to abundant wildlife.

ACCOMMODATION

Artist Residence

Accommodation

Accommodation in London is expensive. Compared with most European cities, you pay over the odds in every category. The cheapest option is to go to one of the independent hostels; going up a notch, even the most basic B&Bs struggle to bring their tariffs below £100 for a double with shared facilities. This is why so many people head for the budget chain hotels – which themselves are not at all cheap. For a really decent hotel room, you shouldn't expect much change out of £150 a night. Most B&Bs and many hotels are housed in former residential properties, which means that rooms tend to be on the small side. That said, even the most basic rooms tend to have TVs, and breakfast is often included in the price. Though hostels normally don't provide breakfast, they do usually have cooking facilities – exceptions are mentioned in the text.

Westminster

ARTIST RESIDENCE MAP PAGE 29, POCKET MAP G10. 52 Cambridge St ⊖ Pimlico ⓦ artistresidence.co.uk. Boutique guesthouse offering relaxed luxury and lifestyle magazine cool. The rooms are gorgeous (though the cheapest are quite small), packed with vintage boho trappings. There's a cocktail bar and a Modern British restaurant, too. ££££

LUNA SIMONE HOTEL MAP PAGE 29, POCKET MAP G10. 47–49 Belgrave Rd ⊖ Victoria ⓦ lunasimonehotel.com. Popular B&B/hotel with very friendly staff and plain, well-maintained en-suite rooms with everything you could possibly need. The breakfasts are big and good value too. £££

ST ERMIN'S HOTEL MAP PAGE 29, POCKET MAP H9. Caxton St ⊖ St James's Park ⓦ sterminshotel.co.uk. A bit of a sanctuary, set back from the street thanks to its long, leafy courtyard, but convenient for Victoria and Westminster, this is a classy four-star. Beyond the theatrical plaster-work reception and grand stairwell, rooms are more contemporary, with marble bathrooms, while some of the larger ones are suitable for families. There's a bar and restaurant on-site. Discounts for prepaying. ££££

SANCTUARY HOUSE MAP PAGE 29, POCKET MAP F19. 33 Tothill St ⊖ St James's Park ⓦ sanctuaryhousehotel. co.uk. A Fuller's hotel above a Fuller's pub, decked out in uncontroversial modern style. Breakfast costs extra, and is served in the pub, but the location by St James's Park is terrific. Rates vary – ask about the special deals. £££

St James's

THE STAFFORD MAP PAGE 35, POCKET MAP D17. 16–18 St James's Place ⊖ Green Park ⓦ thestaffordlondon. com. Tucked into a quiet backstreet off St James's Street, *The Stafford* provides high-class rooms in the main building, the unique Carriage House, a luxuriously converted row of eighteenth-century stables, and in the upmarket Mews Suites. The *American Bar* was founded to provide cocktails for American visitors in the 1930s, and its courtyard terrace remains a delight. ££££

Marylebone

CENTRAL YHA MAP PAGE 46, POCKET MAP D12. 104 Bolsover St ⊖ Great Portland Street ⓦ yha.org.uk. Excellent three-hundred-bed hostel in a quiet West End spot, with a kitchen, a 24hr café and a bar. Dorms are mostly en suite, or with bathrooms near. No groups permitted. Free wi-fi in communal areas. Dorms and doubles £

SUMNER HOTEL MAP PAGE 46, POCKET MAP E6. 54 Upper Berkeley St ⊖ Marble Arch ⓦ thesumner.com. A spruce B&B – with the feel of a boutique hotel – in a Georgian townhouse. The twenty rooms vary in size and style – the best are light and modern, some have tiny balconies, those facing the street can be noisy – but all are tasteful and comfortable, and there's a tranquil sitting room. Breakfast is a buffet. Free wi-fi. £££

Soho and Covent Garden

DEAN STREET TOWNHOUSE MAP PAGE 54, POCKET MAP F15. 69–71 Dean St ⊖ Tottenham Court Road ⓦ deanstreettownhouse.com. This 1730s beauty, owned by the Soho House club, has rooms ranging from "broom cupboard" and "tiny" right up to "bigger", where you'll have plenty of space. All are luxurious with gorgeous details. The restaurant, of the same name, is downstairs. ££££

Booking a room

Demand for beds is so great that London doesn't really have a low season. Most hotels vary their prices considerably depending on demand, so it's worth booking online well in advance to get the best price – you may be able to shave £50–100 off room rates at some of the more upmarket hotels – and if you're flexible with dates you can find some good deals.

London's **tourist offices** (see page 182) operate a room-booking service, for which a small fee is levied (they also take the first night's fee in advance).

Meanwhile, you can book accommodation for free **online** at ⓦ londontown.com; payment is made directly to the hotel and they offer very good discounts. Other useful websites for last-minute offers include ⓦ laterooms.com and ⓦ lastminute.com. ⓦ londonbb.com sources classy **B&B** options. Apartment rentals, such as ⓦ airbnb.co.uk and ⓦ homeaway.com, can be much better value, though the city has some restrictions on short-term rentals, while the Alastair Sawday's site (ⓦ sawdays.co.uk) has a selection of interesting properties in the capital, ranging from B&Bs and hotels to pubs and even apartments and houseboats.

THE FIELDING HOTEL MAP PAGE 54, POCKET MAP H15. 4 Broad Court, Bow St ⊖ Covent Garden ⓦ thefieldinghotel.co.uk. Quietly situated on a traffic-free court, this excellent hotel is one of Covent Garden's hidden gems. Its simple en-suite rooms are a favourite with visiting performers, since it's very near the Royal Opera House. No lift and no breakfast, but hot drinks in rooms. £££

HAZLITT'S MAP PAGE 54, POCKET MAP F146. Frith St ⊖ Tottenham Court Road ⓦ hazlittshotel.com. Located off the south side of Soho Square, this early eighteenth-century building is a hotel of real character and discreet charm, offering en-suite rooms exquisitely decorated with period furniture. Breakfast (served in the rooms) is not included in the rates. ££££

THE RESIDENT SOHO MAP PAGE 54, POCKET MAP F14. 10 Carlisle St ⊖ Tottenham Court Road ⓦ residenthotels.com. Modern hotel offering good value. Rooms are comfy and high-tech, if unexciting (the cheapest are pretty small), and each has a microwave, fridge and kettle – and an espresso machine – so you could effectively self-cater. £££

OXFORD STREET YHA MAP PAGE 54, POCKET MAP E14. 14 Noel St ⊖ Oxford Circus or Tottenham Court Road ⓦ yha.org.uk. The Soho location and relatively modest size mean this hostel tends to fill quickly. The atmosphere is more party central than family-friendly, though kids are welcome. Café and kitchen. Free wi-fi in communal areas. Dorms and doubles £

THISTLE PICCADILLY MAP PAGE 54, POCKET MAP F16. Coventry St ⊖ Piccadilly Circus ⓦ thistle.com. You're in the heart of things here, surrounded by Theatreland – in a no-surprises chain hotel that offers modern, quiet, well-equipped rooms with free (soft drink) minibars, Nespresso machines and rainfall showers. Check for online pay-in-advance discounts. £££

Bloomsbury
ALHAMBRA HOTEL MAP PAGE 68, POCKET MAP J3. 17 Argyle St ⊖ King's Cross St Pancras ⓦ alhambrahotel.com. Clean, friendly, budget hotel a stone's throw from St Pancras. Cheapest rooms have shared facilities and there's no lift, but a generous and good quality breakfast is included. ££

Budget chain hotels
Chain hotels have pretty much got the budget hotel market sewn up. B&Bs may be able to offer a more personal touch and more character in the decor, but the franchises are often in unbeatable central locations. Although they will never really be more than perfunctory places to stay, on the whole they can be guaranteed to provide clean if anonymous rooms.

Bumping along at the bottom are **easyHotel** (ⓦ easyhotel.com), whose summer prices start at just £55 for an en-suite cubbyhole – if you want a window, wi-fi, TV use or room cleaning, it's extra; there are branches in Victoria, South Ken, Paddington, Shoreditch and Croydon. **Travelodge** (ⓦ travelodge.co.uk) has some very handily situated hotels; rooms are unexciting, but if you book online well in advance, en-suite doubles can cost less than £65. **Premier Inn** is generally considered a cut above Travelodge (and it doesn't have quite the online bargains), with rooms from £80; their "hub" hotels offer small pod rooms from £70, with locations including Covent Garden, while the **point.a** chain (ⓦ pointahotels.com) offers smart minimal rooms in Shoreditch, Westminster, Liverpool Street, Paddington, Canary Wharf, Kensington and King's Cross, starting at £80–90.

AROSFA HOTEL MAP PAGE 68, POCKET MAP F12. 83 Gower St ⊖ Goodge Street or Euston Square ⓦ arosfalondon.com. Fifteen en-suite B&B rooms. Some are tiny, but it's clean, comfy and reliable, with contemporary touches. Full breakfast. £££

CLINK 261 HOSTEL MAP PAGE 68, POCKET MAP J3. 261–265 Gray's Inn Rd ⊖ King's Cross St Pancras ⓦ clinkhostels. com. A clean and friendly hostel, with dorms ranging from four to eighteen beds in a converted office block near King's Cross station, with laundry, lounge and kitchen – guests can use the bar at Clink 78. Dorms and doubles £

CLINK 78 HOSTEL MAP PAGE 68, POCKET MAP K3. 78 King's Cross Rd ⊖ King's Cross St Pancras ⓦ clinkhostels. com. This party hostel has funky decor, a lively bar, some pod beds, and plenty of period features from the days when it was a Victorian courthouse – you can even stay in an old cell. Kitchen facilities from noon; four- to sixteen-bed dorms, some girls-only, some en suite. Dorms and doubles £

GENERATOR MAP PAGE 68, POCKET MAP J4. 37 Tavistock Place ⊖ Russell Square ⓦ generatorhostels.com. A huge party hostel, with over eight hundred beds, in a converted police barracks tucked away down a cobbled street. The decor is colourful and hip, and there's a young, sociable atmosphere with a cool late-night bar and regular movie nights. Laundry, but no kitchen; breakfast and snacks available in the café. Groups welcome. Dorms £; doubles ££

GREAT NORTHERN HOTEL MAP PAGE 68, POCKET MAP J3. Pancras Rd ⊖ King's Cross St Pancras ⓦ gnhlondon.com. Grand old Victorian railway hotel offering boutique rooms with a luxe, Deco feel. Generous extras include espresso coffee, pastries and fresh fruit on each floor. £££

THE HOXTON, HOLBORN MAP PAGE 68, POCKET MAP H13. 199–206 High Holborn ⊖ Holborn ⓦ thehoxton.com. The hipster industrial aesthetic of the Hoxton (see page 168) is transplanted to the West End, along with the never-ending buzz of the lobby/bar/café. Cleverly designed rooms, with artworks and faux-vintage furniture, make good use of the spaces (some tiny, rooms start with "shoebox" up to "roomy"). £££

RIDGEMOUNT HOTEL MAP PAGE 68, POCKET MAP F12. 65–67 Gower St ⊖ Goodge Street ⓦ ridgemounthotel. co.uk. Very friendly, old-fashioned, family-run place, with 33 small rooms (half of them with shared facilities), a garden and free hot drinks machine. Full breakfast available. ££

ST PANCRAS YHA MAP PAGE 68, POCKET MAP J4. 79–81 Euston Rd ⊖ King's Cross St Pancras ⓦ yha.org.uk. Popular hostel near the Eurostar terminal on the busy Euston Road; rooms are very clean and bright. Family rooms are available. No groups. They don't have a kitchen but there's a café. Free wi-fi in communal areas. Dorms £; doubles ££

The City

APEX CITY OF LONDON HOTEL MAP PAGE 74, POCKET MAP N6. 1 Seething Lane ⊖ Tower Hill ⓦ apexhotels.co.uk. A four-star hotel on a secluded City street, designed for corporate clientele. Rooms are modern and well appointed; the pricier ones enjoy more light and better views. Rates vary enormously according to availability, so book early. On-site gym, restaurant and bar. ££

THE ROOKERY MAP PAGE 74, POCKET MAP L5. 12 Peter's Lane, Cowcross St ⊖ Farringdon ⓦ rookeryhotel. com. Rambling Georgian townhouse near Smithfield Market that makes a fantastically discreet little hideaway. It's as charming as can be with its panelled walls, flagstone floors and creaky, timeworn floorboards; rooms offer faded Baroque glam with super bathrooms. £££

ST PAUL'S YHA MAP PAGE 74, POCKET MAP L6. 36 Carter Lane ⊖ St Paul's ⓦ yha. org.uk. 215-bed hostel in a superb historic building opposite St Paul's Cathedral (earplugs recommended). There's a lounge and a café for dinner, but no kitchen. Small groups only. Free wi-fi in communal areas. Dorms and doubles £

THE ZETTER HOTEL MAP PAGE 74, POCKET MAP L4. 86–88 Clerkenwell Rd ⊖ Farringdon Ⓦ thezetter.com. A warehouse converted with real style and a dash of vintage glamour. The 59 rooms are funky and colourful, with Penguin paperbacks in many. Ask for a room at the back, overlooking quiet, cobbled St John's Square. Water for guests is supplied from *The Zetter*'s own well, beneath the building; good offers sometimes available. £££

The East End

THE CORNER MAP PAGE 90. 42 Adler St ⊖ Aldgate East Ⓦ thecornerlondoncity. co.uk. Bright, colourful flashpacker place with comfy, eye-popping rooms and fab bathrooms; the cheapest are tiny, though, and you'll pay more for a window. Tea and coffee facilities on each floor. ££

CULPEPER MAP PAGE 90, POCKET MAP 05. 40 Commercial St ⊖ Aldgate East or Liverpool Street Ⓦ theculpeper.com. This welcoming gastropub (see page 95) has five simple but artfully decorated rooms. Cooked or continental breakfast is included and served on the plant-filled roof terrace (weather permitting). It's a good-value choice for those who want a place to stay near the East London scene, but is of course noisy until pub-closing time. ££

HOXTON HOTEL MAP PAGE 90, POCKET MAP N4. 81 Great Eastern St ⊖ Old Street Ⓦ hoxtonhotels.com. The "Hox" brand – now extended to Holborn and Amsterdam – started here, and though it's not as hip as it once was, it's a popular choice. The facilities are good, with flat-screen TVs and duck-down duvets. A light breakfast is delivered to your room. The DJ bar and brasserie are destinations in themselves. £££

ONE HUNDRED SHOREDITCH MAP PAGE 90, POCKET MAP 04. 100 Shoreditch High St ⊖ Liverpool Street Ⓦ onehundredshoreditch.com. Super-slick hipster accommodation. There's lots going on here, with interesting art and music events, DJ nights and pop-ups, and coffee shops, bars, a Modern British restaurant and a club on site. Rooms are quirky and cool, with vintage design touches – the suites

include record players and vinyl – and there's a rooftop lounge with city views. £££

SHOREDITCH ROOMS MAP PAGE 90, POCKET MAP 04. Shoreditch House, Ebor St ⊖ Shoreditch High Street Overground Ⓦ shoreditchhouse.com/hotel. Hip little place with 26 rooms from "tiny" to "small-plus", and larger rooms in a separate building. Lots of tongue-and-groove and fresh, sunbleached colours, old school desks and vintage tiled bathrooms. £££

Tower and Docklands

WOMBAT'S CITY HOSTEL MAP PAGE 100. 7 Dock St ⊖ Tower Hill Ⓦ wombats-hostels. com. This huge (more than five hundred beds) hostel, part of a popular European chain, has light, spacious communal areas, a large kitchen (pasta provided), and a popular, big bar. Dorms – four to eight beds – and doubles are all en suite, and everything is very clean, but very plain. No children. Dorms £; doubles ££

South Bank and around

CAPTAIN BLIGH HOUSE MAP PAGE 105, POCKET MAP K9. 100 Lambeth Rd ⊖ Lambeth North Ⓦ captainblighhouse. co.uk. The former home of Captain Bligh (of *Bounty* fame) is now a nautically flavoured Georgian B&B, a short walk from the South Bank, run by a friendly, unobtrusive couple. There are just a handful of rooms and an apartment, all self-contained and with self-catering facilities. Three-night minimum. ££

MAD HATTER MAP PAGE 105, POCKET MAP L7. 3–7 Stamford St ⊖ Southwark or Blackfriars Ⓦ madhatterhotel.co.uk. Good-value Fuller's hotel with thirty clean and comfy en-suite rooms, above a Fuller's pub in an old hat factory. This is a great location, a short walk from Tate Modern and the South Bank, and staff are friendly. £££

POINT A WESTMINSTER MAP PAGE 105, POCKET MAP K19. 118–120 Westminster Bridge Rd ⊖ Lambeth North or Waterloo Ⓦ pointahotels.com. It's a bit of a stretch to say this smart, no-fuss hotel is in Westminster – it's nearer Waterloo and the South Bank, but still convenient. Rooms are tiny, and the ones with windows are more expensive. £

SAFESTAY MAP PAGE 105, POCKET MAP M10. 144 Walworth Rd ⊖ Elephant and Castle Ⓦ safestay.com/venue/safestay-london-elephant-castle. Reliable hostel in a handsome Georgian building – clean and tidy, with good beds (with curtains) and showers, and spacious common areas. Some of the four- to eight-bed dorms are en suite. Groups welcome. There's another branch in Holland Park. Dorms £; triple £££

SEA CONTAINERS MAP PAGE 105, POCKET MAP L7. 20 Upper Ground ⊖ Southwark or Blackfriars Ⓦ seacontainerslondon.com. This incredibly slick, nautically themed hotel occupies a prime spot right on the south bank of the Thames, in what was once a 1970s office building (known as the Sea Containers building). It features its own Curzon cinema, rooftop bar and well-regarded restaurant. £££

Bankside and Borough

IBIS STYLES LONDON MAP PAGE 112, POCKET MAP M7. 43–47 Southwark Bridge Rd ⊖ London Bridge Ⓦ ibis.com. The *Southwark* branch of this chain is a good central, no-fuss option with colourful design touches that raise the ambience a little above the other bland chain hotels in this area. Rooms are generally comfortable and clean and a buffet breakfast is included in rates, which vary widely depending on availability. ££

THAMESIDE YHA MAP PAGE 112. 20 Salter Rd ⊖ Rotherhithe Ⓦ yha.org.uk. London's largest YHA hostel, with 320 beds, is in a quiet spot near the river. It can feel a bit of a trek from the centre, but it often has space and the riverside pubs round here are good. Self-catering is available, and there's a café-bar serving breakfast and dinner. Free wi-fi. Dorms and doubles £

Kensington and Chelsea

ASTER HOUSE MAP PAGE 120, POCKET MAP D10. 3 Sumner Place ⊖ South

Kensington Ⓦ asterhouse.com. Pleasant, award-winning B&B in a luxurious, white-stuccoed South Ken street with a lovely garden at the back and a large conservatory where breakfast is served. £££

B+B BELGRAVIA MAP PAGE 120, POCKET MAP F9. 64–66 Ebury St ⊖ Victoria Ⓦ bb-belgravia.com. Very close to the train and coach station, this place offers small B&B rooms and self-catering studios. The rooms are comfortable, with original features as well as contemporary touches. Communal spaces are light and well designed, and staff welcoming and enthusiastic. Free bike loan; pet friendly. ££

CARING HOTEL MAP PAGE 120, POCKET MAP C6. 24 Craven Hill Gardens ⊖ Bayswater, Queensway or Lancaster Gate Ⓦ caringhotel.co.uk. This large guesthouse, in a quiet street, is a popular budget choice. Rooms are clean and functional: some have shared facilities, some showers only, and others are en suite. Free wi-fi in public areas and free continental breakfast. ££

COLUMBIA HOTEL MAP PAGE 120, POCKET MAP C7. 95–99 Lancaster Gate ⊖ Lancaster Gate Ⓦ columbiahotel.co.uk. This large hotel, once five Victorian houses, offers a variety of en suites – singles, doubles, triples and quads, some with views over Hyde Park. It's all a bit dated but it has a certain faded charm. Breakfast included. ££

GARDEN COURT HOTEL MAP PAGE 120, POCKET MAP B6. 30–31 Kensington Gardens Square ⊖ Bayswater or Queensway Ⓦ gardencourthotel.co.uk. Unfussy hotel close to Portobello Market; rooms are small, but all (except some singles) are en suite. Rates vary considerably. Buffet breakfast. ££

THE HALKIN MAP PAGE 120, POCKET MAP B19. 5 Halkin St ⊖ Hyde Park Corner Ⓦ comohotels.com. A luxury hotel that spurns the chintzy country-house theme: elegant, East-meets-West minimalism prevails in each of the 41 rooms. The high-end dining options include Michelin-starred Basque restaurant *Amesta*. ££££

KENSINGTON HOUSE HOTEL MAP PAGE 120, POCKET MAP C8. 15–16 Prince of Wales Terrace ⊖ High Street Kensington Ⓦ kensington-house.hotels-of-london. com. Friendly hotel in a nineteenth-century townhouse. The en-suite rooms are smallish and worn in places, but clean and comfy; one has a tiny balcony. Free continental breakfast and a (paid for) snack bar). £££

THE MAIN HOUSE MAP PAGE 120, POCKET MAP A6. 6 Colville Rd ⊖ Ladbroke Grove or Notting Hill Gate Ⓦ themainhouse.co.uk. Three enormous suites that are both homey – thanks to some lovely period furniture – and bohemian. Perfectly placed for Portobello Road, with lots of thoughtful touches. Three-night minimum. No breakfast (but discounts in local deli-café). ££

MEININGER MAP PAGE 120, POCKET MAP C9. Baden Powell House, 65–67 Queen's Gate ⊖ Gloucester Road or South Kensington Ⓦ meininger-hostels.com. Bright and cheerful modern hostel, part of a German chain, secure and clean and located near the South Kensington museums. Free wi-fi. No kitchen; breakfast available. Dorms (4–12 beds), plus private rooms; rates vary depending on demand. Dorms £; doubles ££

THE RESIDENT MAP PAGE 120, POCKET MAP B10. 25 Courtfield Gardens ⊖ Earl's Court Ⓦ residenthotels.com. Excellent-value boutique hotel. The 65 rooms range from singles and "luxury bunks" for two to "deluxe"; all are comfortable, clean and quiet, modern and attractive, with mini-kitchens and bespoke artwork. Good early-bird offers. ££

SAFESTAY HOLLAND PARK MAP PAGE 120, POCKET MAP A8. Holland Walk ⊖ Holland Park Ⓦ safestay.com. With its picturesque location in Holland Park itself, this bright hostel is a good budget choice. The dorms, which sleep four to thirty-three, are clean and tidy (with curtains and reading lights) and showers, though you're stacked three-high in the bigger ones; the private twins (some en suite) have TVs. There's a garden, lounge and pool room,

a café and laundry facilities, but no self-catering. Families and groups welcome. Dorms and twins £

SONDER CHELSEA GREEN MAP PAGE 120, POCKET MAP D10. 35 Ixworth Place ⊖ South Kensington Ⓦ sonder.com. Boutique hotel complete with plants and a stylish glass ceiling. The theme is earthy and serene and a welcome escape from the bustle of Chelsea. The rooms are impeccably decorated in light modern touches and the breakfast is worth waking up for. £££

ST DAVID'S HOTELS MAP PAGE 120, POCKET MAP D6. 14–20 Norfolk Square ⊖ Paddington Ⓦ stdavidshotels.com. Inexpensive, no-frills guesthouse famed for its English breakfast. Most rooms are en suite, and the large family rooms make it a good option for families on a budget. Free wi-fi in lobby (charge in rooms); no lift. ££

VANCOUVER STUDIOS MAP PAGE 120, POCKET MAP B6. 30 Prince's Square ⊖ Bayswater Ⓦ vancouverstudios.co.uk. Good-value, luxurious and well-equipped self-catering suites (from singles to quads, some with balconies) in a stately Victorian townhouse with maid service and a pretty walled garden. Also apartments on site and nearby. £££

Greenwich

NUMBER 16 MAP PAGE 148. St Alfeges Passage ⊖ Cutty Sark DLR Ⓦ st-alfeges. co.uk. Stylish three-room B&B – owned by a flamboyant ex-antique dealer/actor – offering a warm welcome and offbeat touches. ££

Kew and Richmond

THE OLD STABLES MAP PAGE 154. 1 Bridle Lane, Twickenham. St Margarets train station from Waterloo Ⓦ oldestables. com. Three bedrooms and one apartment in a house in a quiet street by the train station; walking distance to Richmond and the Thames. No on-site staff, but the manager is a phone call away and breakfast is provided. £

ESSENTIALS

London transport

Arrival

The majority of visitors arrive in London at one of its five airports, all but one of which can involve an expensive trip to the centre. Those arriving by train or bus are dropped right in the middle of the city, with easy access to public transport.

By plane

Flying into London, you'll arrive at Heathrow, Gatwick, Stansted, Luton or City **airport**, each of which is less than an hour from the city centre.

Heathrow

Heathrow Airport (🌐heathrowairport. com) lies around fifteen miles west of central London, and is the city's busiest airport, with five terminals. The fastest **train** service into London is the high-speed, non-stop Heathrow Express to Paddington station (15min). Cheaper but slower is the Elizabeth Line runs from terminals 2, 3, 4 and 5 to Paddington, with several stops on the way.

A cheaper alternative is to take the Piccadilly **Underground** line, which connects terminals 2, 3, 4 and 5 to numerous tube stations across central London (50min); you can use an Oyster card for both tube options (see page 175). A **taxi** from Heathrow will cost in the region of £50–85, depending on traffic and the time of day.

Gatwick

Gatwick Airport (🌐gatwickairport. com) is around thirty miles south of London, and has a train station at its South Terminal. Non-stop Gatwick Express **trains** run between the airport and London Victoria (30min; 🌐gatwickexpress.com). It's cheaper, however, to take a Southern train to Victoria, or a First Capital Connect train to various stations within London (30–45min), including London Bridge

and St Pancras. National Express buses run from Gatwick direct to central London (1hr 30min). A **taxi** will set you back a ludicrous £100 or more, and take at least an hour.

Stansted

Stansted Airport (🌐stanstedairport. com) is roughly 35 miles northeast of the capital. Stansted Express **trains** run non-stop to Liverpool Street (45min). National Express runs buses 24 hours a day calling at various places in London, including Victoria Coach Station (1hr 30min). A **taxi** will set you back £100 or more, and take at least an hour.

Luton

London Luton Airport (🌐london-luton. co.uk) is roughly thirty miles north of London and mainly handles low-cost flights. A free shuttle bus takes five minutes to reach Luton Airport Parkway station, which is connected by **train** to King's Cross St Pancras (45min) and other stations in central London. National Express runs buses to Victoria Coach Station (1hr 5min–1hr 20min). A **taxi** will cost in the region of £70–80 and take at least an hour to central London.

City

London City Airport (🌐londoncityairport.com), the capital's smallest and used primarily by business folk, is situated in the Royal Albert Docks, ten miles east of central London, and handles almost exclusively European flights. The **Docklands Light Railway** (DLR) takes you straight to Bank in the City (20min), where you can change to the tube; use an Oyster card (see page 175). A **taxi** from the airport to the City's financial sector will cost around £20, and take half an hour or so.

By train and coach

Eurostar (⊗ eurostar.com) trains arrive at the beautifully refurbished St Pancras International train station, next door to King's Cross, which is served by several Underground lines. Arriving by **train** from elsewhere in Britain (⊗ nationalrail.co.uk), you'll come into one of London's numerous mainline stations, all of which have nearby Underground stations linking into the city centre's tube network. Coming into London by **coach** (⊗ nationalexpress.com), you're most likely to arrive at Victoria Coach Station, a couple of hundred yards south down Buckingham Palace Road from Victoria train station and tube.

Getting around

London's transport system is generally efficient and comprehensive, though often overcrowded and can be subject to delays because of upgrade work. It is also one of the most expensive transport systems in the world.

    Transport for London (TfL) provides excellent free maps and information on bus and tube services from its **Visitor Information Centres**. Central ones include Euston, King's Cross, Victoria and Liverpool St, Piccadilly Circus, Heathrow 2 & 3 Underground Station and Gatwick North and South terminals. There's also a **24-hour helpline** and an excellent website (⊗ tfl.gov.uk).

    For transport purposes, London is divided into six concentric **zones** (plus a few extra in the northwest), with fares calculated depending on which zones you travel through: the majority of the city's accommodation and sights lie in zones 1 and 2. If you cannot produce a valid ticket for your journey, or travel further than your ticket allows, you will be liable to a **penalty fare**. Try and avoid travelling during the **rush hour** (Mon–Fri 8–9.30am and 5–7pm) if possible, when tubes can become unbearably crowded and hot, and some buses get so full they literally won't let you on.

Oyster cards, contactless payments and tickets

The cheapest, easiest way to get about London is to use a **Contactless debit or credit card** or **Oyster card**, London's transport smartcard, available from all tube stations and TfL Visitor Centres, and valid on the bus, tube, Docklands Light Railway (DLR), Tramlink, Overground, and almost all suburban rail services, Thames Clipper river boats and the cable car. The simplest way to use an Oyster card is as a pay-as-you-go card – you can top-up your card with credit at all tube stations and most newsagents. As you enter the tube or bus, simply touch in your card at the card reader and the fare will be taken off. If you're using the tube or train, you need to touch out again. Oyster operates daily price-capping when the system will stop taking money off your card, though you still need to touch in (and out). To obtain an Oyster card you must hand over a £5 refundable deposit or you can purchase a non-refundable Visitor Oyster Card for £5, for pay-as-you go travel, which comes with some tourist discounts. If you have a contactless debit or credit card, it works in the same way, though note not all overseas cards work and you may be charged overseas bank charges; weekly capping applies to contactless cards.

    If you don't have an Oyster card, you can buy a paper **Visitor Pass** for two or three days, but Oyster is better value. Paper **Travelcards** from machines and booths at all tube and train stations but really aren't worth the price. Other paper tickets are also roughly double the cost of the Oyster equivalent.

Children under 11 travel for free; children aged 11–15 travel free on all buses and trams and at child-rate on the tube; children aged 16 or 17 can travel at child-rate on all forms of transport. However, all children over 10 must have a Zip Oyster photocard to be eligible for free travel – these should be applied for in advance online; alternatively you can get an Oyster for a child that will charge half-price fares; ask at any station or visitor centre.

The tube

Except for very short journeys, the **Underground** – or tube, as it's known to Londoners – is by far the quickest way to get about. Eleven different lines cross the metropolis, each with its own colour and name – all you need to know is which direction you're travelling in: northbound, eastbound, southbound or westbound (this gets tricky when taking the Circle Line). As a precaution, it's also worth checking the final destination displayed on the front of the train, as some lines, such as the District and Northern lines, have several different branches.

Services are frequent, and you rarely have to wait more than five minutes for a train between central stations. A **Night Tube** core service covers five main lines for Fridays and Saturdays, plus some of the Overground in East London. **Tickets** must be bought in advance from automatic machines, or you can use an Oyster card. Paper ticket single fares are outrageously expensive so if you're intending to make more than one journey, an Oyster card is by far your best option.

Buses

London's famous double-decker **buses** are fun to ride on, with most running

at a frequency of five to ten minutes during the day, and good value. Some stops have live departure information and there are several apps that will do the same for you, like Citymapper. Cash is not accepted on-board buses; you must pay with an Oyster card, Travelcard or contactless payment card. You don't tap out on a bus and as a single fare allows you to change buses for up to an hour (you must tap-in every time you change bus but won't be charged).

A lot of bus stops are **request stops** (easily recognizable by their red sign) – stick your arm out to hail the bus or it will pass you by, and when on board ring the bell to request it to stop. Some buses run a 24-hour service, but most run between 5am and midnight. **Night-buses** (prefixed with the letter "N"), operating outside this period, depart at fifteen- to thirty-minute intervals, more frequently on some routes and on Friday and Saturday nights.

Overground, DLR and trains

The orange **Overground** line is a large network that connects with the tube in an outer loop from Richmond in the west to Stratford in the east. It's particularly useful for East London, where it runs every 5–15min; a night service runs from Highbury & Islington to New Cross Gate on Fridays and Saturdays. There are also **suburban trains**, useful for sights like Hampton Court, Richmond and Greenwich. For enquiries, call ☎ 0345 748 4950 or visit ⓦ nationalrail.co.uk or ⓦ tfl.gov. uk. In East London, the **Docklands Light Railway** (DLR) runs driverless trains to Docklands, Greenwich and beyond. Oyster and Travelcards are valid on all suburban, Overground and DLR trains.

Cycling

Cycling is increasingly popular in London because – in the centre at least – it's the fastest way to get around. Only folding bikes can be taken on public transport, although conventional bikes can go on certain tube and railway lines at off-peak times – check ⓦtfl.gov.uk for details. London's public bicycle sharing scheme, officially **Santander Cycles**, is perfect for short journeys, with over seven hundred docking stations. You need a bank card to use the scheme. Bikes can be **rented** from the London Bicycle Tour Company, 1a Gabriel Wharf on the South Bank (ⓦlondonbicycle.com).

Taxis

Compared to most capital cities, London's metered **black cabs** are an expensive option unless there are three or more of you (take note, they're not always black). After 8pm on weekdays and all day during the weekend, a higher tariff applies, and after 10pm, it's higher still; all cabs accept contactless payments. Tipping is customary. An illuminated yellow light tells you if the cab is available – just stick your arm out to hail it. London's cabbies are the best trained in Europe; every one of them knows the shortest route between any two points in the capital, and they won't rip you off by taking another route.

Minicabs look just like regular cars and are considerably cheaper than black cabs, but they cannot be hailed from the street. All minicabs carry a private hire sticker and all drivers should have TfL ID.

The **Uber** app (ⓦuber.com) is ubiquitous in London, and, despite some initial problems with its operating practices, retains its licence in the city. It's handy if you have a smart phone and internet access. The app connects you to the nearest Uber driver, and it normally takes under five minutes to reach you (you can't book ahead on the basic service). You pay through the app rather than paying the driver, so there's no need for cash. Prices for the standard UberX service can be up to fifty percent cheaper than black cabs. Be aware, though, that "surge" pricing operates at peak times (typically pub closing time), when they can be three times as much, but the app will let you know when this is operating.

Boats

Boat trips on the Thames are a fun way of sightseeing. The **Thames**

Museum tickets and the London Pass

London's big national museums – the British Museum, both Tate galleries, the National Gallery, the South Ken museums and more – are free, though they ask for (voluntary) donations and charge for special exhibits. Others, including the royal palaces, charge an entrance fee, and often ask for an additional donation of £1 or so (which has tax benefits for them). For many sights, it's worth buying tickets online in advance to save a few pounds. If you're thinking of visiting a lot of fee-paying attractions in a short space of time, it's worth considering buying a **London Pass** (ⓦlondonpass.com), which includes entry to a whole host of attractions including Hampton Court Palace, Kensington Palace, Kew Gardens, London Zoo, Westminster Abbey and the Tower of London; it often gives you "fast-track" entry as well. The pass can be bought online or in person from tourist offices and from London's mainline train and principal underground stations.

Clipper service (⊙thamesclippers.com) runs a regular commuter service between the London Eye and Greenwich (including the O2), with some boats going as far as Woolwich. There are piers on both sides of the river, including Embankment, Bankside, Blackfriars, London Bridge and Tower. You can buy tickets at a pier, but there is a discount if you buy online in advance or use an Oyster card. Other companies run boats upstream from Westminster to Kew, Richmond and Hampton Court from April to October (see page 153).

Sightseeing tours and guided walks

Standard **sightseeing tours** are run by several rival bus companies, their open-top double-deckers setting off every thirty minutes from Victoria station, Trafalgar Square, Piccadilly and other conspicuous tourist spots. You can hop on and off several different routes as often as you like with The Original Tour (⊙theoriginaltour.com).

A much cheaper option is to hop on a modern **London double-decker** – the #11 bus from Victoria station, for example, will take you past Westminster Abbey, the Houses of Parliament, up Whitehall, round Trafalgar Square, along the Strand and on to St Paul's Cathedral. Alternatively, you can take an old double-decker **Routemaster**, with open rear platform and roving conductor, on a "heritage" route; #15 from Trafalgar Square to Tower Hill.

Walking tours are infinitely more appealing and informative, mixing solid historical facts with juicy anecdotes in the company of a local specialist. Walks on offer range from a literary pub crawl round Bloomsbury to a roam around the East End. Tours cost approximately £10 and take around two hours; normally you can simply show up at the starting point and join. If you want to plan – or book – walks in advance, contact the most reliable and well-established company, Original London Walks (⊙walks.com). Tours run daily from the City Information Centre by St Paul's.

Directory A–Z

Accessible travel

London is an old city and not well equipped for travellers with disabilities and accessibility considerations, though all public venues are obliged to make some effort towards accessibility. Public transport is improving, with buses now wheelchair accessible, and up to a quarter of tube stations – they're

Congestion charge

All vehicles entering central London on weekdays between 7am and 6pm (and 12noon until 6pm at the weekend and on bank holidays) are liable to a congestion charge of £15 per vehicle. Drivers can pay the charge online or over the phone (☎0343 222 2222), and must do so before midnight the same day. Local residents, disabled drivers, motorcycles, minibuses and some alternative-fuel vehicles are exempt from the charge, but must register in order to qualify. For more details, visit ⊙tfl.gov.uk.

marked with a blue symbol on the tube map. A useful source of information is Ⓦtourismforall.org.uk.

Addresses

London addresses come with postcodes at the end. Each street name is followed by a letter or letters giving the geographical location of the street in relation to the City (E for "east", WC for "west central" and so on) and a number that specifies its location more precisely. Unfortunately, this number doesn't correspond to the district's distance from the centre. Full postal addresses end with a digit and two letters, which specify the individual block.

Cricket

Most years three Test matches are played in London each summer: two at **Lord's** (Ⓦlords.org; ⊖St John's Wood), the home of English cricket; the other at **The Oval** (Ⓦkiaoval.com; ⊖Oval). There are also numerous one-day internationals and Twenty20 matches, some of which are usually held in London.

Crime

Should you have anything stolen or be involved in an incident that requires reporting, go to the local **police station** (Ⓦmet.police.uk) or phone ☏101; the ☏999 number should only be used in emergencies. Central 24hr police stations include: Charing Cross, Agar St ⊖Charing Cross; Holborn, 10 Lambs Conduit St ⊖Holborn; and West End Central, 27 Savile Row ⊖Oxford Circus. The City of London Police (Ⓦcityoflondon. police.uk) are separate from the Metropolitan Police, and have a police station at 182 Bishopsgate ⊖Liverpool Street. If there's an incident on public transport, call the British Transport Police on ☏0800 405040.

Electricity

Electricity supply in London conforms to the EU standard of approximately 230V. Sockets are designed for British **three-pin plugs**, which are totally different from those in the mainland EU and North America.

Embassies and consulates

Australian High Commission Australia House, Strand ☏020 7379 4334, Ⓦuk.embassy.gov. au; ⊖Temple. **Canadian High Commission** Trafalgar Square ☏020 7004 6000, Ⓦunitedkingdom.gc.ca; ⊖Charing Cross. **Irish Embassy** 17 Grosvenor Place ☏020 7235 2171, Ⓦembassyofireland.co.uk; ⊖Hyde Park Corner. **New Zealand High Commission** New Zealand House, 80 Haymarket ☏020 7930 8422, Ⓦnzembassy.com; ⊖Piccadilly Circus. **South African High Commission** South Africa House, Trafalgar Square ☏020 7451 7299, Ⓦsouthafricahouseuk.com; ⊖Charing Cross. **US** 33 Nine Elms Lane, Battersea ⊖Vauxhall ☏020 7499 9000, Ⓦuk. usembassy.gov.

Football

Over the decades, London's most successful club has been **Arsenal** (Ⓦarsenal.com). Fellow London club **Chelsea** (Ⓦchelseafc.com) gave them a run for their money with the arrival of Russian oil tycoon Roman Abramovich in 2003, winning the league five times before the club was seized from him in 2022. Chelsea's closest rivals (geographically) are **Fulham** (Ⓦfulhamfc.com), while Arsenal's are **Tottenham Hotspur** (Ⓦtottenhamhotspur.com). East London's premier club is **West Ham** (Ⓦwhufc.com), based at the Olympic Stadium (see page 92). Tickets for most Premier League games are virtually impossible to get hold of on a casual basis, though you may be able to see one of the Cup fixtures. A better bet is to head to one of London's numerous, less illustrious clubs such as **Crystal Palace** (⊚cpfc. co.uk), **Millwall** (⊚millwallfc.co.uk), **Queens Park Rangers** (⊚qpr.co.uk) or **Charlton Athletic** (⊚cafc.co.uk).

Health

For minor complaints, pharmacists, known as **chemists** in England, can dispense a limited range of drugs without a doctor's prescription. Most pharmacies are open standard shop hours, though some stay open later: Zafash, 233–235 Old Brompton Rd, SW5 (☎020 7373 2798; ⊖Earl's Court), is open 24 hours.

If there's an emergency, you can turn up at the **Accident and Emergency** (A&E) department of your local hospital, or phone for an ambulance (☎999). A&E services are free to all. For non-emergency health concerns you can phone the NHS ☎111 service; they can let you know the nearest place to go, including for dental emergencies.

Internet

Nearly all hotels and hostels in London have internet access. After that, your best bet is a café with **wi-fi**; try the one in Foyles bookshop at 107 Charing Cross Rd (⊖Tottenham Court Road). Alternatively, the Southbank Centre, the British Library, St Pancras station and many museums have free wi-fi.

Left luggage

Luggage storage facilities are available at all airports and major train terminals. The Excess Baggage Company (☎0800 077 4250, ⊚excess-baggage.com) runs

outlets at Heathrow, Gatwick and Luton terminals; and King's Cross, Liverpool Street, Euston, Charing Cross, Paddington, Victoria and Waterloo stations.

LGBTQ+ travellers

Pink News (⊚pinknews.co.uk) is a useful online news site. London LGBTQ Switchboard (☎0300 330 0630, ⊚switchboard.lgbt) runs a helpline for LGBTQ people, including legal advice and counselling.

Lost property

Airports Gatwick ⊚lostproperty.org; Heathrow ⊚missingx.com; London City ☎020 7646 0000; Luton ☎01582 809174; Stansted ☎0330 223 0893. **Eurostar** ☎0344 822 4411. **Transport for London** Lost Property Office, 200 Baker St NW1 ☎0343 222 1234, ⊚tfl. gov.uk.

Money

The basic unit of **currency** is the pound sterling (£), divided into 100 pence (p). Coins come in denominations of 1p, 2p, 5p, 10p, 20p, 50p, £1 and £2; notes come in denominations of £5, £10, £20 and £50. Many shopkeepers may not accept £50 notes – the best advice is to avoid having to use them. For the most up-to-date exchange rates, visit ⊚xe.com.

Credit/debit cards are by far the most convenient way to carry your money, and most hotels, shops and restaurants in London accept the major brand cards – with contactless payment ubiquitous (even in some markets) for small amounts, as well as on public transport. There are ATMs all over the city and every area has a

Emergencies

For **police**, fire and ambulance services, call ☎999.

Eating out price codes

Throughout the Guide, restaurants are categorized according to the following price ranges. This reflects the cost of a two-course meal, including a non-alcoholic drink, per person.

£ under £15
££ £15–25
£££ £26–50
££££ over £51

branch of at least one of the big-four high-street **banks** (NatWest, Barclays, Lloyds and HSBC); opening hours are generally Mon–Fri 9.30am–4.30pm. Outside banking hours go to a **bureau de change**; these can be found at train stations and airports and in most areas of the city centre.

The high **cost** of accommodation, food and drink make London a very expensive place to visit. Staying in a budget hotel and eating takeaways, you'll still need in the region of £85 per person per day. Add in a restaurant meal and tourist attraction, and you are looking at £100–120.

Opening hours

Generally speaking, opening hours are Monday to Saturday 9am or 10am to around 6pm and Sundays noon to 6pm. Some places in central London stay open until 8pm, and later on Thursdays and Fridays (around 9pm).

Phones

Public **payphones** in London are iconic, but are only used for photo opportunities nowadays.

If you're taking your **mobile/cell phone** with you, check with your service provider whether your phone will work abroad and what the call charges will be.

Post

There are lots of post offices in London; to find a convenient branch, visit: ⊙ postoffice.co.uk.

Price codes

Accommodation and restaurant listings throughout this Guide are accompanied by a corresponding price code; see boxes on page 164 and above.

Smoking

Smoking is banned in all indoor public spaces including all cafés, pubs, restaurants, clubs and public transport. These restrictions often also cover e-cigarettes.

Time

Greenwich Mean Time (GMT) is used from the end of October to the end of March; for the rest of the year the country switches to **British Summer Time** (BST), one hour ahead of GMT. GMT is two hours behind South Africa; five hours ahead of the US East Coast; eight ahead of the US West Coast; and nine behind Australia's East Coast.

Tipping

There are no fixed rules for tipping. However, there's a certain expectation in restaurants or cafés that you should leave a tip of ten percent of the total bill – check first, though, that service has not already been included. As a general rule, tip when there is table service, but not when you go to the bar or are served drinks in a pub. Taxi drivers also expect tips – add about 10 to 12.5 percent of the fare – as do traditional barbers. The other occasion when you'll be expected to tip is in upmarket hotels where porters and table waiters rely on being tipped to bump up their often dismal wages.

Toilets

There are surprisingly few public toilets in London. All mainline train and major tube stations have toilets (though you will generally have to pay £0.30). Department stores and free museums and galleries are another good option.

Tourist information

Though there is no large proper, central tourist office in London, TfL Visitor Information Centres can provide information and tickets for attractions. The central **City of London Tourist Information Centre**, on the south side of St Paul's Cathedral (⊕thecityofldn.com/directory/city-of-london-information-centre; ⊖St Paul's) serves the City of London. You can buy tickets to many attractions here, along with Oyster cards, and book guided tours (several walking tours depart from here each day), as well as find information about travel across England. Another useful borough tourist office is in **Greenwich** at the old Royal Naval College (⊕visitgreenwich. org.uk; Cutty Sark DLR).

The weekly **listings magazine** *Time Out* is free and comes out on a Tuesday, but for full listings, you need to visit their website (⊕timeout. com). Other useful **listings websites** include ⊕londonist.com and ⊕.londonnet.co.uk and the website of the free weekday *Evening Standard* (⊕standard.co.uk).

Travelling with children

London is a great place for children and needn't overly strain the parental pocket. The city boasts lots of excellent parks and gardens, public transport is free for under 11s and many of the major museums can be visited free of charge and have exhibtions and events specifically targeted at younger ones. For the most part kids are tolerated in cafés and restaurants – and pubs in the daytime. There are also plenty of cafés in and around London especially for those with children (think ball pits, play areas and kid-friendly menus).

Festivals and events

London Parade

January 1 ⊕lnydp.com.
At noon, a procession of floats, marching bands, cheerleaders and clowns wends its way from Parliament Square to Green Park. Admission charge for grandstand seats in Piccadilly, otherwise free.

Chinese New Year

late January/early to mid-February ⊕chinatownlondon.co.uk.
Soho's Chinatown, Leicester Square and even Trafalgar Square all erupt in a riot of dancing dragons and firecrackers – expect serious human congestion. Free.

Oxford and Cambridge Boat Race

late March/early April ⊕theboatrace.org.
Since 1845 rowers from Oxford and Cambridge universities have battled it out over four miles from Putney to Mortlake. The pubs at prime vantage points pack out early. Free.

London Marathon

third or fourth Sunday in April ⊕tcslondonmarathon.com.
The world's most popular marathon, with around forty thousand masochists sweating their way through the 26.2-mile route. Most of the competitors

are running for charity, often in some ludicrous costume. Free.

IWA Canalway Cavalcade

May Bank Holiday weekend
ⓦ waterways.org.uk.
Lively three-day celebration of the city's inland waterways, held at Little Venice, with scores of decorated narrow boats, Morris dancers and lots of children's activities. Free.

Beating Retreat

early June
ⓦ householddivision.org.uk.
Annual military display on Horse Guards' Parade over two consecutive evenings, marking the old custom of drumming and piping the troops back to base at dusk. Tickets must be booked in advance.

Trooping the Colour

second Saturday in June
ⓦ householddivision.org.uk.
Ticket-only celebration of the Queen's official birthday featuring massed bands, gun salutes and fly-pasts. The royal procession along the Mall allows you a glimpse for free, and there are rehearsals (minus Her Majesty) on the two preceding Saturdays.

Wimbledon Lawn Tennis Championships

first two weeks of July
ⓦ wimbledon.com.
This Grand Slam tournament (played on grass) is one of the highlights of the sporting and social calendar.

Pride London

late June or early July
ⓦ prideinlondon.org.
A month of LGBTQ+ events – performances, film-screenings and so on – culminates in a colourful, whistle-blowing march through the city streets followed by a rally and concert in Trafalgar Square.

Henry Wood Promenade Concerts

mid-July to mid-September
ⓦ bbc.co.uk/proms.
Commonly known as the Proms, this series of nightly classical concerts at the Royal Albert Hall (and elsewhere) is a well-loved British institution with themed nights from Doctor Who to disco.

Notting Hill Carnival

last bank holiday weekend in August
ⓦ nottinghillcarnivalguide.com.
World famous two-day street festival established nearly fifty years ago, Carnival is a tumult of imaginatively decorated floats, eye-catching costumes, thumping sound systems, live bands, irresistible food and huge crowds. Free.

Open House

third weekend in September
ⓦ londonopenhouse.org.
A once-a-year opportunity to peek inside over 750 buildings around London, many of which don't normally open their doors to the public. You'll need to book in advance for some of the more popular places. Free.

London Film Festival

late October ⓦ bfi.org.uk/lff.
A two-week cinematic season with scores of new international films screened at the BFI Southbank, some West End venues and beyond.

Bonfire Night

November 5
In memory of Guy Fawkes – who tried to blow up King James I and the Houses of Parliament in 1605 – effigies are traditionally burned on bonfires. Today, the council-run celebrations tend to stick to fireworks displays. Some free; some are ticketed. Alexandra Palace is a good vantage point.

Public holidays

You'll find all banks and offices closed on the following days, while everything else pretty much runs to a Sunday schedule (except on Christmas Day when everything shuts down; museums and sights are often closed Dec 24–26): New Year's Day (January 1); Good Friday (late March/April); Easter Monday (late March/April); Spring Bank Holiday (first Monday in May); May Bank Holiday (last Monday in May); August Bank Holiday (last Monday in Aug); Christmas Day (Dec 25); Boxing Day (Dec 26). Note that if January 1, December 25 or December 26 falls on a Saturday or Sunday, the holiday falls on the following weekday.

Lord Mayor's Show

second Saturday in November
Ⓦ lordmayorsshow.london.
Big ceremonial procession from Mansion House to the Law Courts on the Strand and back again. Some 140 floats and military bands followed by the new Mayor in his gilded coach and a whole train of liverymen in carriages.

After dark, there's a fireworks display on the Thames. Free.

New Year

New Year's Eve Ⓦ london.gov.uk.
New Year is seen in by a spectacular fireworks display centred on the London Eye. TfL runs free public transport all night. Advance tickets required for access to riverside areas.

Chronology

43 AD Romans invade and establish a permanent military camp by the Thames called Londinium.

c.61 Queen Boudica, leader of the Iceni tribe, burns Londinium to the ground.

c.100 Londinium becomes the capital of the Roman province of Britannia, boasting a vast basilica, a forum and an amphitheatre.

410 The Romans abandon Londinium and leave the place at the mercy of marauding Saxon pirates.

871–1066 The Danes and Norwegians fight it out with the kings of Wessex over who should control London.

1066 Following the defeat of the English King Harold at the Battle of Hastings, William the Conqueror, Duke of Normandy, is crowned king in Westminster Abbey.

1290 King Edward I expels London's Jewish population.

1348 The Black Death wipes out a third of London's population of 75,000.

1381 During the Peasants' Revolt, London is overrun by the rebels who lynch the archbishop, plus countless rich merchants and clerics.

1532–39 The Reformation: King Henry VIII breaks with the Roman Catholic church, establishes the Church of England, dissolves the monasteries and executes religious dissenters.

1553–58 The religious pendulum swings the other way as Elizabeth's fervently Catholic sister, forever known as "Bloody Mary", takes to the throne and it's the Protestants' turn to be martyred.

1558–1603 During the reign of Elizabeth I, London enjoys an economic boom and witnesses the English Renaissance, epitomized by the theatre of William Shakespeare.

1603 James VI of Scotland becomes James I of England, thereby uniting the two crowns and marking the beginning of the Stuart dynasty in England.

1605 The Gunpowder Plot to blow up the Houses of Parliament (and King James I along with it) is foiled and Guy Fawkes and his Catholic conspirators executed.

1642–49 English Civil War between the Parliamentarians and Royalists ends with the victory of the former under the leadership of Oliver Cromwell. King Charles I (1625–49) is tried and beheaded in Westminster.

1660 The Restoration: Charles I's son, Charles II (1660–1685), returns from exile to restore the monarchy and encourages the development of the arts and sciences.

1665 The Great Plague kills some one hundred thousand Londoners, around a fifth of the population.

1666 The Great Fire rages for four days, kills just seven people but destroys four-fifths of the City.

1714–1830 The Georgian period: from the reign of George I to George IV, London's population doubles to one million, making it Europe's largest city. The period is one of boom and bust, gin drinking, rioting and hanging.

1750 Westminster Bridge opens, the first rival river crossing to London Bridge in over seven centuries.

1836 London gets its first railway line from London Bridge to Greenwich.

1837–1901 During the reign of Queen Victoria, London becomes the capital of an empire that stretches across the globe. Its population increases to nearly seven million, making it the largest city in the world. Industrialization brings pollution, overcrowding and extreme poverty.

1851 The Great Exhibition is held in a giant glasshouse known as the "Crystal Palace", erected in Hyde Park.

1855 The Metropolitan Board of Works is established to organize the rapidly expanding city's infrastructure.

1914–18 During World War I, London experiences its first aerial attacks, with Zeppelin raids leaving some 650 dead – a minor skirmish in the context of a war that takes the lives of millions.

1939–45 During the course of World War II, London suffers a lot of bomb damage, with sixty thousand killed and many thousands more made homeless.

1948 The SS *Windrush* brings the first postwar immigrants to London from the West Indies; over the next two decades, thousands more follow from former colonies.

1951 The Festival of Britain is held on the south bank of the Thames in an attempt to dispel the postwar gloom. The Royal Festival Hall is its one lasting legacy.

1960s Pop music and fashion helps turn London into the centre of the

"Swinging Sixties", with King's Road and Carnaby Street the hippest places to be seen.

1980s Under the Conservative Thatcher government, the gap between rich and poor grows. London's elected governing body is abolished.

2000 London gets to vote for its own Mayor (Ken Livingstone) and its elected assembly. London's national museums introduce free entry; the London Eye and Tate Modern open.

2005 A day after London is awarded the 2012 Olympics, on July 7, the city is hit by four suicide bombers who kill themselves and over fifty commuters in four separate explosions.

2008 Conservative candidate Boris Johnson defeats Ken Livingstone and becomes Mayor.

2012 London hosts the Olympic games for the third time.

2016 London elects Labour candidate Sadiq Khan as mayor. Seven weeks later the UK votes to leave the EU (though in London a majority voted to remain).

2017 Three separate terror incidents (Westminster, London Bridge and Finsbury Park) shake the city. In June, the UK votes in a "snap" general election. The Conservatives come first, but without a majority. In London, the Labour Party increases its dominance.

2019 Two key ministers, including Foreign Secretary Boris Johnson, resign in protest at government's plans for a free trade area with the European Union. Boris Johnson becomes Prime Minister later this year.

2020 Covid-19 sweeps London as it does the rest of the UK and the world, causing travel restrictions, national lockdowns, school closures and the cancellation of public events.

2022 Queen Elizabeth II passes away in September at the age of 96; a reign of over 70 years makes her Britain's longest reigning monarch. She is succeeded by her eldest son, Charles III. Also this year, Boris Johnson is succeeded as Prime Minister by Liz Truss, who is Prime Minister for a total of 50 days before she resigns and Rishi Sunak takes her place.

2024 The cost of living crisis that has been happening since 2021 continues on; both King Charles and his daughter-in-law Princess Katherine (Kate Middleton) are diagnosed with cancer.

Publishing Information
Sixth edition 2024

Distribution
UK, Ireland and Europe
Apa Publications (UK) Ltd; sales@roughguides.com
United States and Canada
Ingram Publisher Services; ips@ingramcontent.com
Australia and New Zealand
Booktopia; retailer@booktopia.com.au
Worldwide
Apa Publications (UK) Ltd; sales@roughguides.com

Special Sales, Content Licensing and CoPublishing
Rough Guides can be purchased in bulk quantities at discounted prices. We can create special editions, personalised jackets and corporate imprints tailored to your needs. sales@roughguides.com. roughguides.com
Printed in China
This book was produced using **Typefi** automated publishing software.

A catalogue record for this book is available from the British Library
The publishers and authors have done their best to ensure the accuracy and currency of all the information in **Pocket Rough Guide London**, however, they can accept no responsibility for any loss, injury, or inconvenience sustained by any traveller as a result of information or advice contained in the guide.

Rough Guide Credits
Editor: Beth Williams
Cartography: Carte
Picture editor: Piotr Kala
Picture Manager: Tom Smyth
Layout: Ankur Guha

Original design: Richard Czapnik
Head of DTP and Pre-Press: Rebeka Davies
Head of Publishing: Sarah Clark

Author
Annie Warren is an editor, writer and translator, as well as the proud creator of the Rough Guide to LGBTQ+ Friendly Places in Europe, the first book of its kind. Having lived in London, France, Italy and Austria, she now lives on a canal boat in her native Midlands. She loves wild swimming, film photography and strong margaritas. You can follow her @notanniewarren and find her work at annie-warren.com.

Acknowledgements
Huge thanks go to Ruth Pritchard and to Michael Cook and Claire Fitzpatrick, for offering me places to stay so often that it feels like I never truly left London.

Help us update

We've gone to a lot of effort to ensure that this edition of the **Pocket Rough Guide London** is accurate and up-to-date. However, things change – places get "discovered", opening hours are notoriously fickle, restaurants and rooms raise prices or lower standards. If you feel we've got it wrong or left something out, we'd like to know, and if you can remember the address, the price, the hours, the phone number, so much the better.

Please send your comments with the subject line "**Pocket Rough Guide London Update**" to mail@uk.roughguides.com. We'll credit all contributions and send a copy of the next edition (or any other Rough Guide if you prefer) for the very best emails.

Photo Credits

(Key: T-top; C-centre; B-bottom; L-left; R-right)

Alamy 50, 63, 64, 71, 72, 76, 82, 86, 87, 94, 96, 97, 138, 139
Flesh & Buns 62
iStock 2BL, 2BC, 5, 12T, 15T, 17B, 31, 53, 66, 85, 92, 99, 102, 111, 115, 147, 149, 150, 151, 172/173
Mandarin Oriental Hotel Group 131
Mark Thomas/Rough Guides 17T, 18B, 45, 59, 60, 98, 104, 107, 144
Museum of Brands, Packaging and Advertising 127
Natascha Sturny/Rough Guides 152
Patricia Niven/Anchor & Hope 108
Paul Massey 162/163
Rough Guides 18C, 19T, 19C, 19B
Shutterstock 1, 2TL, 2MC, 4, 6, 10, 11T, 11B, 12B, 13T, 13B, 14T, 14B, 15B, 16T, 16B, 18T, 20T, 20C, 20B, 21T, 21C, 21B, 22/23, 24, 27, 28, 30, 32, 33, 34, 36, 37, 39, 40, 42, 44, 46, 47, 48, 49, 51, 52, 56, 57, 61, 65, 67, 69, 70, 73, 77, 78, 80, 83, 84, 89, 91, 93, 103, 106, 109, 110, 114, 116, 117, 118, 119, 122, 123, 124, 125, 126, 128, 129, 130, 132, 133, 134, 137, 140, 141, 146, 155, 156, 157, 158, 160, 161
Spencer House, London 38
Suzanne Porter/Rough Guides 43, 153
The National Gallery, London 25
Trustees of the Geffrye Museum, London 88
Vivi Pham/Pidgin 95
ZSL 136

Cover: Tower Bridge **Jane Rix/Shutterstock**

Index